Jewish and Christian Views on Bodily Pleasure

Jewish and Christian Views on Bodily Pleasure

Their Origins and Relevance in the Twentieth-Century

ROBERT CHERRY

Foreword by Donna Schaper and Valerie Holly

WIPF & STOCK · Eugene, Oregon

JEWISH AND CHRISTIAN VIEWS ON BODILY PLEASURE
Their Origins and Relevance in the Twentieth-Century

Copyright © 2018 Robert Cherry. All rights reserved. Except for brief quotations in critical publications or reviews, no part of this book may be reproduced in any manner without prior written permission from the publisher. Write: Permissions, Wipf and Stock Publishers, 199 W. 8th Ave., Suite 3, Eugene, OR 97401.

Wipf & Stock
An Imprint of Wipf and Stock Publishers
199 W. 8th Ave., Suite 3
Eugene, OR 97401

www.wipfandstock.com

PAPERBACK ISBN: 978-1-5326-4744-4
HARDCOVER ISBN: 978-1-5326-4745-1
EBOOK ISBN: 978-1-5326-4746-8

Manufactured in the U.S.A.   10/02/18

This book is dedicated to my grandchildren: Daniela, Gita, Jacob, Kentaro, and Kazuhiro.

Contents

Foreword by Donna Shaper and Valerie Holly — xi
Preface and Acknowledgments — xiii
Illustrations — ix

1. The Religious Setting — 1
2. Jewish Beliefs before the Common Era — 14
3. Jewish Renewal Movements at the Beginning of the Common Era — 30
4. Jesus' Ministry — 51
5. Paul: The Beginnings of Christian Anti-Pleasure Views — 72
6. The Triumph of Ascetic Values — 89
7. The Emergence of Rabbinic Judaism — 110
8. Ascetic Values Confront Roman Society — 126
9. Bodily Pleasures: Foundational Jewish Values — 144
10. Forward through the Nineteenth Century — 161
11. Relevance in the Twentieth Century — 176
12. Judeo-Christian Myth — 197

Appendix — 201
Bibliography — 207
Index — 217

Illustrations

page 23   Figure 2.1: Kingdoms of Israel and Judah, 9th Century BCE Kingdoms_of_Israel_and_Judah_map_830.svg
page 32   Figure 3.1: Jerusalem at the Time of Jesus https://jesusreigns.wordpress.com/2009/07/13/jerulalem-at-the-time-of-jesus-map/
page 33   Figure 3.2: Model of Second Temple, 1st Century CE Israeli Museum
page 42   Figure 3.3: Necropoli del Crocifisso del Tufo, scavi Bizzarri, tomb. no. 26. Museo Archeologico, Orvieto, Italy

Art Resource Incorporated: ART190171

page 42   Figure 3.4: The Rape of Ganymede, Museo Archeologico, Ferrara, Italy

Art Resource Incorporated: ART128251

page 43   Figure 3.5: Red figure cup, 510-500 BCE Musée du Louvre, Paris, France

Art Resource Incorporated: ART162763

page 54   Figure 4.1: Map of Israel, 1st Century CE. https://www.pinterest.com
page 76   Figure 5.1: Paul's Second Journey Biblestudy.org
page 80   Figure 5.2: Marble bas-relief, Imperial Roman, 1st century CE. From a tavern in Pompeii. Museo Archeologico Nazionale, Naples, Italy

Art Resource Incorporated: ART383545

page 80   Figure 5.3: Fresco from Pompeii. Museo Archeologico Nazionale, Naples, Italy

Art Resource Incorporated: ART81253

page 163   Figure 10.1: Spanish, said to be from convent of Santa de Astudillo, Copy of the 8th century Lucca cross. Metropolitan Museum of Art 47.100.54
page 163   Figure 10.2: Central Plaque of a Cross 1185–95 Limoges, France Metropolitan Museum of Art 17.190.409a
page 177   Figure 11.1: Mulligan's Guard Harrigan & Hart (1873) Brown University Library
page 178   Figure 11.2: Maggie Cline Performing "T'row Him Down McClosky" American Vaudeville Museum
page 184   Figure 11.3: Theda Bara in *Sin* (1915) https://froMatthebygone.wordpress.com
page 187   Figure 11.4: Dorothy Day, 1934 New York World Telegraph & Sun Collection
page 193   Figure 11.5: Al Jolson Sheet Music for "Swanee," 1919 https://www.bing.com

page 202 Figure AP.1: Map of Babylonia Academies, 5th Century CE. http://www.moellerhaus.com
page 205 Figure AP.2: Page from the Babylonia Talmud

Foreword

To FULLY GAIN AN understanding of Jewish and Christian attitudes, both historically and currently regarding sex and intimacy, Mr. Cherry, the author of this book, takes the reader through Jewish and Christian theological and Christological beginnings. Readers of Mr. Cherry's book are initially presented with an extensive and clearly researched amount of significant material that describes in detail Jewish and Christian communities from their inception. Mr. Cherry paints a vivid picture of Jewish life Before the Common Era and into the first four centuries of the Common Era. In addition, this author's use of the biblical texts, both Old Testament and New Testament, substantiates his assertions specifically the impact of religion and spirituality regarding sexual pleasure. Mr. Cherry's book includes plenty of background concerning Jesus and Jesus' ministry. Thus readers are able to gain valuable knowledge of the cultural and social dynamics impacting the first four centuries in the Common Era.

After Mr. Cherry presents the intensive historical and biblical overview of the Jewish and Christian communities for his readers, he next details Jewish and Christian views regarding intimacy and sexual gratification. The author provides documented historical data that reveals how both of these religious communities developed and changed their attitudes and spiritual positions towards sexual intimacy. At different stages, these religious communities were not opposed to women and men engaging in sex for pleasurable purposes as well as for purposes of procreation. Mr. Cherry discloses the variables that affected .the changing views. Specifically, he details the impact ascetic religious beliefs had on Jewish and Christian views regarding sexual intimacy.

Finally, Mr. Cherry informs his readers on the unique and specific ways Judaism differed from Christianity in its historical and evolving attitudes on bodily pleasures. He identifies aspects of the biblical texts, religious

FOREWORD

beliefs from the founding Christian fathers, and spiritual interpretations from other theologians to ascertain the reasons for these changing views.

Mr. Cherry concludes his book with an overview on nineteenth and early twentieth century attitudes regarding sexual intimacy within the Jewish and Christian communities: he examines their similarities and their differences.

Reading Mr. Cherry's book will expose the reader to extensive biblical, cultural, and historical material that informs the reader of the Jewish and Christian beliefs and attitudes regarding bodily pleasures.

Donna Schaper, Senior Minister Judson Memorial Church

Rev. Dr. Valerie Holly, Prison Chaplin and Senior Community Minister Judson Memorial Church

Preface and Acknowledgments

THE CORE OF THIS book is about the history of Judaism and Christianity during the first four centuries of the Common Era, with a special emphasis on how each religion's views on bodily pleasures evolved. The two religions started off with very similar views, but as we shall see, by the end of the time period, they were dramatically different.

One can surely ask how I became interested in this topic. I am an economist, specializing in the study of US poverty and economic discrimination. I am a secular Jew, who before six years ago had little interest in religious history. However, before explaining the journey that led me to this project, let me explain what sustained my efforts sufficiently to write this book.

As I began researching the topic, the first thing that struck me was the skills religious historians possess. I entered a world in which erudite scholars, fluent in many dead languages, had scoured the archives to find shreds of evidence of this ancient world. Piecing together these fragments, they built narratives for first-century Jewish renewal movements. I was overwhelmed by the seminal work of Peter Brown, *The Body & Society*. Indeed, chapter 8 is substantially a condensation and paraphrasing of his work.

It also became clear that this religious scholarship had to make sense of a puzzle of small bits of information when all of the pieces aren't available. The resulting speculation that is inherent in this detective work is often not done by disinterested investigators. Many have religious or political motivations that shape the narratives they present. As an academic, I was fascinated by the nature of the intellectual inquiry and ferreting out fact from fantasy.

I was also struck by the ongoing tension within Judaism and Catholicism between concerns for social justice and the drive for religious piety.

Preface and Acknowledgments

The ebbs and flows of the priority given to one or the other is a lasting story that is still relevant.

By far the most important motivation, however, was to gain an understanding of how these two religions flourished after experiencing near extinction. Jesus was crucified around 32 CE. Within twenty years, his ministry was failing. The Galilean peasantry among whom he had proselytized had turned their backs. There were no Christian communities in the land of Israel save for that of his original apostles now residing in Jerusalem.

Another twenty years later, an unsuccessful revolt against Roman rule was launched and its defeat led to the destruction of the center of Jewish religious life, the Second Temple in Jerusalem. Now Jews had neither their political sovereignty nor a religious infrastructure. Without kings or temple priests, it was unclear how Judaism could survive.

I marveled at how these two religions were reborn because of revolutionary transformations engineered by true visionaries. Paul re-centered Christianity toward Christ's saving grace away from the moral sayings of the living Jesus; from a Jewish sect attempting to focus on the Israel countryside into an all-inclusive religion, devoid of Jewish requirements, that recruited Gentile converts throughout the Mediterranean basin.

No less revolutionary were the efforts of the remnants of the first-century Jewish renewal movement, the Pharisees. Escaping Jerusalem during the revolt, they set up a religious academy distant from Jewish life to develop practices that would transform Judaism. Over the next centuries, these rabbinic sages were able to move Judaism toward religious study in local academies, replacing sacrificial offerings and holiday pilgrimages to the Jerusalem Temple.

Finally, I found it compelling to learn about the process by which each navigated through uncertain waters. Paul and the evangelists had an apocalyptic vision. However, once it became clear that the end-time was not near, Christianity had to begin making decisions concerning organizational structure and texts. Similarly, the rabbinic sages had to create new texts and respond to the increasing Hellenist imprint of Roman rule. Moreover, since Judaism and Christianity did not hold state power, competing views could be sustained and how leaders were able to gain consensus on important religious principles is itself a remarkable story.

Now that I have explained what energized my efforts that culminated in this book, let me describe the journey that led me to this enterprise. More than ten years ago, my reading of Neal Gabler's *An Empire of Their*

Preface and Acknowledgments

Own: How the Jews Invented Hollywood set in motion this current project. Exquisitely written, the book sets out to document how the Jewish movie moguls overcame the Edison-led Protestant monopoly of the silent film industry. Gabler's portrait of these larger-than-life figures emphasized their ingenuity and their marketing and management skills, but did not consider the possibility that the content of their films had anything to do with their success.

The early Protestant moviemakers were intent on Americanizing the unwashed immigrants to Victorian values. A similar group of Progressives, led by Edward Franklin Albee and Benjamin Keith, had the same goal for their big-time vaudeville circuit which dominated the industry. Gabler totally ignored how the movie moguls, as well as Jewish vaudevillians, might have been successful because they effectively countered the Victorianism that dominated popular culture. Jewish entrepreneurs emphasized the pursuit of personal pleasures and presented a positive view of modern women and female sexuality.

I looked further into the religious culture of Eastern European Jewry and found that the eighteenth-century Hasidic movement reasserted joyfulness in Jewish lives. It not only expanded the role of music but also reestablished the positive role of bodily pleasures, including sexual relations. Together with the Enlightenment, it created the anti-Victorian attitudes that Jewish immigrants brought to America.

As I pursued my research, I realized that part of the story must be the ebb and flow of Irish American involvement in popular culture. After all, in the 1880s, Irish Americans were the most prominent group in vaudeville and one would have expected that to continue. Strikingly, however, their role declined substantially while the Jewish role ascended.

It became clear that the evolution of Irish Catholicism held the answer. The Irish immigrants who came to the US during the Great Famine were individuals who had little religious training. Successful vaudeville performers came from this cohort. After the Famine, there was a religious revival in Ireland that harkened back to Augustinian notions of human sinfulness and the resulting devotional movement deplored personal indulgences. Irish-trained priests and nuns brought these anti-pleasure views to America. As a result, succeeding generations of Irish Americans increasingly frowned on commercial vaudeville, making it difficult to continue to participate in the industry.

Preface and Acknowledgments

When I published an article, "Jewish Displacement of Irish Americans in Vaudeville: The Role of Religious and Cultural Values," in the *Journal of Religion and Popular Culture* in 2013, one reviewer thought I should include more material on the religious roots of contrasting beliefs on bodily pleasures. I had read a bit on the views of the rabbinic sages and Church Fathers at the beginning of the Common Era on bodily pleasures. This suggestion, however, led me to look further into the evolution of early Jewish and Christian thought that became the subject of this book. Thus, my interest in the origins of religious differences derived from a desire to better understand the contrasting patterns of Irish American and Jewish immigrant involvement in early twentieth-century popular culture. It was further stimulated by the recent renewed promotion of the notion of a unified Judeo-Christian tradition. These contemporary issues will be discussed in the closing chapters.

I make no claims for original research. My strength, if I have one, is to synthesize published works in interesting and sometimes insightful ways. One example is my 2017 *Contemporary Jewry* article, "Jesus and the Baal Shem Tov: Similar Roles but Different Outcomes." Hopefully, you will agree after reading this book.

As should be obvious, my initial ignorance of the scholarly literature on the variety of religious topics this book covers required me to seek out experts who generously gave of their time to help guide me along. I gained an understanding of nineteenth century Catholic revivalism in Ireland through the suggestions made by Mary Daly, Maria Luddy, Joseph Lee, and Kevin O'Neill. My interactions with Moishe Rosman, Ada Rapoport-Albert, and David Berger enriched my understanding of the dynamics within the first century of the modern Hasidic movement. Without the guidance of my colleagues Brian Sowers and Lauren Mancia my understanding of the evolution of Christianity would have suffered greatly. My knowledge concerning the origins and evolution of rabbinic Judaism can be attributed in no small measure to my interactions with Syd Leiman, Daniel Boyarin, and Rabbi Reuven Boshnack.

Finally, this book is meant for a general audience not those in religious studies so its readability is just as important as its scholarship. For someone who has been an academic writer for his entire professional career, this was a daunting task. To the degree that I have been successful transformed my writing style, I have to thank those who had the thankless task of providing editorial guidance. These includes some friends like Anita Podrid,

Preface and Acknowledgments

Marilyn Horan, Noson Yanofsky and Paul Moses, but most importantly Arthur Goldwag and Ruth Mullen, professional editors who did the best they could to put clarity and energy into my writing. And, of course, I must thank the staff at Wipf & Stock, headed by Matthew Wimer, who masterfully transformed the manuscript into the book you are reading.

1

The Religious Setting

Increasingly, Republican politicians point to the "Judeo-Christian tradition" to rally the nation to their view of America's uniqueness. During his 2012 presidential campaign, Mitt Romney credited America's world stature to "our Judeo-Christian tradition, with its vision of the goodness and possibilities of every life."[1] This association only grew with the 2016 presidential campaign and Trump presidency. Not surprisingly, candidate Ted Cruz claimed his policy proposals were based on Judeo-Christian traditions but so did the more moderate John Kasich. In a 2015 speech to the National Press Club, he said,

> US public diplomacy and international broadcasting have lost their focus on the case for Western values and ideals and effectively countering our opponents' propaganda and disinformation. I will consolidate them in a new agency that has a clear mandate to promote the core, Judeo Christian Western values and ideals that we and our friends and allies share: the values of human rights, the values of democracy, freedom of speech, freedom of religion and freedom of association.[2]

In his July 2017 speech in Poland, President Trump spoke more generally about defending Western values but his then chief political advisor, Steve Bannon, has often explicitly stated that its source are Judeo-Christian

---

1. Preston, "Judeo-Christian Tradition."
2. Collins, "Kasich Calls."

JEWISH AND CHRISTIAN VIEWS ON BODILY PLEASURE

values.³ By tracing the evolution of foundational Christian and Jewish beliefs, this book forceful questions the very notion of a unifying Judeo-Christian tradition.

There are certainly many similarities between the foundational tenets of Judaism and Christianity but the attitude towards bodily pleasures is not one of them. At the end of the fourth century, the Babylonian Talmud completed the religious transformation into rabbinic Judaism. It firmly rejected ascetic behavior, presenting a positive view of festive activities and female sexuality. At the same time, Augustine was finalizing the foundational doctrines of Christianity. He labeled the Jews "carnal Israelites" because Augustine believed that Jews were "of the flesh" rather than "of the spirit;" they satisfied bodily pleasures at the expense of enhancing the spirituality of their souls.

Both rabbinic Judaism and Christianity evolved through their understanding of the history and traditions of biblical Israel. From the Dead Sea through the Sea of Galilee, an Israelite kingdom was carved out a millennium before the Common Era. This backwater fiefdom was of little consequence to the various empire builders that contested for domination in the greater region. As a result, for most of the following centuries, except for the sixty-year Babylonian captivity, Israelites were able to select their own Jewish rulers complemented by religious leaders in charge of their Great Temple in Jerusalem.

The situation changed substantially with the Roman conquest of Judea in 63 BCE, ending Jewish rule. Now an administrator selected by Rome governed. The Jewish populace first looked to the priestly class for leadership. That segment, however, lost favor when Jews witnessed its siding with the wealthy-owning class instead of impoverished farmers and tradesmen. Many looked towards Jewish renewal movements that offered alternatives to the priestly class. The two most significant were Jesus' ministry and the Pharisees.

This book will trace the evolution of these two movements through the end of the fourth century, particularly their views on bodily pleasures. It will indicate how the eighteenth century Hasidic movement in Eastern Europe and the nineteenth century devotional movement in Ireland reestablished these contrasting bodily pleasures beliefs. The book concludes by exploring how these religious differences help explain why Jewish immigrants rather than Irish Catholics came to dominate early twentieth

---

3. Beinart, " Racial and Religious Paranoia."

century popular culture and how they contrasting views bring into question contemporary notions of unifying Judeo-Christian values.

THE CHRISTIAN PROJECT

Twenty years after Jesus' death, the Christian sect was struggling. Despite the determined effort of committed evangelists who spread Jesus' prophetic sayings, the Jewish people had turned their backs. Outside Jerusalem, there were no Christian communities in the land of Israel, not even in the Galilee, Jesus' birthplace and where he proselytized. Christianity consisted of a small group who lived in Jerusalem and a limited number of Diaspora Jews who had been converted during their pilgrimages to the Great Temple in Jerusalem. These converts formed isolated, small communities in the Mediterranean basin, whose faith in Jesus was nourished by the evangelists who periodically visited.

This stagnating Christian movement was transformed by Paul. He diagnosed its problems and offered solutions. First, remaining a Jewish movement was a loser! Few Jews were sympathetic to Jesus' ministry and still fewer to the message of his evangelist disciples. The Christian message must be brought to the Gentiles and this could only be successful if circumcision was abandoned, as well as the dietary requirements based upon the Mosaic laws.

Recently, Reza Aslan gained widespread visibility following the publication of his best-selling book, *Zealot: The Life and Times of Jesus of Nazareth*. For Aslan, Jesus was the "Galilean peasant and Jewish nationalist who donned the mantle of the messiah and launched a foolhardy rebellion against the corrupt Temple priesthood and the vicious Roman occupation."[4] This stance was changed by Paul and his allies, Aslan argues:

> The task of defining Jesus' message fell instead to a new crop of educated, urbanized, Greek-speaking Diaspora Jews who would become the primary vehicles for the expansion of the new faith. As these extraordinary men and women, many of them immersed in Greek philosophy and Hellenistic thought, began to reinterpret Jesus' message so as to make it more palatable. they gradually transformed Jesus from a revolutionary zealot to a Romanized demigod, from a man who tried and failed to free the Jews from

---

4. Aslan, *Zealot*, 169.

Roman oppression to a celestial being wholly uninterested in any earthly matter.[5]

The image of Jesus as a social justice warrior has inspired some Christian movements to combat the inequities brought forth by the capitalist system. In the late nineteenth century, Protestants in the Midwest formed the Social Gospel movement to defend farmers against the avaricious behavior of bankers and grain traders. A century later, South American Catholics espoused liberation theology in support of land-less peasants. In the 1980s, Jesus' condemnation of economic inequality led the US Council of Catholic Bishops to call for strong redistributionist policies, and this perspective continues to resonate in the pages of the Catholic journal *Commonweal*.

While religious scholars do not doubt the authenticity of Jesus' social justice sayings, few consider him a revolutionary who sought redistribution. For Jesus, it would be God that punished the uncaring members of the wealth-owning class, and the punishment would be their inability to enter the gates of heaven: "It is easier for a camel to go through the eye of a needle than for a rich man to enter the kingdom of God" (Mark 10:25, Matt 19:24). Moreover, there is no evidence that Jesus' ministry focused on freeing Jews from Roman oppression. The Romans executed a number of leaders in the Jewish renewal movement who, like Jesus, did not confront Roman rule. For example, John the Baptist urged Jews to go into the wilderness to lead ascetic lives in preparation for the end-time; and yet the Romans executed him.

To the extent that Jesus had revolutionary zeal, it was to challenge the priestly class who controlled the Second Temple. We are told in the Gospels that Jesus entered the Temple and "overturned the tables of the money changers and the seats of those who sold doves" (Matt 21:12-17, Mark 11:15-19). This action has nothing to do with Roman rule but with Jesus' belief that the priestly class was polluting the Temple.

The revolutionary nature of his actions, however, is undercut by a number of factors. While Jesus is crucified, no other member of his ministry is harmed. This suggests that rather than organizing a collective revolt, Jesus alone engaged in a symbolic action that was a nuisance to the priestly class and its Roman overlords. Indeed, in a scathing *Washington Post* review of *Zealot*, Stephen Prothero rejects Aslan's claim that Jesus was a "'revolutionary zealot who walked across the Galilee gathering an army

---

5. Ibid., 171.

The Religious Setting

of disciples' to rain 'God's wrath ... down upon the rich, the strong, and the powerful.'" Prothero points out:

> What about the obvious problems with the argument that Jesus was not just a political revolutionary—as biblical scholar John Dominic Crossan and others have argued—but a violent one? What are we to make of Jesus' apparent lack of interest in doing anything practical whatsoever to prepare for holy war? If he has come to fight for "a *real* kingdom, with an *actual* king," where are his soldiers and their weapons? And why no battle plan? The short answer to these questions is that Aslan is more a storyteller here than a historian.[6]

Aslan also undermines his claims when he discusses the situation of the Jerusalem Christian community, which he believes faithfully followed Jesus' ministry. Yes, there were persecutions, notably the murder of the evangelist Stephen three years after Jesus' crucifixion, but Aslan notes: "The Jerusalem assembly continued to thrive under the shadow of the Temple for decades after Stephen's death." According to Aslan, its leader, Jesus' brother James, called "James the Just," was a well-respected member of the Jerusalem religious community. Some thirty years after Jesus' crucifixion, James was executed by a renegade high priest, Ananus. In response, according to the Jewish historian Josephus, the Jewish religious community in Jerusalem rebelled. So universal was the condemnation of James's execution, the installed but yet-to-arrive Roman governor, Albinus, wrote a "seething letter to Ananus, threatening to take murderous vengeance upon him the moment he arrived."[7] This is hardly the experience one would expect of a revolutionary movement dedicated to the overthrow of the religious order and Roman rule.

What is most remarkable is that Aslan ignores what was Jesus' truly revolutionary activity: bringing the good news to the destitute and despised. Like Jesus' ministry, virtually all of the other renewal movements believed the land of Israel was entering a messianic period. They all referenced the imagery in Isaiah:

> The Spirit of the Lord God is upon me; because the Lord hath anointed me to preach good news unto the meek; he hath sent me to bind up the brokenhearted, to proclaim liberty to the captives, and the opening of the prison to them that are bound. (Isa 61:1)

6. Prothero, "Book review."
7. Aslan, *Zealot*, 199.

Jewish and Christian Views on Bodily Pleasure

Jesus' ministry, however, was unique. Other renewal movements stressed that only a select few would receive the messianic banquet. For some, it required scrupulously following the Mosaic laws while, for others, it required living in isolated ascetic communities.

By contrast, Jesus opened the doors to all. In particular, he desired to rehabilitate the image of the Galilean peasantry, the *ammei ha'aretz*. They were denigrated by the Pharisees and other renewal movements for not observing the Mosaic laws of purity. The Gospels note that Jesus sat with tax collectors and sinners, and sought companionship with the wicked sinner Mary Magdalene. If Jesus believed that these despised individuals had a place at the messianic banquet, then surely the *ammei ha'aretz* would.

Paul certainly differed with the Jerusalem leaders on the role of the Mosaic laws. However, he amplified Jesus' core thesis: God's grace is open to all who embrace Christ. Aslan also wrongly claims that Paul abandoned social justice concerns. Like Jesus, Paul rejected struggling for redistributive policies to reduce economic inequities. However, Paul did not abandon the ideal of equality. His most famous statement reads:

> There is neither Jew nor Greek, neither slave nor free, there is neither male nor female; for you are all one in Christ Jesus. (Gal 3:28)]

This goal of equality was not simply in the afterlife. As will be documented in future chapters, Paul's own practices and authentic epistles promoted equality of all within Christian communities. In particular, Paul traveled with female evangelists, some of whom had leadership positions in their home communities. So pronounced were his efforts that narratives of Paul's travels with the mythical Thecla were widely circulated for at least two centuries after his death.

In the second century, these narratives were threatening to the leading bishops. In response, these church leaders circulated "newly found" documents, the Pastoral Letters allegedly written by Paul, in which he is firmly committed to the patriarchal family and rejects allowing women to have any voice within the church. At the end of the century, church leaders began to circulate new versions of the Thecla narratives that eliminate her leadership role. Thus, as we shall see, the patriarchal church only arises after Paul's voice for gender equality is silenced.

Aslan points to "Greek-speaking Diaspora Jews . . . many of them immersed in Greek philosophy and Hellenistic thought" as a reason for the movement away from social justice concerns. He is correct to speak of the Diaspora Jewish community. Until the second century, the majority of Christian recruits were likely either Diaspora Jews or "God-fearers," those sympathetic to Judaism but unwilling to accept all its religious requirements. In every city that Paul visited, he would go to the local synagogue for Sabbath services. His purpose was not primarily to recruit the Jewish congregants but rather the God-fearers who would come.

What explains Paul's recasting of Christianity's social justice message, however, was not his immersion in Hellenistic thought but his immersion in Hellenist society. This was a society in which the degradation of poor women, particularly those who were enslaved, was pervasive. One could not walk down a street in Rome or other Hellenized towns in the Mediterranean basin without passing a house of prostitution staffed by women working under unbearable conditions. Paul's reaction to what he labeled *porneia* is what drove him to focus his proselytizing efforts on the struggle for equality for women and slaves within Christian communities.

Unfortunately, Paul came to believe that the only way to end this degradation was to severely limit the sexual act. Passionless sex became his counsel for married households, with lifelong virginity his ideal. By contrast, Jesus roamed the Galilee at a time when there was virtually no penetration of Hellenism. Even Sepphorus and Tiberias, where Jesus likely worked as a carpenter, were devoid of Greek cultural institutions and manifestations of Hellenist society. As a result, constraint on the sexual act was not a consideration in the land of Israel.

Interestingly, Aslan neglects to mention the role of pagan converts with no relationship to Jewish communities in the evolution of Christianity. Steeped in Hellenistic philosophies, these pagan converts believed there was a fundamental conflict between the evil body and the spiritual heart. The need to starve the body became the basis for promoting ascetic behaviors within the Christian movement. These men were not necessarily against Paul's equality project. Like Paul, they believed that gender equality could be achieved between celibate men and women. One such leader was Tatian. In his Asia Minor communities, women held leadership positions equal to men. He claimed:

> Only by demanding that men and women renounce the marriages that had previously held them together, and even by dissolving the ties that bound children to parents, could true Christians come

together in a freely chosen communion not undermined by preexisting family bonds, loyalties, and habits.[8]

Over the three centuries after Paul's death, there were many decisions that the Christian movement had to make as it was transformed from a small sect waiting for the end-time into a large institution that had to navigate the real world. Among many tasks, it had to select church officials who would replace traveling evangelists as spiritual leaders, choose its core texts, and make sure that married householders were not perceived as lesser Christians. As these topics are explored, we will realize the crucial role that ascetic behavior played; its centrality to understanding early Christianity is one story this book will tell.

THE JEWISH PROJECT

At the same time that Paul's converts were putting Christianity on the road to success, Judaism was in deep crisis. Responding to the increasing Roman intrusion into Temple practices, a rebellion arose in 66 CE. After four years of fighting, the Jewish rebels were defeated and the community suffered brutal reprisals. Tens of thousands of Jews died, the Great Temple was destroyed, and the majority of the priestly class was killed. A century earlier, the Israelites had lost their sovereignty and now they lost their central religious institution.

It cannot be overemphasized how important the Second Temple was to Jewish life. As Aslan noted,

> The Temple ... is the center of commerce for all Judea, its chief financial institution and largest bank. The Temple ... not only houses the sacred writings and scrolls of law that maintain the Jewish cult, it is the main repository for the legal documents, historical notes, and genealogical records of the Jewish nation.
>
> Unlike their heathen neighbors, the Jews do not have a multiplicity of temples scattered across the land. There is only one cultic center, one unique source of the divine presence, one singular place and no other where a Jew can commune with the living God.[9]

---

8. Brown, *Body & Society*, 89.
9. Aslan, *Zealot*, 7.

The Religious Setting

Without its two core pillars, it was unclear how Judaism could survive. Into the breach stepped the surviving Pharisee leadership. Escaping the ravages of the struggle in Jerusalem, its leader, Yohanan ben Zakkai, set up a religious academy in the coastal town of Yavneh, near present-day Tel Aviv. He was just as determined as Paul to put Judaism on a new footing. Far from the Jewish population centers in Judea, the first generation of rabbinic sages began to devise a strategy to move Jewish practices toward religious study in local academies and away from sacrificial offerings and holiday pilgrimages to the Jerusalem Temple.

Because they had neither communal stature nor manpower, their initial efforts were futile. It would take an even more devastating defeat—the second-century Bar Kochba revolt—to convince the Jewish people that they could not return to the old ways with an independent Judea once again anchored by a central temple.

In response to this second rebellion, the Roman governor leveled Jerusalem and forced the surviving population to disperse from its environs. The Jewish population in Palestine now numbered less than one million, whereas it had been 2.5 million before the destruction of the Second Temple. Migrating north, Jews made Galilee the center of their decimated, despondent community.

At this nadir of Judaism, the rabbinic sages moved their academies to the Galilee and slowly convinced the populace to embrace their revolutionary religious program. The Pharisees had long contended that when Moses received the written Torah at Mount Sinai, he also transmitted an Oral Torah that gave guidance to its applications. Now the sages began to compile competing and contrasting commentaries on the application of the Mosaic laws to a variety of actual and hypothetical situations, similar to what today is standard law school training. As we shall see, this work led ultimately to the production of the most important treatise for Orthodox Jews: the Babylonian Talmud.

Both the Pharisees and some of the leaders of the Palestinian sages embraced some ascetic behavior. Seizing on these examples, a few scholars find strong similarities to Christian asceticism. Eliezer Diamond contends that "extreme devotion to study and practice of Torah on the part of some of the rabbis resulted in self-denial indistinguishable behaviorally, *if not motivationally*, from that of the classic ascetic."[10] Michael Satlow claimed similarities to Greek-inspired asceticism:

---

10. Diamond, *Holy Men*, 12. Emphasis added.

> *Talmud torah* was the means by which the soul was made pure or whole, thus bringing the individual closer to the divine, or into the "spiritual condition." *Talmud torah* required the same mental and physical discipline demanded by the non-Jewish study of philosophy. Body and soul, working together in a disciplined (i.e., ascetic) fashion, can help a man overcome his evil inclination.[11]

Just as Paul prescribed to the Christian faithful, the second century Palestinian sage Rabbi Meir engaged in passionless sex with his wife, and another sage, Ben Azzai, was a lifelong virgin. David Biale suggests,

> Perhaps Ben Azzai, the one avowedly celibate rabbi, represented the tip of an ascetic iceberg. . . . Ben Azzai may have represented a real threat, a temptation that few followed but that had to be actively resisted.[12]

What these researchers ignore is that virtually all of the sages' ascetic practices reflected a deep sense of mourning following the death and destruction visited upon Palestinian Jewry. In Judaism, when a blood relative dies, mourners are required to desist from joyful behavior for a prescribed period. Mourning begins at the funeral where flowers are not allowed. During the first week—called the Shiva period—the mourner is required to stay within the confines of the house of mourning, sit on the ground or on a low stool, and refrain from engaging in business, work, Torah study, or marital intimacy.

For the rest of the first month, the mourner must refrain from taking a bath or shower for pleasure; using lotions, cosmetics, or perfumes; and cutting his or her hair. There are also prohibitions against wearing new clothes, buying a new home, and redecorating or purchasing new furniture. The mourner may not listen to music or go on pleasure trips, attend parties or wedding celebrations, send gifts, or get married. These restrictions extend for a year in the case of the death of a parent.

After the destruction of the Great Temple, some sages claimed, "It is forbidden for a person to fill his mouth with levity in this world."[13] Rabbi Meir adopted his behavior after witnessing the killing of his mentor, Rabbi Akiba, and of Meir's father-in-law during the Bar Kochba revolt. However, as Roman atrocities became a distant memory, joyfulness returned to the

---

11. Satlow, "You Shall Sleep," 213.

12. Biale, *Eros*, 35-36.

13. Friedman and Friedman, *God Laughed*, 108.

The Religious Setting

Palestinian Jewish community. While gluttony and opulence were frowned upon, by the middle of the third century a festive atmosphere dominated Jewish life. This return to a positive view of pleasure was reflected in the religious texts that were being compiled. Particularly as the more prosperous Babylonian community gained influence, the total rejection of ascetic practices was complete.

The Jewish marriage contract encourages lustful lovemaking by requiring that partners be unclothed: "One who says I do not desire it unless she is in her clothing, I in mine, must divorce his wife and pay her the marriage settlement."[14] Indeed, there was no recoil from romantic passion:

> One was wont to say: "When our love was intense, a bed the width of a blade was room enough for both of us to lie upon. Now that our love is less intense, a [king-size] bed the width of sixty cubits does not suffice."[15]

By the end of the fourth century, the contrast between Christian and Jewish attitudes toward bodily pleasures was transparent. It was aptly summed up in 386 by John Chrysostom, a popular Christian preacher. He accused Jews of bringing into their Antioch synagogue troupes of actors and dancers. He condemned the use of drums, lyres, harps, and other musical instruments, probably at weddings or Purim celebrations. Chrysostom warned his congregants of the dangers they presented:

> The festivals of the pitiful and miserable Jews are soon to march upon us one after the other and in quick succession . . . I am afraid that, because of their ill-suited association and deep ignorance, some Christians may partake in the Jews' transgressions . . . [When] the devil summons your wives to the feast of the Trumpets and they turn a ready ear to this call, [I fear] you will not restrain them [and] let them be dragged off into licentious ways. For, as a rule, it is the harlots, the effeminates, and the whole chorus from the theater who rush to that festival.[16]

---

14. Boyarin, *Carnal Israel*, 48.
15. Lichtenstein, "Of Marriage," 14.
16. John Chrysostom, *Eight Homilies Against the Jews*, I.I 4; I.IV 1; II.II 4, 5.

CONTEMPORARY RELEVANCE

The next eight chapters detail the background of Jewish renewal movements at the beginning of the Common Era, the emergence of Rabbinic Judaism and Christianity, and how these two movements evolved. By the end of the fourth century, the fundamental structures and scriptures of these two religions were in place, including deeply contrasting views on bodily pleasure and female sexuality.

Chapter 10 describes the evolution of Jewish and Christian ascetic beliefs from the fifth through the nineteenth century. Among Christians, there was an increased emphasize of Jesus' suffering. As a result, depictions of Christ on the cross were transformed during the medieval period from a triumphant to an emaciated figure. This new emphasis led many devout Christians to engage in acts of self-mortification and other ascetic practices, as well as spawning increased enmity towards those who killed Christ, the Jews.

Ascetic practices among Irish Catholics had always been more pronounced and it became even more so with a shifting from Benedictine to Cisterian practices among Irish monastic orders. This anti-pleasure stance was further strengthened in the eighteenth century by the training Irish priest received in France where the Jansenist movement was influential. By the second half of the nineteenth century, under the leadership of Cardinal Cullen, Catholicism in Ireland was steeped in ascetic behaviors that harkened back to the Augustinian era. These religious practices were brought to the United States in the last quarter of the century by the priests and nuns trained there.

The chapter also discusses the Jewish transition from the Middle East to Europe. By the sixth century, Babylonia had become the home of the majority of the Jewish population as their numbers in Palestine and the Mediterranean basin were decimated. Jewish communities in Babylonia prospered under Islamic rule, becoming urbanized and gaining leading commercial roles. As Islam spread, Jews followed their conquest to Europe where Jewish middlemen gained prominent positions in commercial enterprises, especially in Spain and Eastern Europe.

Christian anti-Semitism led to the Spanish expulsion and the Ukrainian massacres. These calamities led Jewish religious leadership to encourage mournful ascetic practices, similar to those embraced after the destruction of the Second Temple. During the eighteenth century, however, these practices in Eastern Europe were countered by the Hasidic movement that arose under the leadership of the Baal Shem Tov. It reinvigorated festive activities, particularly weddings and holiday celebrations; and was a catalyst for secular activities, including the dramatic growth of Yiddish theaters and popular music venues. Thus, by the end of the nineteenth century, Irish and Jewish immigrants to the New World once again had starkly contrasting views on bodily pleasure and female sexuality similar to earlier times.

Chapter 11 explores the impact on the twentieth century of these contrasting views, as well as the tensions between religious piety and concerns for social justice that were present at the beginning of the Common Era. As anti-pleasure beliefs came to again dominate Catholic teachings in the United States, it became increasingly difficult for Irish performers to enter or remain in commercial vaudeville. They were replaced by Jewish immigrants whose positive attitudes towards bodily pleasures and female sexuality enabled them to become star performers and venue owners. Similarly, Jewish movie moguls, by presenting anti-Victorian content, came to dominate the silent film industry at the expense of the Protestant monopoly lead by Thomas Edison.

In addition, during the twentieth century, both Catholic and Jewish organizations and activists reinvigorated social justice efforts that had been an important part of Jesus' ministry and the exhortations of the Jewish prophets. The activities of Dorothy Day in the 1930s and the US Council of Bishops in the 1980s exemplified these efforts. Similarly, Jewish philanthropists substantially funded black organizations in the 1920s, as well as educational and anti-lynching activities in the 1930s, while Jewish activists played an outsized role in subsequent civil rights efforts. Unfortunately, the chapter ends with a retreat from social justice concerns as substantial shares of both Christians and Jews have somewhat shifted their focus to religious piety.

The book concludes with a short chapter describing the origination in the 1930s of the concept of a Judeo-Christian tradition. While well-intentioned, during the postwar era it evolved into a chauvinistic narrative that had little to do with the complex role that religion has played in American society. In addition, the narrative deflected attention away from the substantial differences between the two religions or anti-Jewish behaviors that have sometimes been animated by broadly-held interpretations of Christian teachings.

2

Jewish Beliefs before the Common Era

AT THE BEGINNING OF the Common Era, Judaism was in crisis, generating a number of renewal movements, including Jesus' ministry and the Pharisees. However, before we explore the separate and contrasting paths chosen by these two groups, it is important to understand the legacy, traditions, and rituals of biblical Judaism, for in their own way, these new religion movements built upon them.

CONQUERING CANAAN—A SECULAR RENDITION

Judaism as an organized religion began a millennium before the Common Era. Central to Judaism is the exodus-from-Egypt narrative and the conquest of Canaan under the leadership of Joshua. Indeed, the Passover celebration, which commemorates the exodus, is perhaps Judaism's most valued ceremony. For both religiously observant and secular Jews, the Passover seder is the product of extensive preparation and is laden with symbolism.

While these foundational stories, as well as their attendant rituals, continue to have a profound effect on the beliefs and norms of Judaism, archaeological evidence suggests that they are legends with at most a kernel of verifiable historical truth. It is certainly possible, if not probable, that a core group had endured severe oppression. However, no archaeological findings have evidenced a massive slave revolt in Egypt or a military conquest of Canaan. Indeed, excavations have found that most of the sites listed among

Joshua's conquests were abandoned over a long period, and almost none reveal signs of military conquest.

Regarding the fall of Jericho, the Bible recounts that the family of the woman who hid Joshua's spies was saved but that Joshua's armies "exterminated everything in the city by the sword; man and woman, young and old, ox and sheep and ass" (Josh 6:21). Next, they conquered Ai:

> Joshua did not draw back . . . until all the inhabitants of Ai had been exterminated . . . and the body of the king of Ai was hanged on a gallows . . . Then Joshua burned down Ai and turned it into a mound of ruins for all time. (Josh 8:26-29)

Excavations did indeed uncover a mound of ruins on the site of Ai, but the pottery and other artifacts are from a time well before Israelite settlement, as is the case with similar objects found at Jericho. Only at Hazor has evidence consistent with the Joshua narrative been found. There, the city was apparently destroyed suddenly, and its ruins can be dated to roughly the time of Israelite entry into Canaan.

Defenders of the veracity of the Biblical narrative have pointed to the Hazor ruins even though that site presents virtually the only one of Joshua's conquests that is consistent with archaeological excavations. Moreover, the Joshua narrative stands in substantial conflict with the material in the book of Judges, wherein the Israelites are described as being unable to conquer many of the Judean cities. It is noted that the Israelites "took possession of the hill country; but they were not able to dispossess the inhabitants of the plain, for they had iron chariots" (Judg 1:19). Elsewhere, Judges (1:29) lists numerous cities where the Israelites "did not dispossess the Canaanites . . . so they dwelt in their midst."

While the narratives consistently claim the Canaanites had to perform forced labor, Judges strongly suggests that the alleged Israelite conquests were much more limited, less violent toward the Canaanites, and more contested. (See Judg 1:26-35). Most telling, Judges laments what transpired in the next generation:

> The Israelites did what was offensive to the Lord. They worshiped the Baalim and forsook the Lord. They followed other gods, from among the gods of the peoples around them, and bowed down to them. (Judg 2:11-12)

Archaeological evidence indicates that during the relevant time period—1300 to 1100 BCE—there was a large and continued influx of settlers to the Judean highlands. A growing number of small, self-sufficient communities formed on previously uninhabited land. These settlements can be classified as nascent Israelite communities, because, unique to their surroundings, they contained no pig bones.

In the sturdy walled Canaanite cities we find splendid homes filled with fine art and pottery. By contrast, proto-Israelite settlements were on the most inferior land and contained the most primitive pottery and household implements. This suggests that they were poor and marginalized, not what would be expected of conquerors. Moreover, the lack of fortification around settlements further suggests a peaceful integration of Israelites into the Canaanite landscape. Finally, an arriving group intermingling with the indigenous population is consistent with the presentation in Judges.

Several alternatives to the Joshua narratives have been proposed during the twentieth century to explain the advent of these new communities. The two most prominent are the "peaceful integration theory," proposed by Albrecht Alt and Yohanan Aharoni, and the "peasant revolt theory," developed independently by George Mendenhall and Norman Gottwald. The peaceful integration theory contends that pastoral tribes roamed the sparsely populated highlands of western Canaan. At some point, they formed permanent settlements and started to produce food staples instead of trading for them. The housing pattern of the earliest settlements seems to mimic the style associated with formerly pastoral communities.

By contrast, Mendenhall and Gottwald contend that these early Israelite settlements were populated by a displaced urban and peasant underclass. At the time, Canaanite city-states were highly stratified, comprising extreme inequalities. Local rulers depended upon support from Egypt. The thirteenth century BCE Amarna letters describe both the tribute paid to Egypt in slaves and concubines as well as the mistreatment of the communities under royal control. Archaeological evidence, including burial sites, shows the concentration of impressive wealth and status symbols in the hands of a very few. The Amarna letters also note a group of outsiders, the Apiru, who would rob the elite and flee into uninhabited areas, somewhat in the manner of Robin Hood and his Merry Men. These Apiru are generally identified as Hebrews. In a letter to the Egyptian court, one Canaanite prince wrote:

> Let the king, my lord, learn that the chief of the Apiru has risen against the land which the god of the king, my lord gave me . . . it is I and Abdu-Heba who fight against the chief of the Apiru. And

Jewish Beliefs before the Common Era

Zurata, prince of Accho, and Indaruta, prince of Achshaph, it was they who hastened with fifty chariots—for I had been robbed by the Apiru—to my help. [1]

These letters were written just when Canaanite city-states were beginning to collapse. Trade throughout the Mediterranean basin and agricultural production within Canaan were evidently declining. The once-powerful myths of religion found in Canaanite texts no longer seemed credible in the face of overwhelming challenges from the declining economy and the increasing oppression that the populace faced. In response to this crisis, Mendenhall argues that the Apiru, together with displaced peasants, initiated the first Israelite settlements in the Judean highlands.

The Biblical wilderness narrative and the presence of goat and sheep but not pork bones strongly suggest that some pastoralists were part of the early settlements. However, the rapid expansion of the highland settlements over the eleventh century BCE cannot be completely explained by pastoralists shifting to a sedentary life. Moreover, the farming technology used required prior agricultural experience, and the pottery styles are consistent with those found in urban Canaan.

Both theories do agree that this nascent Israelite community eventually rose up militarily and was triumphant only after it destroyed Hazor. This violent confrontation, however, is much more consistent with the peasant revolt explanation than with the peaceful integration theory. The central role that the Bible places on support for the underclass in its conflict with elites also favors the theory of a peasant revolt led by the Apiru.

The Old Testament highlights the concern for the poor and dispossessed in a number of ways. For example, it requires land-owners not to harvest a portion of their crops, which could be picked by the poor. It also requires the designation of cities of refuge for the protection of individuals from the retribution of families whose kin the refugees had killed inadvertently.

Judaism is considered the first religion to have a single, all-powerful God. This characterization may be true, but is at best incomplete. What may be more revolutionary about Judaism is the way in which people had to serve this God. In virtually all other contemporary religions, the way to curry favors and benefits from the gods was by making sacrifices to them. Indeed, the willingness of Abraham to sacrifice his son Isaac reflected the "old" ways of serving one's god. The Jewish God's rejection of this most

---

1. Dever, *Early Israelites*, 171.

valuable offering, however, relegated sacrifices to a symbolic level at important celebrations and in the Holy Temple.

Just as with early Christianity, there were various existing narratives. In the case of Christianity, there were many gospels, of which four were included in the New Testament. Critical textual analysis, begun by German Christians in the nineteenth century, identified four distinct writing styles in the Old Testament. Just as with the gospels, sometimes there are conflicting accounts, as we have already seen with the contrasting presentations in the books of Joshua and Judges.

RELIGIOUS BELIEFS DURING THE FIRST TEMPLE PERIOD

The Old Testament tells us that Canaan had been the home of the first three patriarchs—Abraham, Isaac, and Jacob. When the Israelites resettled Canaan after the exodus from Egypt, it was divided among twelve tribes, each named for one of Jacob's sons. This new religious formation sought the liberation of individual men from tyranny and voiced the responsibility of society to care for the less fortunate.

The fear of all-powerful rulers remained. Facing external threats, we are told, the tribes beseeched the prophet Samuel to appoint a king. Reflecting these fears, he forewarned:

> This will be the practice of the king who will rule over you: He will take your sons and appoint them as his charioteers and horsemen, and ... they will have to plow his fields ... He will take daughters as perfumers, cooks, and bakers. He will seize your choice fields and vineyards. He will take a tenth part of your grain. He will take your male and female slaves and your choice young men, and your asses, and put them to work for him. He will take a tenth part of your flocks and you shall become his slaves. The day will come when you cry out because of the king whom you yourselves have chosen. (ISam 8:11-18)

Whatever the origins of the Israelite communities in Canaan, by 1000 BCE the Jewish state was formed and Saul had been anointed king, to be followed by David, whose son Solomon built the First Temple in Jerusalem. The Bible detailed the splendor of Solomon's sumptuous court:

> Provision for one day was thirty cors of fine flour [about 335 bushels] and sixty cors of meal, ten fat oxen and twenty pasture-fed

cattle, a hundred sheep, besides harts, gazelles, roebucks, and fatted fowl. (1 Kgs 4:22-23)

No longer pastoral, the vast majority of Israelites were engaged in agricultural endeavors. After tending their fields and orchards, most went home to towns that lay in the orbit of fortified cities. Just as Samuel had forewarned, Solomon confiscated a portion of production to support his lifestyle and public works projects. As a result, these agriculturalists generally lived in tightly spaced houses that offered only small family living areas with virtually no furniture.

Unlike Solomon, most Israelites had a basic diet dominated by cooked wheat and barley. Meat was only included on festive occasions. The housewife would grind the grain into cakes that she would garnish with lentils, cucumbers, and other vegetables. Fresh and dried fruit sweetened the meals. From the beginning, Israelite communities abstained from pork. On the infrequent occasions when meat was consumed, it was either lamb or poultry.

Samuel's forewarning also signaled a tension between those voices that emphasized religious piety and those that emphasized solving societal inequities. A focus on religious piety was understandable during the First Temple period, since the Israelites had not fully freed themselves from pagan gods. These deviations were the result of the initial decentralization of religious activity. Shrines and altars existed throughout Judea and sacrifices to the God of Israel could be offered anywhere.

In 622 BCE, King Josiah "discovered" the book of Deuteronomy that contained the Mosaic laws. Until then, only the Ten Commandants were known. Now the full *mitzvot* (guiding principles) to lead an ethical live, generally numbered at 613, were available. There was no immediate attempt, however, to translate these requirements into behavioral changes that would affect Jewish daily life. For example, one of the principles is "do not cook a kid in its mother's milk" (Deut 14:21). As we shall see, this came to mean that you could not eat meat and dairy products together and this affected the cooking and eating utensils used. Religious regulations over the purity of utensils and the separation of meat and dairy products, however, would have to wait almost a millennium. Even the maintaining of the Sabbath had not been regularized. Thus, the religiosity of the Israelites was much more limited than it would become in the Common Era.

Instead, Josiah used the discovery of the scroll to begin undertaking a series of reforms. He centralized religious practices by decreeing that now the only place to make sacrifices was at the Temple in Jerusalem. Just as important, he turned the nation away from widespread idolatrous practices. An emerging reformist party exhorted the nation to repent. It was led by the rural prophet Jeremiah, who expressed God's displeasure:

> What fault did your ancestors find in me, that they strayed so far from me? They followed worthless idols and became worthless themselves," declares the Lord. (Jer 2:5)

Jeremiah proclaimed that if Israel did not repent, the nation would face famine and be plundered and taken captive by foreigners who would exile the people:

> And when your people say, "Why has the Lord our God done all these things to us?" you shall say to them, "As you have forsaken me and served foreign gods in your land, so you shall serve foreigners in a land that is not yours." (Jer 5:19)

Only after Jeremiah resided in Jerusalem, where he witnessed gaping inequities, did he see more than religious deviations. When the king used forced labor (as Samuel had forewarned), Jeremiah condemned him:

> Woe unto him that buildeth his home by unrighteousness,
> And his chambers by injustice;
> That useth his neighbour's service without wages. (Jer 22:13)

The stress on regaining religious piety was even more pronounced in the teachings of Ezekiel, another rural prophet. With very graphic metaphorical flourish, he deplored the ungratefulness of the Israelites to the Lord: "You took your beautiful things, made of the gold and silver that I had given you, and you made yourself phallic images and fornicated with them" (Ezra 16:8-22). Unlike Jeremiah, however, Ezekiel never focused on unequal human relations. As the biblical scholar Louis Finkelstein concluded, "Ezekiel, the rural prophet, knew but one manner of loyalty to YHWH, being devoted to His sole worship; he knew but one sin, the worship of idols. Nothing else mattered."[2]

In contrast to these rural prophets, Finkelstein pointed to the urban-based prophets and their shepherd allies, who saw more clearly the unethical social relationships between the powerful and the powerless. The most important representative of such prophets was Isaiah. Though from aristocratic origins, Isaiah grew up in Jerusalem and witnessed the struggles

---

2. Finkelstein, *Pharisees*, 325.

between rich and poor. He relentlessly attacked greed and oppression, condemning the wealthy:

> It is ye who have ravaged the vineyard;
> That which was robbed from the poor is in your houses.
> How dare ye crush My people,
> And grind the face of the poor? (Isa 3:14-15)

He also condemned those who manipulated the legal system for their personal gain:

> To rob of their rights the needy of My people;
> That widows may be their spoil,
> And fatherless children their booty! (Isa 10:1-2)

These differences among the three major prophets—Isaiah, Jeremiah, and Ezekiel—were also present among the minor prophets. The shepherd prophet Amos railed against the wealthy: "[They] sell the righteous for silver, and the needy for a pair of shoes.... For they know not to do right, sayeth the Lord, who store up violence and robbery in their palaces" (Amos 2:6, 3:10). By contrast, the rural prophets Hosea and Nahum focused solely on religious piety.

THE BABYLONIAN EXILE

The contrast between Ezekiel and Jeremiah grew as Judah faced the Babylonian threat. In around 604 BCE, Judah became a vassal state to Babylonia. Whereas the pious nationalists led by Ezekiel favored fighting against this arrangement, Jeremiah sought to accommodate Babylonia. When King Jehoiakim sided with the nationalists, Jeremiah was jailed and threatened with death.

Believing that Egypt would support an independent Judah, Jehoiakim miscalculated and revoked his vassal treaty with Babylonia. King Nebuchadnezzar decided to make an example of Judah and personally led a campaign that resulted in Jehoiakim's death and the taking of his son, Jehoiachin, as a captive back to Babylonia with thousands of other Judeans. When the installed King Zedekiah rebelled, Nebuchadnezzar destroyed the First Temple and took even more captives, including the prophet Ezekiel.

Nebuchadnezzar's actions were not meant to destroy Yahweh, only the nationalist sentiment. Indeed, he appointed the Judean Gedaliah to administer Judah, and Jeremiah chose to stay in order to help rebuild the society that remained in Israel. At the time of the destruction of the First Temple, probably one-quarter of the 80,000 Judeans were taken captive. Another one-quarter had dispersed, leaving about 40,000 Jews remaining in Judah.[3]

Gedaliah's primary goal was to provide bread and jobs for the remaining population as quickly as possible. He had the complete support of the Babylonians, who assigned to the poor the abandoned property of the departed upper and middle classes. Gedaliah also expressly approved the occupation—by force if necessary—of the deserted villages by groups of refugees returning to Judah from neighboring lands.

This extraordinary and controversial redistribution of property provoked outrage among the exiled former owners as voiced by Ezekiel (Ezra 11:14-21; 33:23-29). It is likely that Gedaliah saw this redistribution as the biblical social justice that the reform party had fought for during the reign of Josiah. Thus, Gedaliah's supporters saw the breakdown of the structures of national government and deportations as a great opportunity to establish a more egalitarian society.[4]

Gedaliah's reforms lasted only a few years as he was killed in 582 BCE by a disgruntled former army officer from a royal family. This led to more Judeans being taken into captivity and the house arrest of Jehoiachin, who would not be released for another twenty years. The yoke on the Jewish remnants in Judah hardened and this increasingly oppressive situation is captured in Lamentations 5:

> We have become orphans, without fathers;
> our mothers are like widows.
> We pay money to drink our own water,
> our own wood comes at a price.
> With a yoke on our necks, we are driven
> we are worn out, but allowed no rest.
> Our skin heats up like an oven,
> from the searing blasts of famine.
> Women are raped in Zion,
> young women in the cities of Judah.

---

3. Albertz, *Israel in Exile*, 90.
4. Ibid., 92.

Jewish Beliefs before the Common Era

The most remarkable aspect of the Babylonian conquest, however, was its impact on Jewish religiosity. After King Solomon's death in 931 BCE, ten of the twelve tribes rejected his successor and split away, forming the Northern Kingdom of Israel. As it was located on important trade routes, the Northern Kingdom was desirable and was conquered by the Assyrians in 732 BCE. The victors captured the most influential members of the Jewish community and took them back to the Assyrian capital. All evidence suggests that these captives fully assimilated into their new environment and their ties to Judaism were entirely lost. By contrast, Jewish religiosity was strengthened among the exilic community in Babylon.

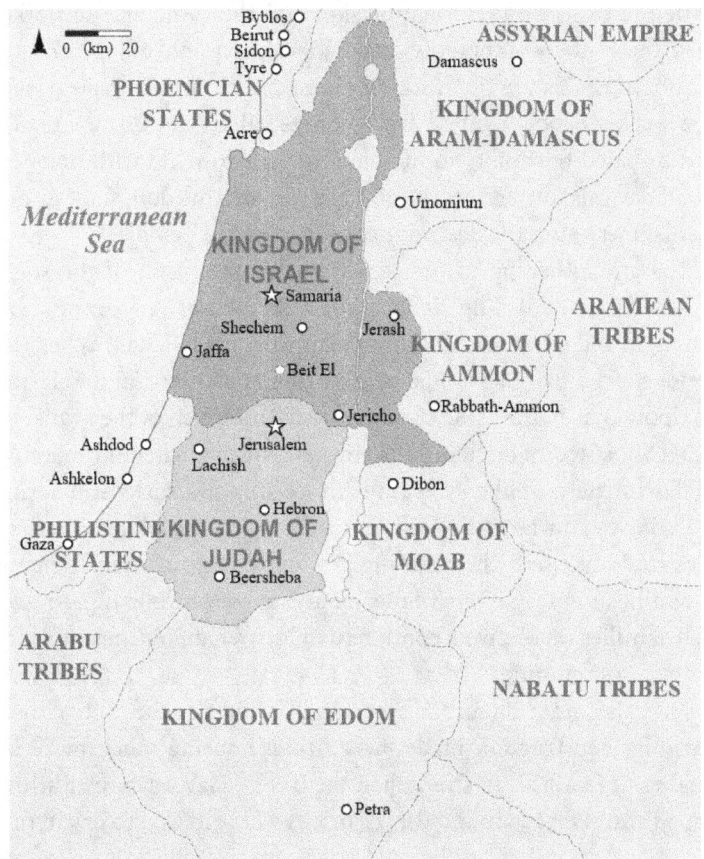

Figure 2.1: Israel and Judah, 9th c. BCE

In part, this reflected the extraordinary efforts of the Jewish prophets in Babylonia, most especially Ezekiel. It is likely, however, that the key factor was timing. When the Assyrians carted off the defeated Jews, Northern Kingdom Judaism was predominantly a temple cult. That is, it focused almost exclusively on ritual obligations performed at its temples. Moreover, Northern Kingdom Judaism had not decisively rejected other gods as its temples were often adorned with symbols of the god of fertility, Baal.

The situation was dramatically different when the religious and economic elite were transported to Babylonia. King Josiah's reform movement had successfully suppressed the worship of other gods, especially among the elites. Just as important, the discovery of the full set of Mosaic laws gave the exilic community a means of worship other than temple rituals.

Before exile, besides circumcision and the avoidance of pork, there were virtually no forms of individual behavior required of Judeans. At most, the Sabbath rituals were performed once each month. In exile, observance of the weekly Sabbath now became universal, as did dietary regulations that eliminated the ability to maintain table fellowship with non-Jews. As we shall see, this turn to the Mosaic laws was also the dominant response of religious Jewry after the destruction of the Second Temple.

The strengthening of Judaism was also the result of the somewhat sympathetic views of King Nebuchadnezzar. He was very accommodating to Jeremiah and to Jehoiachin until the murder of Gedaliah. When the Jewish refugees came to Babylonia, he gave them parcels of land to farm.

Upon arrival, the exilic community found much of the available rural housing consisted of circular huts covered with thatch and cemented with mud. Fortunately, unlike in Judea with its hills and rocky soil, farming in Babylonia was on large flat spaces where primitive ploughs rather than spades could be used. The resulting productivity gains enabled many Israelite families to escape harsh housing and subsistence living. In addition, Jewish families were given contiguous plots, enabling them to maintain close-knit communities.

Jews also moved to urban areas. In Babylon and the other cities, brick rectangular construction made basic urban housing much more accommodating to families. To strengthen the bricks, clay was mixed with finely chopped straw. Placed in molds, the bricks were allowed to dry in the open air.[5]

This method had its pitfalls. Dried bricks can shrivel when exposed to prolonged heat and disintegrate during flooding. Baked bricks are much longer lasting but the baking process requires fuel. Since fuel was expensive,

---

5. Contenau, *Everyday Life*.

baked bricks were only used to build the homes of the more prosperous Babylonians. Fortunately, Jewish refugees faced little discrimination so a large number of them were able to provide services to the wealthy Babylonians, enabling them to rise above poor urban laborers. Indeed, some even came to hold important government positions. Thus, many of the refugees, particularly the next generation, were able to attain prosperous positions in a society in which they faced few impediments because of their religion.

RETURN OF THE EXILES

In 539 BCE, King Cyrus of Persia conquered Babylonia. One of his first acts was to allow Jews to return to Palestine. At the time of the return, Jerusalem was a small town of about 1,500 inhabitants. It was the only true urban site in Judea; the bulk of the province's population lived in small unwalled villages.

The first wave of returnees was led by Sheshbazzar, who very well may have been the grandson of the late King Jehoiachin. He, however, had faded from the narrative by the time the Second Temple was completed twenty years later. Instead, Israel was governed by a Sanhedrin, an assembly of seventy elders and religious leaders who decided civil and religious cases.

While they still sustained a strong allegiance to the Jewish faith and the centrality of the Jerusalem Temple, half of the exiles chose to remain in Babylonia. It is likely that those who stayed had become more prosperous while returnees were disproportionately poor. A millennium later, this prosperous Babylonian community provided a lifeline to a beleaguered Palestinian Jewish community.

Gender imbalance was an unintended consequence of the return, leading many of the poorest Jewish men to marry women from the surrounding Palestinian communities. Intermarriage was also practiced by the priesthood. When Ezra came to lead the Jewish community in 458 BCE, he was outraged by this practice and demanded that Jewish men abandon their non-Jewish wives. He was opposed not only by the general populace but also by the prophet Malachi. After all, Ezra's demand contradicted the book of Ruth, which defended the marriage of Israelites to Moabite women. As gender balance emerged in succeeding generations, the need for marriage to outsiders was eliminated.

Most important for future developments, Ezra instituted public Torah readings, which took Torah study out of the exclusive hands of the priestly class, enabling Jewish writers who were neither priests nor prophets to produce works on religious issues. These included the books of Daniel and Job, and the writings of Ben Sira. Second Temple Judaism became a religion of the book, so that there was a canonization of texts, resulting in the Tanakh, the Old Testament Bible.

Ezra's actions also created the potential for a new type of authority figure—the scribe, whose stature was derived neither from pedigree and institutional affiliation (like the priests) nor from charismatic personality who had direct contact with God (like the prophets). Rather, it was derived from knowledge of the sacred scriptures and traditions.

The position of the scribe was elevated by Simeon the Righteous, the leader of the priestly class at the time of Alexander the Great. "The spiritual world," he said, "depended upon three things: Torah, ritual, and acts of loving-kindness."[6] By placing the study of Torah before rituals, Simeon strengthened the position of the scribes, who then became members of the Sanhedrin. The Jewish community, however, remained under the leadership of the priestly class. It eventually became dominated by a faction known as the Sadducees and increasingly reflected the interests of the wealth-owning class. The Sadducees tried to shape writings to emphasize religious piety and minimize concerns for social inequities.

FOREIGN DOMINATION AND THE MACCABEE REVOLT

After Alexander the Great died in 323 BCE, his empire was divided among his senior generals. Ptolemy was given Egypt and the surrounding area, including Judea. While the imprint of Hellenism began, Ptolemy had little interest in the Jewish backwater. The Ptolemaic dynasty allowed Jews to manage their own affairs, without significant intervention. Leadership continued to reside with the high priest, as is found in an account written around 300 BCE: "The Jews never have a king, and authority over the people is regularly vested in whichever priest is regarded as superior to his colleagues in wisdom and virtue."[7]

After the death of Ptolemy IV in 205 BCE, the Seleucid regime sought to spread south and successfully invaded Egyptian territory. Its leader, Antiochus III, captured Jerusalem after a series of battles that severely

---

6. Pirke Avot 1:2.

7. *Diodorus Siculus*, 40.3.1-40.3.3, referenced in Grabbe, *A History of Judaism*, 35.

damaged the community, including the Temple. He looked favorably on improving conditions, facilitating resettlement by giving a three-year tax exemption and allowing a reduced rate thereafter. He exempted from the toll tax all materials imported for restoration of the Temple. Antiochus III also exempted the priests and all Temple personnel from taxation.

At the time, the Seleucid regime was spreading Hellenistic culture throughout its empire. It reached Judea in 175 BCE, under efforts of the high priest Jason and the new Seleucid ruler, Antiochus IV. Greek-style athletic activities began and a gymnasium and men's club (*ephebrion*) were built where the Jewish elite could educate their sons to the Greek ways. Jason was seeking a way for Jews to live within the wider Hellenistic world without abandoning the age-old traditions of Israel.

After Menelaus replaced Jason, many among the wealth-owning class embraced Greek culture. They introduced foreign deities into the Temple, setting off conflicts among Jerusalemite Jews. Antiochus IV chose to quell the unrest by persecuting the forces opposed to Menelaus. In addition, in 167 BCE, he rescinded the extensive rights of religious freedom decreed by Antiochus III. Moreover, we are told, "throughout Palestine, the Sabbath and festivals were to be violated, outdoor shrines were built where unclean animals were to be offered, circumcision was outlawed, and the dietary laws could not be observed."[8]

When the Jerusalem priestly class equivocated, a rural Jewish priest, Mattathias sparked a revolt against the Seleucid Empire. He refused to worship the Greek gods and killed a Hellenistic Jew who then stepped forward to offer a sacrifice. Mattathias and his five sons fled to the Judean wilderness. After Mattathias's death in 166 BC, his son Judah Maccabee led an army of Jewish dissidents.

At first their efforts were directed against Hellenized Jews. The Maccabees destroyed pagan altars in the villages, and circumcised boys. After two years of fighting, the Maccabees were victorious. In 165 BCE, the Temple was liberated and consecrated so that ritual sacrifices could begin again. The festival of Hanukkah was instituted by Judah Maccabeus and his brothers to celebrate this event (1 Macc 4:59).

Jerusalem grew in size, population, and wealth. Pilgrimages to the city intensified, drawing an influx of people from both home and abroad. A merchant class and others to serve these visitors increased its residential population. City limits expanded and the government built new fortifications,

---

8. Schiffman, *Maccabean Revolt*, 3.

palaces, and institutions. For the first time, Jerusalem came to reflect its status as a national capital.

While Jerusalem may have become more prosperous, the conflict with the Seleucids brought to the fore questions of God's attitude toward the faithful. Throughout the Old Testament, God provided a bountiful land and guidance, through the Mosaic laws, on how to conduct a moral life. While he might intervene to aid the survival of the Israelites, more often he is a vengeful God, punishing Jews for their transgressions. Prophets pronounced that the Babylonian captivity occurred because the Israelites had forsaken their one God. During Antiochus IV's rule, however, it was the pious Jews who were oppressed without an expectation of an afterlife. This situation troubled many of the faithful.

Ancient Hebrews had no idea of an immortal soul living a full life beyond death, nor of any resurrection or return from death. Human beings, like the beasts of the field, are made of "dust of the earth," and at death they return to that dust (Gen 2:7; 3:19). When faced with injustices, the prophets did not counsel the Israelites to take comfort that they would be in God's hands in the afterlife. Instead, the prophets wished a Messiah would bring peace and justice to earthly existence.

The book of Ecclesiastes was written well before Seleucid rule. Like the prophets, it voiced outrage at the senseless abuse that humankind experienced. Its author, Koheleth, grieves at the idea of the wicked flourishing while the righteous are afflicted. He comes to the conclusion that men are not judged in this world as he had previously hoped. After reaching a point of despair, Ecclesiastes opens the door to the possibility of an afterlife:

> Man's fate is like that of the animals; the same fate awaits them both: As one dies, so dies the other.... All go to the same place; all come from dust, and to dust all return. *Who knows if the spirit of man rises upward* [emphasis added] and if the spirit of the animal goes down into the earth? (Eccl 3:19-21)

This equivocation, however, disappears in the last section, Ecclesiastes 12, which many scholars believe was added by a religious writer soon after the Seleucid tyranny. In it, we find an expectation of an afterlife: "man goeth to his long home, and the mourners go about the street." Even more supportive, Ecclesiastes states, "And the dust returneth to the earth as it was, and the spirit returneth unto God who gave it."

The existence of an afterlife gained legitimacy among religious leaders and eventually became universally accepted. The successful Maccabean revolt, however, did not resolve the tensions between the goals of religious piety and economic equality. Nor did it sustain long-term freedom from foreign control. As a result, within a century, Jewish renewal movements arose in response to the religious and economic crises. This is the subject of the next chapter.

3

Jewish Renewal Movements at the Beginning of the Common Era

From the mid-second to the mid-first century BCE, Israel was once again an independent state, ruled by successive representatives of the Maccabean family. Even when Rome defeated the state of Israel in 63 BCE, it chose to appoint Jewish administrators. The most important, Herod the Great, administered Judea from 37 BCE until his death in 4 CE.

Considering himself "King of the Jews," Herod was vengeful and ruthless toward those who were a threat to his rule. He could, however, be sympathetic to Jewish interests. When Israel experienced hunger and disease after a drought, he imported grain from Egypt and waived one-third of the taxes. Later, he supported the Jews in Anatolia and Cyrene (present-day Libya). Most of all, he completely rebuilt the Second Temple in Jerusalem.

While there was not universal support for Herod, he was tolerated as long as he seemed to promote Jewish interests. However, after the death of Herod's son, Archelaus, the Jewish people lost complete trust in the Roman governors. Instead, many turned to the priestly class, whom they believed were the true leaders of the Jewish people.

The priestly class held only a fragile leadership position. During the two centuries before the Common Era, the land of Israel experienced bitter intra-Jewish factionalism. There developed an intolerable discrepancy between the ideals of God's rule of justice and the oppressive rule of native high priests in collaboration with the wealth-owning class. As a result, new religious movements questioned the legitimacy of the Jewish Temple leaders.

In the Psalms of Solomon, a distinction is made between those who live by the Mosaic laws and sinners who (in the eyes of the devout) compromised religious dictates for personal gain.[1] This intra-Jewish conflict is present in *The Wisdom of Ben Sira*, a second-century BCE collection of ethical teachings. Ben Sira counseled readers on the duties of man toward others, especially in view of the increasing gulf between the rich and the poor:

> How should there be peace between hyena and dog?
> How should there be peace between rich and poor?
> Wild asses of the wilderness are food for the lion:
> So the poor are the prey of the rich.[2]

Apocalyptic visions offered world-weary individuals a means of resolving the tension between brilliant hopes and bleak realities: a glorious future through the resurrection of the dead and the coming of the Messiah to rescue His people.[3] Major themes included an emphasis on personal piety, reward and punishment, resurrection, immortality and the Messiah. These ideas encouraged some to form separate communities so that they could better prepare themselves for the apocalypse.

Becoming a cornerstone of Jewish hopes for a better future, many in the Jewish renewal movements pointed to the proclamations in Isaiah:

> And the almighty Yahweh will prepare for all the nations on this mountain a banquet of the best foods and the finest wines. And on this mountain he will swallow up death forever. And the Lord Yahweh will wipe clean the tears from upon all faces. He will remove the reproach of His people from upon all the earth. For Yahweh has spoken. (Isa 25:6-8)

While the righteous remnant of Israel will enjoy the bountiful provisions of the messianic age, the enemies of Israel will be destroyed.

Despite these tensions, the center of Jewish religious life remained the Great Temple in Jerusalem. All Jews were expected to give a half shekel

1. Dunn, *Jesus Remembered*, 283.
2. *The Wisdom of Ben Sira*, chapter 13, 18-19.
3. Hanson, *Dawn of Apocalyptic*, 30.

annually for its support. Diaspora Jewish communities set up banking centers to collect these funds. In Babylonia, two cities were designated as collection centers. Periodically the monies would be transported to the Holy Land in guarded caravans. At least once, Herod relocated a military contingent to provide protection.

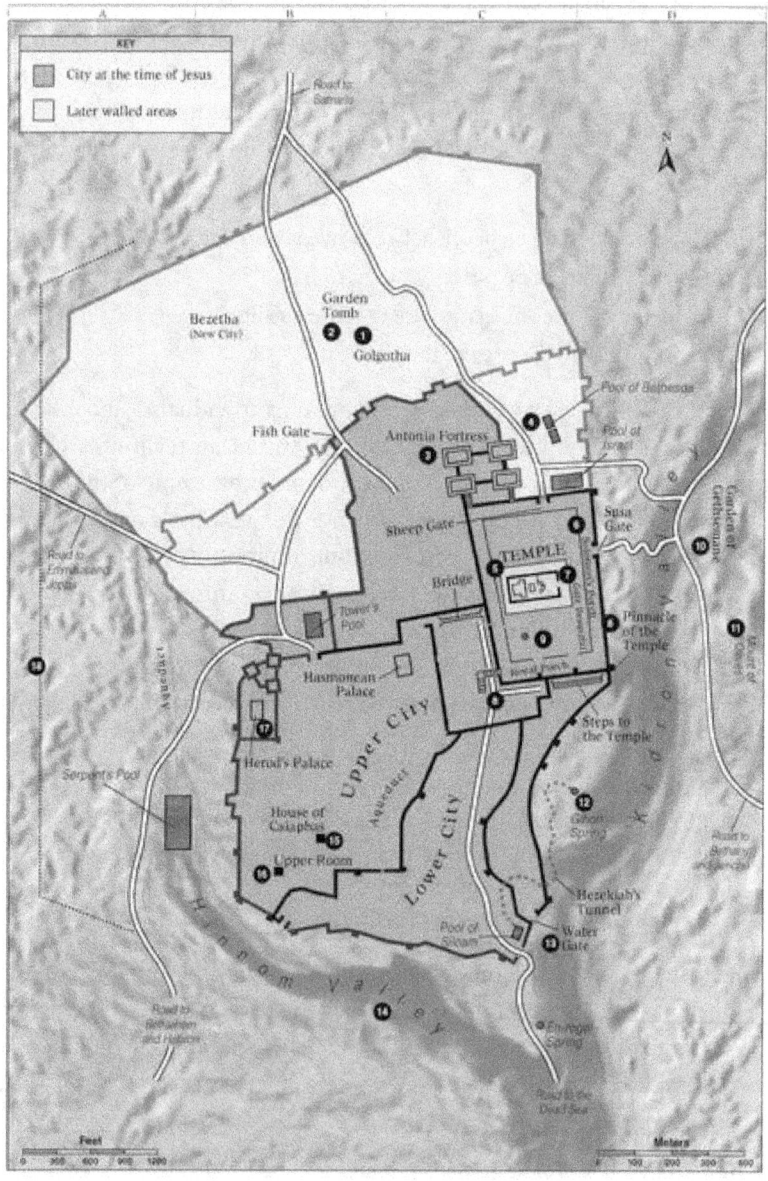

Figure 3.1: Jerusalem at the time of Jesus

Jewish Renewal Movements at the Beginning of the Common Era

These donations helped pay for the maintenance of the Temple, the purchase of animals for the required daily offerings, renovation of the city walls and towers, upkeep of the water supply system, and other municipal needs. It also provided generous payments to the priestly class, particularly its senior members. In addition, there was a widely held tradition for the Judean farming community to "bring their first fruits to Jerusalem annually, a ritual often accompanied by pomp and ceremony."[4]

Figure 3.2: Model of Second Temple, 1st Century CE

4. Levine, *Jerusalem*, 248.

Huge numbers of pilgrims, perhaps as many as a half million, filled the city streets during the thrice-annual pilgrimages: at Passover to celebrate the exodus; at Shavuot to celebrate Moses giving the Torah; and at Sukkot to commemorate the forty years in the wilderness before entering the land of Israel. One of the leaders of Alexandrian Jewry, Philo, noted:

> For innumerable companies of men from a countless variety of cities, some by land and some by sea, from east and from west, from the north and from the south, came to the Temple at every festival.[5]

By the first century, a growing number of Jews began to observe the Mosaic laws, in particular the separation of meat and dairy products. This required the thorough cleaning of utensils and earthenware after meat use before they could be used for dairy. These laws of purity, however, were suspended at the pilgrimages in order to enable unconstrained transactions of goods and services. To discourage exploitation of the visitors, the local population was exhorted to exhibit generous hospitality, including food and lodging. Indeed, landlords were forbidden to charge money for lodging and instead were compensated by the hides of animals sacrificed at the Temple.[6]

The Temple was pyramid-shaped, with a series of tiered courtyards. The first and largest was open to all and was where the faithful purchased offerings. Only Jews with their offerings could ascend to the next smaller courtyard, where oils and wood for the sacrifices were stored. Only males climbed one courtyard further, where the faithful handed over their offerings to priests who would take them to the sacred altar. Not surprisingly, the slaughters taking place on the uppermost courtyard created a foul atmosphere. Even the use of sweet-smelling incense did not mask the insufferable stench.

Only priests and Temple officials entered the last of the tiered courtyards, where the offering were prepared for sacrifice. The priests carefully dismembered the carcasses so that the prime meats and hide could be taken away for the enrichment of the Temple staff. The remains were then carried up a ramp to be placed on the eternal fire.

Next to the eternal fire was the Holy of Holies—a gold-plated sanctuary. It had previously housed the Ark of the Covenant containing the

---

5. Philo, *Special Laws*, 1:69.
6. Levine, *Jerusalem*, 250.

commandments of God. Following this tradition, in the front of every present-day synagogue is an ark that houses a Torah scroll. After the Ark was lost, however, the Temple sanctuary remained empty and assumed a purely symbolic role as the place where the spirit of God resided.

Jewish renewal movements were in opposition to the priestly class and its leaders, the Sadducees, who could trace their lineage back to King David. They saw themselves alone as protectors of the Mosaic covenant, the "sons of light," the "house of perfection and truth in Israel," the chosen ones.[7] Many renewal movements preached in the Galilean countryside, including the *haberim* and Pharisees.

The *haberim* wanted to sanctify the entirety of life, to make common life as holy as the Temple, filled with the presence of God. They agreed to handle, sell, and eat food in virtually the same state of purity as that which the Bible prescribes for the priests who serve in the Temple.[8] However, the *haberim* were solely focused on their own rigorous observation of the laws, which they did not believe the masses should follow.

Unlike the *haberim*, the Pharisees believed that the masses should also be expected to strictly observe these religious requirements. In addition, the Pharisees formed a political party that sought to seize control of the religious affairs of the Jewish people as they had done briefly during the post-Maccabean period.[9]

There were also a number of individuals who preached Jewish renewal. Theudas persuaded people to take their possessions and follow him to the Jordan River, telling them that he would, by his own command, divide the river, and afford them an easy passage over it (Acts 5:36-38). The first-century historian Josephus identified another false prophet he labeled the Egyptian, who also claimed godlike powers: to collapse the walls of Jerusalem at his command.

ASCETICISM IN JEWISH THOUGHT

Other renewal movements chose to live in isolated communities in the Judean wilderness and stressed ascetic practices to better prepare for the coming apocalypse. For the breakaway Qumran community, the solution was to provide an alternative priestly class. Mimicking the Temple, the Qumran

7. Dunn, *Jesus Remembered*, 282
8. Sanders, *Jesus and Judaism*, 20.
9. Neusner, "Josephus' Pharisees," 274-292.

community set itself up with a surrogate sanctuary, the *yahad*. That community included dissident priests who had fled Jerusalem and were chosen as prospective candidates for senior office. The Dead Sea manuscripts discovered in 1947 describe some of the activities of the Qumran community:

> Each member of the Community had vowed "that they should seek God with a whole heart and soul . . . and no longer stubbornly follow a sinful heart. . . . He will refine for himself the human frame, by rooting out the spirit of falsehood from the bounds of the flesh."[10]

In their messianic vision, patterned after Isaiah 61, they believed that the Messiah would release the captives held by Israel's enemies and comfort all other afflicted members of the community. He would also give sight to the blind, heal the wounded, resurrect the dead, and feed the hungry. However, there was no universal salvation, for only the true remnant of Israel that aligned itself with the Qumran community would survive.[11]

The Essenes formed another group of ascetic communities. For them, "Jews from birth . . . turn away from the joys of life as if from an evil thing and embrace continence as a virtue."[12] The Essenes believed that "whoever renounces marriage is neglecting an essential task in life, namely the begetting of offsprings." However, they rejected sexual intimacy during pregnancy, "which goes to show that they do not marry for reasons of lust, but for the blessings of children."[13]

An important participant in the renewal movement was John the Baptist. The Gospels point to John's stature: "Assuredly, I say to you, of those born of women there has not risen among you one greater than John the Baptist" (Matt 11:7-11; Luke 7:24-28). Similarly, Josephus reported:

> He was a good man and had exhorted the Jews to lead righteous lives, to practice justice toward their fellow and piety towards God, and so doing to join in baptism. In his view this was a necessary preliminary if baptism was to be acceptable to God. They must not employ it to gain pardon for whatever sins they committed, but as a consecration of the body implying that the soul was already thoroughly cleansed by right behavior.[14]

10. Brown, *Body & Society*, 37-38.
11. Steffen, *Messianic Banquet*.
12. Ranke-Heinemann, *Eunuchs*, 18.
13. Ibid., 18-19.
14. Dunn, *Jesus Remembered*, 348.

Jewish Renewal Movements at the Beginning of the Common Era

Like the Essenes and members of the Qumran communities, John lived an ascetic life:

> Now John himself wore clothing made of camel's hair, with a leather belt around his waist. His food was locusts and wild honey. (Matt 3:4)

At first glance, it would appear that Judaism is fundamentally in opposition to ascetic behavior. After all, at the beginning of Genesis, God commanded, "Be fertile and increase; fill the earth, and master it" (Gen 1:28). The goal of fertility is consistent with the clinging of many Israelites to the Canaanite god, Baal. It is also reflected in Psalm 128:3-4, when God proclaimed:

> Your wife shall be like a fruitful vine within your house;
> Your sons, like olive saplings around your table.
> So shall the man who fears the Lord be blessed.

Though there are Levitical laws that restrict specified sexual relations, the Old Testament makes clear that even some of these taboos can be overridden to secure future generations. Lot's daughters' seduction of their father, Ruth's seduction of her cousin, and Tamara's seduction of her father-in-law are looked upon favorably in the Bible because the products of those unions ensured future generations and the continuity of favored lineage. While the subterfuge used by David to marry Bathsheba was condemned, the Bible emphasized the positive fruit of their procreation—Solomon, the greatest of all kings. Reflecting on this context, the rabbinic sage Resh Lakish said: "Come and let us give thanks to our ancestors, for had they not sinned, we would not have come into the world."[15]

Despite these guiding principles, ascetic behaviors did have a place in biblical Israel, which helps explain why many first-century Jewish renewal movements embraced them. An important foundation is the behavior expected of individuals when they are in the presence of God. In preparation for His giving of the laws, God tells Moses:

> Let them be ready for the third day; for on the third day the Lord will come down, in the sight of all people on Mount Sinai.... And Moses said to the people, "Be ready for the third day: do not go near a woman." (Exod 19:11-15)

---

15. Biale, *Culture of Jews*, 43.

For Moses, moreover, the command was stronger. If God desired the Israelites to abstain from sexual relations in preparation for their one-time encounter with the Almighty, how much more so should he—Moses—abstain! For *at any moment*, he was expected to be ready to accept God's direct commands.[16]

In the biblical period, the demand that Moses maintain abstinence for the rest of his life was unique. After all, none of the prophets who claimed a direct relationship with God were asked to maintain celibacy, nor were Moses's siblings, to whom God often spoke. Indeed, this issue arose when Moses' siblings, Aaron and Miriam, discovered that Moses was no longer having sexual relations with his wife, Zipporah. The Bible reports: "They said, 'Has the Lord not spoken through us as well?'" (Num 12:1-2).

This understanding, that whenever interacting with God, one must abstain from sexual intercourse, was applied broadly. It was a requirement for the priestly class to undergo a ritual purification process after sexual activity before they could enter the sanctuary of the Temple to make sacrificial offerings to God. Soldiers during a time of war, or perhaps when "trouble loomed" and heavenly intervention was desired, would remain apart from the camp until they had undergone such purification after sexual relations. When discussing asceticism in the Old Testament, Louis Finkelstein described the author of the book of Esther as a ritualist from the patrician class "to whom fasting, sackcloth, and ashes are essential when trouble looms."[17]

A second motivating force was the large gap between the lifestyles of the rich and the commoners. One of the Dead Sea scrolls, the Zadokite document, denounced gluttony as a sin of the rich and their priestly supporters. A century later, the most revered Pharisaic leader, Hillel, demeaned luxurious lifestyles: "The more flesh, the more worms; the more property, the more anxiety." Josephus claimed that the Pharisees "lived meanly and despised delicacies in diet."

By contrast, the priestly class lived in luxury. Their spacious homes on the hills above the Second Temple were furnished with rare glass and private baths; they could afford opulent burial sites where their ossuaries were placed. Later rabbinic literature preserved a taunt that the Pharisees received from the leaders of the priestly class, the Sadducees: "The Pharisees

---

16. Tuchman and Rapoport, *Moses' Women*, 199-200.
17. Finkelstein, *Pharisees*, 216.

are bound by tradition to deny themselves the pleasures of this world; yet in the future world they will also have nothing."[18]

JEWISH DISPERSION

At the beginning of the Common Era, only about half of the 5 million Jews worldwide lived in the land of Israel as a result of a substantial outward migration into the Mediterranean basin. At least 1.5 million Jews resided there, the majority in Egypt and North Africa. Another million Jews lived in Mesopotamia and Persia, descendants of those who chose to remain in Babylonia after captivity ended. As we shall explore later in this book, the Mediterranean communities were an important source of Christian converts while the Babylonian communities were crucial to long-term Jewish survival.

Remembering the warm treatment Abraham received when he entered Canaan, Judaism had a welcoming attitude toward outsiders. Jewish law allowed a stranger sojourning among the Jews to keep the Passover with the congregation of Israel (Ezra 6:21). Leviticus exhorts: "The stranger who sojourns with you shall be to you as the homeborn among you, and thou shalt love him as thyself" (Lev 19:34). So, too, Isaiah announces, "My house shall be called a house of prayer for all people" (Isa 56:7). This welcoming stance enabled Jewish immigrants to smoothly integrate into their new environs.

Mediterranean Diaspora communities were proud of the Jewish tradition and produced works of literature that glorified Jewish history. They also produced a Greek version of the Old Testament, called the Septuagint. These Jews wished to integrate themselves into their adopted communities so they incorporated Hellenistic terms into their thinking and reasoning.[19] Jews adapted genres and transformed legends to articulate their own legacy in modes congenial to a Hellenistic setting. They recreated their past, retold stories in different ways, and amplified the scriptural corpus itself through the medium of the Greek language and Greek literary forms.

Jews tapped into a rich vein of legendary materials, both pagan and Jewish. Audiences happily absorbed hybrid products that grafted pagan folktales onto the Scriptures or set fables and fictions in historical contexts.[20]

---

18. Ibid., 186.

19. Van Groningen, *First Century Gnosticism*, 63.

20. Gruen, *Heritage and Hellenism*, xvi.

While these writings were predominantly for a Jewish audience, they also tried to present Judaism in the positive way to pagans by emphasizing parallels to Hellenistic philosophies.

Diaspora Jews, however, were appalled by the sexual excesses in Hellenist society. Wealthy Alexandrians travelled down the canal to Canopus for sex holidays where they would engage in orgies of drinking, dancing, and sexual indulgences. As the geographer Strabo noted, "Every day and every night Canopus is crowded with people on the boats who play the flute and dance unrestrainedly, with the greatest licentiousness."[21] Erotic representations on pottery and household artifacts enabled them to remember these experiences in their homes.

What must have made Alexandria's Jewish community most upset was that these activities took place in a town dominated by some of the holiest religious sites in Egypt. It is in this environment that Strabo paints "a vivid picture of the erotic effect of an emotionally charged religious atmosphere on the collective mind."[22] Indeed, many observers associated Egyptian festivals, if not Egyptian culture, with sexual activities that had gotten out of control. The Roman historian Tacitus branded the province "contentious and mercurial because of superstition and sexual license."[23]

This behavior occurred because Egyptian regeneration myths stressed the centrality of the sexual act. The Nile bursting its banks and pouring over the fields was compared to a lover mounting a woman and impregnating her. To honor the goddess Bastet, it was said that certain gods left their shrines to sail up the Nile Delta and join in the great festival at Bubastis. The fifth century BCE historian Herodotus described the bawdiness of the women on the boat journey to Bubastis: "While some of the women mock the women of the towns that they pass, others dance, and others stand up and expose their genitals."[24]

In this environment, it was not surprising that many Jews embraced Hellenistic philosophies that stressed the need for men to control their sexual impulses. As Peter Brown summarized:

> For many well-to-do Jewish aristocrats some dualistic attitudes of Hellenistic philosophies came naturally. The body had physical needs that troubled the pious. Upright Jews expected sexual

21. Montserrat, *Sex and Society*, 164.
22. Ibid., 165.
23. Ibid., 167.
24. Ibid., 169.

temptation to bulk large in the life of young males. They did not approve of the "love of pleasure" associated with "the power of procreation," for it "leadeth the young as a blind man to a pit and as a beast to the precipice."[25]

Reflecting this viewpoint, *The Wisdom of Solomon* embraced Hellenistic dualism: "Wisdom will not ... dwell in a body held in a pledge of sin: For a corruptible body weigheth down the soul."[26]

Philo of Alexandria was the most important Hellenized Jew attempting to respond to these sexual excesses. He fully embraced the dualism found in Plato and other Hellenistic philosophies:

> The soul is first aroused by the stimuli of sensual pleasures ... It becomes devoted to the body, and begins to lead an intolerable life. It is inflamed and excited by irrational impulses. ... All the higher aspirations after God and virtue are stilled. The end is complete moral turpitude, the annihilation of all sense of duty, the corruption of the entire soul: not a particle of the soul that might heal the rest remains whole. ... Sensual things are placed above spiritual; and wealth is regarded as the highest good.[27]

For Philo, man must strive to control his sensual impulses. For this reason, Philo speaks approvingly of the Therapeutae community that was situated just outside Alexandria. These were individuals who led a Platonic contemplative life consisting of ascetic practices: fasting, solitary prayers, and the study of the scriptures in their isolated cells.

While never proselytizing, Jews broadly interacted with the pagan populace, many of whom sought to learn about the Jewish religion. As a result, many pagans were attracted to the Jewish culture, even attending synagogue services and other communal events. Many of these so-called "God-fearers" remained polytheists and simply added the Jewish God to their other deities.

THE HELLENIST ENVIRONMENT

Sexual concerns were deeply embedded in Hellenist societies. The lives of freeborn women were totally controlled by men: first by their fathers and

---

25. *Testament of the Twelve Patriarchs* as quoted in Brown, *Body & Society*, 34.
26. Urbach, *Sages*, 235-36.
27. Toy, Siegfried, and Lauterbach, "Philo Judaeus."

then by their husbands. Young girls were married soon after puberty and then were housebound during their childbearing years. They were considered only a vessel for procreation and tight control was required to make sure that any children conceived were fathered by husbands, and not the result of illicit affairs. Indeed, rape laws existed not to protect women from degradation but to protect each man's property and his bloodlines. Erotic artifacts were widely distributed among the elite.

Figure 3.3: Erotic Scene 5th Century BCE

Figure 3.4: The Rape of Ganymede, 5th Century BCE

Figure 3.5: Erotic Scenes, Red Figure Cup

Much of the literature that survives focused on the actions of the cultured elite. It presents sexual relations in a civilized manner with little of the base exploitation of the powerless by the powerful. Those in the elite who favored women invariably chose slave women for their sexual outlet. But here, too, there was a refinement projected. In the Greek plays, the slave paramour was well cared for and was able to lead a life of intrigue. And the wife, too, despite her confinement, lived a luxurious lifestyle.

Hellenist writers, however, were nearly all misogynists, and succeeded in coloring many parts of Homeric poems with women's perverse immorality. While some writers, including Socrates, Aristophanes, Plato, and Xenophon, took a more nuanced position on freeborn women, they did not triumph. Aristotle threw his full support to the misogynists.[28]

The Greek city-state, even at its most highly developed point, remained a men's club; a closed masculine society from which the opposite sex was absent, but where pederasty—a passionate attachment between adult males and adolescent boys—was acceptable, if not desirable.[29] The mythological Menelaus, husband of Helen of Troy, "extoled the sharp, if brief, pleasure of boys, whose very evanescence makes the pleasure so much greater."[30] Virgil was fonder of boys than girls "because a beautiful body arouses

---

28. F.A. Wright, *Feminism in Greek Literature*, 4.
29. Flaceliere, *Daily Life*, 110.
30. Harper, *From Shame to Sin*, 23.

sexual desires."[31] In Greek society, pederasty was perceived as noncoercive behavior toward adolescent boys based on an intellectual bonding first and sexual intimacy second.[32]

When Roman society made even voluntary unions with freeborn boys illegal, slaves provided a ready outlet. "In Roman pederasty, elaborate courtship before the act was replaced by the master's authority . . . and the physical mechanics of pleasure. . . In the Roman context, pederasty was recentered around the bare fact of dominance."[33]

In the dense, urbanized Roman Empire, sex was a most basic and readily available commodity. Girls stalked the streets. Taverns, inns, and baths were notorious dens of venal sex. When Christian proselytizing came to the Mediterranean basin, brothels were visible everywhere.

Much amorous literature romanticized venal sex and even the erotic art in brothels idealized the sexual encounter between professional and customer. There certainly were women who became high-priced prostitutes or courtesans of the wealthy who led lives of luxury and intrigue. But the profession was much more populated with droves of poorly paid women who were forced to become prostitutes in the Roman Empire. In an economy with relatively few respectable employments for women and no social safety net, sudden adverse changes in personal circumstances could render women hopelessly vulnerable.

The defining feature of prostitution in the Roman era, however, was the pervasive influence of slavery. While many slaves were the bounty from military conquest, other women entered slavery as abandoned infants. At the beginning of the Common Era, there was an abnormally high rate of childless couples, especially among the well-to-do. While abortion and contraception were known, it is unlikely that those practices alone could be responsible. Instead, there was a well-established practice of getting rid of unwanted infants by exposing them to die.

Some of the most famous tales of ancient literature, including the stories of Oedipus and of Romulus and Remus, concerned abandoned infants who were rescued. In Rome, however, the vast majority of those rescued, especially female infants, ended up in slavery. Slave women were hired out by their owners as an important source of revenue. Together with poor women, they populated the lower rungs of the sex trade.

---

31. Ibid., 28
32. Ibid., 111.
33. Ibid., 26.

The brothels in which they worked were often exceedingly dirty and poorly ventilated, so that patrons left "reeking still of the soot of the brothel." The lingering stench, the atmosphere of violence, the cramped concrete "evil-smelling" cribs, and the systemic abuse: these were the reality of the flesh trade. Disease surely followed in the wake of such exploitative drudgery.[34]

Sex was stunningly inexpensive. The most common rate in a neighborhood brothel seems to have been "about the price of a loaf of bread." Fellatio cost even less. As a result, women had to service fifteen to twenty men per day just to net a subsistence wage. So overworked, "the prostitute's body became, little by little, 'like a corpse.'"[35] This was the environment in which Christians proselytized and, as we shall see, substantially shaped Saint Paul's views on sexuality.

THE ASCENDANCY OF THE PHARISEES

A number of factors enabled the Pharisees to gain political strength during the decades leading up to the Great Revolt in 66 CE. First, they made use of the local synagogues. Starting with Ezra's pronouncement that there should be public readings of the Torah, there was a movement to eliminate the monopoly that Jerusalem held over prayer and religious discourse. This may explain why Mattathias, the leader of the Maccabee revolt, has been described as a rural priest.

These public readings, however, were probably quite infrequent as there is no record of synagogues until the Hasmonean era. In particular, in the early second century BCE writer Ben Sira's detailed "description of contemporary Jewish religious leadership and institutions," he never mentions the presence of synagogues.[36] Instead, a square near the town gate served local communal needs and probably hosted the occasional Torah reading.

Given hostility toward the priestly class for their unwillingness to confront the Hellenist rulers, Pharisaic influence grew during the Hasmonean era. In a period of general prosperity, it is likely that some towns moved the role of town squares to newly constructed synagogues. These first synagogues continued to serve primarily secular uses: they provided lodging to strangers and assisted in the collection of charity for the poor.

34. Wikipedia, "Prostitution in Ancient Rome."
35. Harper, *From Shame to Sin*, 49.
36. Levine, *Ancient Synagogue*, 25.

By the first century of the Common Era, the Pharisees were able to use the growing number of synagogues to advance their claim of being the true interpreters of the Mosaic laws. Their position was further strengthened by the religious edict, promulgated by Joshua ben Gamla, that a religious education should be available to all male children. Finally, the Pharisaic movement gained prestige by having, we are told, exceptional leaders during this period: first Hillel and then Rabbi Gamaliel.

At the time, the population of the land of Israel was marked by extreme class divisions. The fertile plains were divided into large estates, some of which were owned by members of the priestly class. Land was tilled by slaves, and the owners lived in lavish mansions. As a result, the priestly class showed little concern for the economic problems faced by the Jewish poor.

A modest number of wealthy landowners did support the Pharisees. To accommodate them, the Pharisees had two poles of leadership: the titular leader, or Nasi, and the head of its legislative body, the Av Beit Din. These two leaders—most often one from the patrician class and one from the plebeian—are sometimes labeled *zugot* (pairs).

Disputes between the two wings often arose because of different interpretations of what was called the Oral Torah. According to the Pharisees, at the same time that Moses handed down the written laws, he also orally communicated an interpretative methodology, to be given orally to future generations, that explained how those laws should be understood and applied to emerging situations:

> Moses received the (Oral) Torah from Sinai and gave it over to Joshua. Joshua gave it over to the Elders, the Elders to the Prophets, and the Prophets gave it over to the Men of the Great Assembly.[37]

According to the Pharisees, this oral tradition was then transmitted through the scribes and received ultimately by the first identified zugots: Hillel, representing the plebeian wing, and Shammai, representing the patrician wing. These legendary figures were active during the reign of Herod through the first decade of the Common Era.

The Oral Torah became an important component of Pharisaic understanding of the Mosaic laws, particularly when there was a movement to spread observance beyond the religious elite. As we have seen, the separation of meat and dairy consumption arose from an interpretation of a single

37. Pirkei Avot 1:1

biblical injunction to not cook a kid in its mother's milk. According to the Pharisees, it is through this oral tradition that one determines the application of this law: which utensils had to be cleaned and which did not; how long after eating meat is one allowed to eat dairy; when can the rules be suspended.[38]

By contrast, the priestly class rejected the notion of an Oral Torah, instead claiming that all interpretation must be based solely on the words of the written Torah. As we shall see, the Pharisees solidified their preeminence after the destruction of the Second Temple by transcribing the Oral Torah, first into the Mishnah and then into the more expansive Babylonian and Jerusalem Talmuds.

Whether or not they actually existed, Hillel and Shammai have an honored position in rabbinic literature written generations after they lived. It tells us little about the life of Shammai except that he was a prosperous builder. By contrast, legend claims that Hillel was born in Babylon and was a poor laborer. At the age of forty years old, he decided to migrate to Israel to study Torah and worked as a woodcutter. In the land of Israel, Hillel is said to have lived in such great poverty that he was sometimes unable to pay the admission fee to study Torah, and because of him that fee was abolished.

A second tradition held by the Pharisees, particularly by its plebeian wing, was that guiding the strict interpretation of the Mosaic laws—the *halakah*—were the ethical principles underpinning them—the *aggadah*. The most important of these ethical principles was loving-kindness. Thus, to the extent possible, the Mosaic laws must be interpreted to afford loving-kindness, especially to the poor and powerless. While Shammai was known for his rigorous interpretations, Hillel was known for his loving-kindness. One of his most famous sayings, recorded in Pirkei Avot (1:14), is "If I am not for myself, then who will be for me? And if I am only for myself, then what am I? And if not now, when?"

The following tale emphasizes this distinction between Hillel and Shammai. A certain non-Jew came first to the home of Shammai, then to the home of Hillel, making a request of each: "Teach me the Torah while I am standing on one foot." He was a laborer who claimed he had no time to study. Shammai dismissed him forthwith. Hillel, however, responded: "Don't do unto your neighbor what you would find distasteful if done to

---

38. For the separation of meat and dairy, see http://www.shamash.org/lists/scj-faq/HTML/faq/06-16.html

you. All else is commentary. Now, go and study." According to Jewish tradition, the visitor was so impressed with Hillel's response that he began to study the Torah seriously and converted to Judaism.

Hillel considered his actions to be part of his general philosophy: "Be among the disciples of Aaron [the first head priest of the Temple], loving peace and pursuing peace, loving G-d's creatures, and bringing them close to the Torah."[39] Elsewhere, the rabbinic literature highlights Hillel's concern for the welfare of the individual. For example, with regard to the remarriage of a woman whose husband is not known with certainty to be alive or dead, the view of Hillel was that she can remarry, even on the basis of indirect evidence of the husband's death. By contrast, Shammai required that witnesses come forth with direct testimony before she can be permitted to remarry. Hillel also stated, "Do not judge your fellow man until you reach his place." This infers that it is fundamentally impossible for one human being to judge another because no two people ever occupy the same "place." Thus, while one might rule that an individual did not follow the Mosaic law, we cannot make judgment on the transgressor's ethics.[40]

The balancing of ethical behavior with legal rulings became a norm of Pharisaic handling of disputes. The institution of the *zugot* signaled that when scholars differ as to interpretation, both the dominant and minority opinions must be respected. All learned men within the Jewish community were free to offer their interpretation of how the Mosaic laws could be applied. Indeed, Hillel's successor, Rabbi Gamaliel, vigorously defended the Christian evangelist Peter when he was brought before the Sanhedrin. While rejecting Peter's interpretations, Rabbi Gamaliel claimed the right of Christian Jews to voice their religious opinions without fear of reprisal. This tradition continued so that when the Oral Torah was transcribed, minority opinions were included.

Though Sanhedrin leadership was given to the priestly class, it is said that Rabbi Gamaliel's prestige enabled him to become its most powerful member. Indeed, he was so greatly respected that his son, Simeon ben Gamaliel, succeeded him as Nasi. As the zugot tradition dictated, Johanan ben Zakkai was appointed head of the Beit Din. Such was the Pharisaic leadership on the eve of the Great Revolt.

The Great Revolt began in the year 66 CE, when the Roman governor plundered the Jewish Temple, arresting numerous members of the priestly

---

39. *Pirkei Avot* 1:12.
40. *Pirkei Avot* 2:5.

class. This prompted rebellion. The Roman military garrison was quickly overrun, led by the remaining members of the priestly class allied with a substantial portion of the Pharisee leadership. The Romans brought in the Syrian army to quell the rebellion. However, despite initial advances, the Syrian Legion retreated after it was defeated by Jewish rebels at the Battle of Beth Horon, with 6,000 Romans massacred.

The revolt spread to the Galilee under the leadership of the Zealots, who in the past had sporadically attacked Romans and Greeks. When the Romans regrouped, they successfully regained the Judean countryside. As the Romans seized the Galilee, they retreated to Jerusalem. Upon entering Jerusalem, the Zealots placed all blame for the failure of the revolt on the shoulders of the moderate Jerusalem leadership, which they purged and replaced.

The Roman effort to retake Jerusalem was delayed by political conflicts in Rome. In addition, Jerusalem was a well-fortified city. The Romans had constructed a series of walls, the third completed just before the revolt. The army breached the first two walls quickly but a stubborn rebel standoff prevented them from breaking through the third and thickest wall. In response, a siege was undertaken.

The Zealots were unwilling to surrender and murdered dissenters. Josephus contended that their savagery included torching the city's food supply in an attempt to force inhabitants to fight for their lives. When the Roman army finally conquered Jerusalem in 70 CE, they leveled the Second Temple and razed to the ground virtually all of Jerusalem's infrastructure: the archives that kept all business and household records, the council building, and the entire Lower City. One can still see evidence of the severe fire that consumed much of the Upper City.

The remnants of the Zealots fled south to the hilltop plateau of Masada, where they held out against the Roman army for three years. When the end was near, rather than surrendering, almost a thousand survivors chose martyrdom. All told, hundreds of thousands of Jews perished in the revolt.

In subsequent chapters, we will describe the ascendancy of the Pharisees to communal leadership in the land of Israel after the devastating losses resulting from the failed revolt, and establish how the rabbinic sages were able to replace the temple cult and rituals with an emphasis on religious study. We will also explore the reasons for the shifting of religious leadership from the land of Israel to Babylonia.

At the same time that these changes within Judaism were occurring, another of the Jewish renewal movements blossomed; this one led by Jesus of Nazareth. Absorbing the followers of John the Baptist, Jesus' ministry gained a following in the Galilee and a Christian movement arose after his death. Under Saint Paul's leadership, the Christian movement spread in the Diaspora where Hellenist culture was dominant. These Christian beginnings are the subject of the next two chapters.

4

Jesus' Ministry

AT THE BEGINNING OF the Gospel of Mark, we are told that Jesus, like others who came to John the Baptist, experienced a "baptism of repentance and remission of sins" (Mark 1:4). This presentation created a dilemma for Christians as it implied that John, at least at first, was a superior figure. Written two decades later, the Gospel of Matthew somewhat corrected this by indicating that John recognized Jesus as the "one coming after me" and only baptized him after Jesus insisted that he do so. In the third New Testament Gospel, Luke minimized the baptism, while in the last, the Gospel of John, there is no baptism mentioned.

Though the Gospels change the nature of the baptism, they all suggest that some of Jesus' first disciples came from the circle of John's followers, that Jesus modeled his own ministry after John's, and that their ministries overlapped. Jesus carries on the ministry after the Baptist is imprisoned and then put to death by the Roman-appointed governor, Herod Antipas. Jesus, however, had a different message. The Baptist promoted ascetic behaviors, like others in the renewal movement. An ascetic approach was conducive to a movement that would be open to only the meritorious few.

By contrast, Jesus desired a mass renewal movement open to all, so he rejected ascetic practices. As Luke noted:

> John the Baptist came neither eating bread nor drinking wine [while] . . . the Son of Man came eating and drinking and [the masses] say, 'Look a glutton and a winebibber . ' (Luke 7:33)

Jesus' rejection of ascetic practices was noted by the Pharisees. When he abstained from demanding voluntary fasting for his followers, Jesus was admonished by the Pharisees: "Why did the disciples of John and the Pharisees fast, but your disciples do not fast?" (Mark 2:18) Finally, his decision to let his disciplines pluck grain on the Sabbath rather than remain hungry (Mark 2:24) also indicated that voluntary neglect of bodily needs was not part of his program.

Even more than the Baptist, Jesus brought his preaching to the wicked.[1] In the call of Levi (Matt 9:9-13, Mark 2:13-17, Luke 5:27-32), Jesus sits with tax collectors and sinners, as is the case in Luke's three parables of the Lost Sheep, the Lost Coin, and the Prodigal Son (Luke 15:1-32). When confronted by the Pharisees, Jesus says, "I desire mercy not sacrifice. For I did not come to call the righteous, but sinners, to repentance" (Matt 9:13).

As Christianity developed, Jesus' approach to sinners became an important part of religious lore. His friendship with Mary Magdalene would certainly have drawn the ire of the religious establishment as she may have been the wicked sinner described in Luke; a judgment made by the sixth century Pope Gregory the Great.[2]

Most telling, however, was Jesus' attitude toward the adulterous wife, found in many copies of the second-century Gospel of John. A woman, we are told, has committed adultery and is being held by the Pharisees in order to test Jesus. They argue that the Mosaic law demands that she be stoned to death and ask Jesus what should be done. If he is lax toward the law, then he would be condemned. But if he holds a strict line, then he opens himself to trouble from the Romans, for he will be held responsible if the stoning proceeds. Jesus, however, turns the table by announcing, "He who has not sinned, cast the first stone." This ensures there is no stoning, for none of the accusers want to take responsibility for it; and it causes them to reflect on their own sinfulness before God.

Jesus is left alone, sitting on the ground with the woman standing before him. Jesus says to her, "Neither do I condemn you. Go, and from now on no longer sin" (John 8:11). Here is mercy, as the sin but not the sinner

---

1. Sanders, *Jesus and Judaism*, 178.

2. As quoted in Hooper, *The Crucifixion of Mary Magdelene*. Gregory stated, "She whom Luke calls the sinful woman, whom John calls Mary, we believe to be the Mary from whom seven devils were ejected according to Mark. And what did these seven devils signify, if not all the vices? It is clear, brothers, that the woman previously used the unguent to perfume her flesh in forbidden acts."

Jesus' Ministry

is condemned.[3] These examples demonstrate that central to Jesus' mission was bringing a loving God to the lost and the sinners.

Mark places Jesus at the center of Jewish renewal. After being designated at his baptism as the chosen agent of God, he then spends forty days in the wilderness (like Elijah) and immediately calls protégés (as Elijah called Elisha). He commissions twelve disciples, symbolic representatives of the twelve tribes, to continue his missionary work.

Mark then presents stories of Jesus' healings that reflect the healing of the Jewish people. A woman who has been hemorrhaging for twelve years approaches Jesus. She "had suffered many things from many physicians. She had spent all that she had and was no better, but rather grew worse." However, after she touched Jesus' garment, "immediately the fountain of her blood had dried up and she felt in *her* body that she was cured of her affliction" (Mark 5:23-43).

At the same time, one of the leaders of the local synagogue pleaded with Jesus to aid his dying daughter. When he got to the girl, the people were weeping and wailing, thinking her dead. Jesus said, "Why make a commotion and weep? The child is not dead, but sleeping." Despite being ridiculed, Jesus took the parents into the room where their daughter lay. With a touch of his hand, "immediately the girl arose and walked for she was twelve years old." The woman who had been hemorrhaging for twelve years and the twelve-year-old girl who was almost dead were representatives of an Israel hemorrhaging and almost dead but given new life through Jesus.

In addition to carrying out sea crossings and feedings reminiscent of Moses leading the exodus and performing Elijah-like healings, Jesus taught about a renewal of the covenant for the families and village communities in the nascent movement. He declared in clear terms that the "brothers and sisters and mothers" of the movement are those who do the will of God (Mark 3:31-35). Later, in a sequence of four dialogues (Mark 10:2-45), he renewed Mosaic covenantal teachings about the integrity of marriage and family, community membership, economic relations, and political leadership.[4]

Jesus traveled through the Galilee countryside, avoiding the major cities. He preached to those who were oppressed by the Temple taxes and Roman tribute. During Jesus' ministry, the Galilean peasantry, the *ammei*

---

3. Augustine *In John* 33.6.
4. Horsley, *Jesus and the Powers*, 90-91.

ha'aretz, were subjected to three layers of taxation. One was the tithes due the Temple priests. Second were the levies instituted by Herod Antipas to support his Galilean building projects. Finally, there was the tribute paid to Rome. Together, these taxes came to more than one-third of all produce and income.[5]

Figure 4.1: First Century Map

5. Dunn, *Jesus Remembered*, 296–97.

Unfortunately, there has been a tendency to conflate the wicked and the *ammei ha'aretz*. The *ammei ha'aretz* did not follow the laws of purity and had a tense relationship with the Pharisees, who expected more rigorous observance. When the rabbinic sages reorganized the Jewish community, some claimed that those who were ignorant of the law, the *ammei ha'aretz*, would have no place in the world to come.[6]

During the time of Jesus' ministry, however, the Pharisees believed that the *ammei ha'aretz* were sufficiently religious to have a place in the world to come. As a result, the Pharisees would not have opposed Jesus simply because he ministered to the common people and the economically impoverished; the charge against Jesus was that he extended grace and charity to the wicked *before* they engaged in the appropriate acts of restitution and changed behavior.

THE GALILEAN COMMUNITY

At the time of Jesus' birth, Nazareth was a poor city of mud and brick homes that flanked a single paved road. Only the most prosperous could afford wooden furniture and the entire town had to use a single public bath. The more successful artisans had to ply their trades in the bigger towns. For those from Nazareth, that meant a day-long walk to the Galilean capital, Sepphorus.

Sepphorus was then a thriving metropolis with wide avenues and two-story private homes complete with courtyards. It was served by two large aqueducts providing ample bath facilities for all its residents. Before the Common Era, it had numerous Roman villas, featuring colorful mosaics depicting nude hunting scenes and other provocative images that were typically found in Hellenized households throughout the Mediterranean basin. It had a large Roman theater at which Greek plays and musical concerts were performed.[7]

This situation changed dramatically soon after Herod's death in 4 BCE. A Galilean revolt against his successor, Herod Antipas, was defeated and, in response, Sepphorus was razed. When Sepphorus was rebuilt a few decades later, it was downgraded to a garrison town and became, along with neighboring Tiberias, a mere administrative site on the local trade

---

6. Sanders, *Jesus and Judaism*, 180.
7. Aslan, *Zealot*, cf. 38.

route. While the two towns did contain theaters and temples, there were too few Greeks and Romans for Hellenistic culture to be as significant as in the major cities of the Mediterranean basin. By contrast, there is plenty of archaeological evidence in these cities of Jewish religious identity: "stone vessels, *miqwaoth* (ritual baths), absence of pork remains, and burial in *kochim* (shafted tombs with ossuaries)."[8]

Some researchers believe Jesus' Galilee faced a severe social and economic crisis, one that grew worse day by day. However, the region, including Nazareth, may have experienced relative prosperity when the Romans rebuilt Sepphorus and Tiberias. It not only increased the demand for craftsmen, like Jesus, but also for locally-produced goods and products, like pottery. In these urban centers, the Galilean peasantry was exposed somewhat to Hellenism but decisively retained its allegiance to Jerusalem. They willingly paid the Temple tithing but deeply resented the Roman tax.

Jesus ministry, however, comes after these projects were virtually completed.[9] A subsequent economic contraction may very well have caused Galilean small landholders to be victimized by a "tightening noose of institutionalized injustices such as double taxation, heavy indebtedness, and loss of land." Peasant families "fell ever more heavily into debt under the steady economic pressures of double taxation."[10] The wealthy lent them money that they could not repay. The resulting foreclosures enabled estates to become larger while more people were forced off the land.

Given Jesus' Galilean audience, many of his sayings voiced concern for the oppressive conditions the people faced. In Luke, we find a rich man "clothed in purple and fine linen and fared sumptuously every day" (Luke 16:19-31). The beggar Lazarus was "full of sores" and "laid at his gate," fighting with wild dogs for "the crumbs [which] fell from the rich man's table." However, when Lazarus died, he "was carried by the angels to Abraham's bosom." The rich man also died but was left "in torments in Hades." The rich man cried, "Father Abraham, have mercy on me, and send Lazarus that he may dip the tip of his finger in water and cool my tongue for I am tormented in the flame." But Abraham said, "Son, remember that in your lifetime you received your good things, and likewise Lazarus evil things, but now he is comforted and you are tormented."[11]

---

8. Dunn, *Jesus Remembered*, 299-300.

9. Edwards, "Socio-Economic and Cultural Ethos."

10. This characterization is found in Sanders, "Jesus in Historical Context."

11. Bultmann, *Synoptic Tradition*, 203. He contends that some of the synoptic

Jesus' Ministry

The parable of the day laborer (Matt 20:1-16) describes the interaction between a landowner and his workforce. In the morning, the owner easily found workers willing to work a full day for one penny, the typical subsistence wage. As the day progressed, the owner was able to hire additional workers without even making a definite promise. When the owner shows seeming generosity by also paying those who only worked part of the afternoon one penny, those who had worked the full day had little recourse: the owner had to pay them only what they had agreed to work for.

Matthew shaped this parable to convey two meanings. The paying of a necessary subsistence wage to all echoed Deuteronomy's injunction: "Thou shalt not oppress a hired servant that is poor and needy, whether he be of thy brethren, or of thy strangers if they are in thy land within thy gates" (Dt 24:14-15). More generally, Matthew indicated that whether they were faithful for an entire life or only for the last days, everyone has an equal place in the world to come. This is summarized by the conclusion: "So the last will come first, and the first last. For many are called, few are chosen" (Matt 20:16).

Note that Matthew ignored any judgment based on the efforts of the day laborers. By contrast, a similar story found in the Babylonian Talmud emphasizes the workers' efforts: one who worked fewer hours was paid the same wage because he was so industrious that he produced the same amount as the others.[12] Most important, Matthew is silent on the unequal relationship between the rich landowner and the destitute day laborers and instead puts the entire focus on God's grace.

Matthew's intentions, however, may not have been Jesus' view. After all, Matthew was writing at the end of the first century and was among well-to-do Christian leaders in Antioch, distant from the travails of the Galilean day laborers of Jesus' ministry. For Jesus, it is quite likely that just as with the beggar Lazarus, the day-laborer parable could have served to highlight the ongoing inequality between the wealthy and displaced peasantry. Their abundant labor supply created a situation where day laborers had no control over the pitiful wages that they received.[13]

---

similitudes have "been taken from the Jewish tradition by the Church and put into Jesus' mouth." And he singled out the Lazarus story as "one example of very high probability."

12. Vermes, *Religion of Jesus the Jew*, 105. He ignores the distinction between merit and grace in the two stories. On this point, also see Bultmann, *Synoptic Tradition*, 201.

13. This perspective on the parable is found in Herzog, "Why Peasants Responded."

Just as important, siding with the poor against their exploitation was a staple of the Jewish prophets, a tradition that Jesus surely embraced. It began with Samuel's forewarnings when he was beseeched by the populace to appoint a king so that the tribes could be united to better combat their adversaries. Similarly to the Lazarus parable, Amos 5-8 condemned the wealthy rulers for their conspicuous consumption and luxurious living while "trampling on the needy and bringing the poor to ruin." Micah 2:2 condemned the wealthy and powerful rulers who "covet fields and seize them ... and oppress the householders [robbing them] of their inheritance." Isaiah also cries out against the ruling elite for systematically exploiting the poor, getting them into debt and then taking over their lands and houses. Finally, Nehemiah lamented:

> Here we are, slaves to this day—slaves in the land that you gave to our ancestors to enjoy its fruits and its good gifts. Its rich yield goes to the kings whom you have set over us because of our sins; they have power also over our bodies and over our livestock at their pleasure, and we are in great distress. (Neh 9:36-37)

CONTEMPORARY APPLICATIONS

Not surprisingly, protest movements based upon Jesus' sayings (and the Jewish prophetic tradition) arose in modern times within some Christian communities. Jesus did not seek to lead a revolt against these injustices, for it was God that would take retribution against the rich for their transgressions, particularly in the afterlife. Many readers, however, were inspired by his exhortations against inequalities to undertake social justice actions.

At the end of the nineteenth century, a Social Gospel movement harnessed the protests of Midwestern farmers who were experiencing difficult economic conditions. Technical innovations made large-scale, mechanized farms more cost effective than smaller, less mechanized farms. Credit to purchase the needed equipment, however, became increasingly difficult to obtain. The United States was on the gold standard so that credit expansion required increased gold supplies. With no new gold discoveries after the Civil War, banks were unable to significantly increase their loans. This gold shortfall caused a series of banking crises that resulted in economic contractions that lowered grain prices, further harming the less competitive family farmers.

Jesus' Ministry

Midwestern farmers believed that unproductive urban bankers and middlemen were exploiting their productive labor. One of the leaders of the Social Gospel movement, Protestant minister Charles Sheldon, lamented, "The horrible blunder and stupidity of our whole industrial system that doesn't work according to any well-established plan of a Brotherhood of men, but is driven by forces that revolve around some pagan rule of life called supply and demand." [14] This situation harkened back to the lack of bargaining power of the day laborers in Matthew.[15]

The Social Gospel movement had sufficient strength in the Democratic Party that it nominated William Jennings Bryan to be its 1896 presidential candidate. If elected, he pledged to enact a bimetallic gold-silver standard that would ease credit restraints and the stranglehold big-city banks had over those who produce. In his acceptance speech, Bryan demanded:

> You shall not press down upon the brow of labor this crown of thorns;
> You shall not crucify mankind upon a cross of gold.[16]

While the Klondike gold discoveries that year enabled credit markets and the economy to eventually recover, it was too late to stem the bankruptcies of many family farms.

In the late nineteenth and first half of the twentieth century, the day laborer imagery perfectly captured the situation of Southern black communities. Without receiving "forty acres and a mule" after the Civil War, the vast majority of black families continued to be tied to the plantation owner. When they refused to work in the gang labor system that typified antebellum life, the sharecropper system was introduced.

The exploitive situation was reflected in their requirement to buy provisions from company stores and to sell their cotton at the price the landowner offered. Compounding those problems, black sharecroppers had to deal with bad crop years that caused them to be further indebted to the landowner.[17] Finally, government agricultural policies during the Great Depression forced many to become day laborers.

---

14. Sheldon, *Charles Sheldon*, 81.

15. Spector, "A Meal for the Poor." A Yiddish tale which shows that if the supply of the poor is less than the demand for them, they will strike for a better deal.

16. History Matters: Bryan's Cross of Gold Speech. http://historymatters.gmu.edu/d/5354/

17. Cherry, *Who Gets the Good Jobs?* Chapter 4.

In particular, when faced with cotton prices falling to one-fourth their pre-Depression level, the Roosevelt Administration's Agricultural Adjustment Act (AAA) paid cotton producers to keep some land out of production. Supplies were reduced, enabling the market price to rise. However, virtually all government payments went to the plantation owners rather than to those who worked the land.

Cotton acreage in production fell by 46 percent between 1932 and 1940, creating a substantial excess supply of farm labor. Funds for mechanization and cheap labor enabled plantation owners to replace the sharecropper system. In the Mississippi Delta, tenancy went from comprising 81.9 percent of cotton production in 1930 to 58.2 percent by 1940. Many sharecroppers, who could not survive on their share, hired themselves or family members out as day laborers during the picking season. By 1936, 36 percent of owner-operator cotton acreage in plantations was picked by day laborers, and this percentage continued to increase.[18] The burden of displacement fell on black workers disproportionately as Jim Crow practices enabled Southern white workers to monopolize the industrial jobs which increased dramatically after New Deal policies brought electrification to the Deep South.

What role did Christianity play for the exploited black peasantry whose destitution increased with their transformation from sharecroppers to day laborers? Unlike the Social Gospel movement, Southern Christian churches embraced the Matthew transformation where grace for the sinful was the central message. This is most clearly represented by the role that the spiritual "Amazing Grace" played in black communities. The words, "Amazing Grace, how sweet the sound / That saved a wretch like me," may have encouraged many among the black peasantry to focus on their own sinfulness and God's loving grace rather than on the exploitation they faced.[19] What is even more amazing is that this hymn was written by a slave trader, John Newton, after he was miraculously saved when one of his ships capsized. Thus, the sinfulness of a slaver is transposed into the sinfulness of the descendants of the people he had enslaved.[20]

18. Wright, *Old South, New South*, 235.

19. Heilburt, *The Gospel Sound*, 21-22. According to Heilburt, the verse black congregations prefer is:
Through many dangers, toils and snares, I have already come; 'Tis grace has brought me safe thus far, And grace will lead me home."

20. The sinfulness that John Newton lamented was not his being a slaver but other personal defects. Indeed, despite his religious conversion after the shipwreck in 1748, he

JESUS' CRUCIFIXION

There is some question as to whether or not Jesus had significant support in the Galilean countryside. Parts of the Gospels undercut the view that Jesus had a large following. In Luke, Jesus lamented that the people rejected the proselytizing of either the Son of Man or John the Baptist:

> They are like children sitting in the marketplace and calling to one and other saying: "We played the flute for you, and you did not dance, we mourned to you, and you did not weep." (Luke 7:32)

It is even less likely in Jerusalem. In the three Synoptic Gospels of Matthew, Mark, and Luke, Jesus only travels to Jerusalem once. For most observers, this confirmed that Jesus had little presence in Judea and was unlikely to have had more than a small band of followers in Jerusalem. By contrast, the Gospel of John, written much later, has Jesus' ministry exclusively in Judea, including Jerusalem. In this environment, John documents an extensive discourse between Jesus and the Pharisees, strengthening claims that Jesus had a strong following in the capital and was a serious threat to the Pharisees if not to the Temple leadership.[21]

Jesus becomes particularly threatening when he enters Jerusalem just before the beginning of Passover. As Mark relates:

> Jesus went into the temple, and began to cast out them that sold and bought in the temple, and overthrew the tables of the moneychangers, and the seats of them that sold doves. My house shall be called of all nations the house of prayer? But ye have made it a den of thieves. And the scribes and chief priests heard it and sought how they might destroy Him: for they feared Him, because all the people were astonished at his teachings. (Mark 11:15-18)

As described earlier, an important function of the Temple was to allow the Jewish people to provide offerings during important religious holidays, most prominently Passover. So important were these events, the Pharisees

---

continued as a slaver until illness forced him to retire from the sea; and then he continued to invest in slave vessels. In 1764, he became an ordained minister and remained silent on the evils of slavery. Finally, in 1788, Newton for the first time publicly denounced slavery in his influential pamphlet, "Thoughts about the Slave Trade." For more on Newton's life and the history of "Amazing Grace," see Turner, *Amazing Grace*.

21. Fredriksen, *Jesus of Nazareth*. She believes the Gospel of John gives a more accurate picture of Jesus' ministry but does not believe it resulted in a large and threatening movement.

suspended strict adherence to the purity laws so that the *ammei ha'aretz* could participate. Only at these times did the Pharisees permit the sharing of utensils and the trading of goods with one another.[22]

The moneychangers were crucial for pilgrims from the Diaspora as transactions for doves and other products could only be made in local currencies. If Jesus did in fact act as Matthew claimed, he would have been opposed, not so much by the scribes and priestly class, but by the public who had come to make their offerings or to trade their wares. It is more than problematic, however, to link Jesus' transgressions with the desire of Jews to want him crucified.

After the destruction of the Second Temple, the Sanhedrin was comprised of only the Pharisee scribes. They strongly rejected applying the death penalty even in cases in which it was prescribed. Already the bar was set high for executing one who committed murder: there had to be two witnesses who actually saw the act. Now the Pharisee Sanhedrin added the requirement for two more witnesses who could testify that before the act had been committed, they had warned the person and told him: "Know that what you are about to do is forbidden by Torah law, and know that if you do it, you will be sentenced to death."

For all practical purposes, this abolished the death penalty. Indeed, it was now said, "Had we been in the Sanhedrin during Second Temple times, no person would ever have been put to death."[23] In addition, as already mentioned, the Pharisees respected differences of interpretation of the Mosaic laws and after Jesus' death, they protected the rights of the evangelist Peter. Thus, it is extremely unlikely that the Pharisee members of the Sanhedrin would have supported significant punishment for Jesus' transgressions, let alone a death sentence.

The Gospels, all written well after Jesus' crucifixion, picture the Roman governor, Pontius Pilate, as a reluctant executioner, forced to follow the will of the Jewish populace. Other contemporary accounts paint a different picture. Philo characterized Pilate's "vindictiveness and furious temper." Referring to Pilate's governance, Philo further describes "his cruelty, and his continual murders of people untried and uncondemned, and his never ending, and gratuitous, and most grievous inhumanity."[24]

---

22. Oppenheimer, *'Am Ha-aretz*, 159-160.

23. Cohn, *Human Rights*, 21.

24. Philo, *On the Embassy to Gaius,* Book XXXVIII, 299–305.

Jesus' Ministry

The first-century historian Josephus recounted another incident in which Pilate spent money from the Temple to build an aqueduct. Pilate had soldiers hidden in the crowd of Jews while addressing them. When Jews again protested his actions, Pilate gave the signal for his soldiers to randomly attack, beat, and kill—in an attempt to silence Jewish petitioners.[25] As a result, it is not credible to believe that Pilate took into consideration the opinion of the Jewish populace. Instead, as in the cases of Theudas and the Egyptian, Pilate simply killed any leader who made a public display, no matter how small his following. Consistent with this perspective, the fact that Jesus was crucified while his disciples went free "showed that the Romans regarded him as dangerous on one level but not at another: dangerous as one who excited the hopes and dreams of the Jews, but not an actual leader of an insurgent group."[26]

THE FIRST FOLLOWERS

The first Christians did not understand their faith as a new religion or their community as a religious fellowship which, like the people of Qumran, kept its distance from other Jewish communities. The new movement "was by no means a group of pious observants with a private devotional tradition."[27] Rather than withdrawing, Christians wished to remain Jews and live in diverse Jewish communities.[28]

The first apostles saw Christianity as "the community of God's chosen ones in the end-time."[29] They "dreamed of future acts and revelations of God that would transform the older Judaism into a religion of the spirit . . . [but] there was no thought of founding a new religion apart from Judaism."[30]

Like those who produced the Dead Sea scrolls, Jesus' first followers believed that God would soon redeem the world and bring in a new kingdom in which there would be no more sin, suffering, or death. The clearest expression of this belief is in the words of Jesus: "Truly I tell you, some of you standing here will not taste death until you see the kingdom of God having come in power" (Mark 9:1). Later, Mark forewarned:

25. Josephus, *Antiquities of the Jews*, 18.3.2.
26. Sanders, *Jesus and Judaism*, 295.
27. Carrington, *Early Christian Church*, 54.
28. Conzelmann, *History of Primitive Christianity*, 43.
29. Ibid., 48-49.
30. Ibid., 50

Jewish and Christian Views on Bodily Pleasure

> After the tribulations, the sun will be darkened, and the moon will not give its light, and the stars will be falling from heaven ... And then they will see the Son of Man coming in clouds with great power and glory. (Mark 13:24-26)

This vision is reflected in Isaiah: "For the stars of the heavens and their constellations will not give their light; the sun will be dark at its rising, and the moon will not shed its light" (IS 13:10). Similarly, the apocalyptic vision found in Daniel 7:13 is transmitted into the words of Jesus. Matthew reported: "Then the sign of the Son of Man will appear in heaven ... and they will see the Son of Man coming on the clouds of heaven with power and great glory" (Matt 24:30).

In the first decades of the Christian movement, Jesus is treated as a great prophet, even a Messiah, with the focus on his sayings. The early oral tradition substantially reflected a continuation of his wisdom teachings. The vast majority of scholars believe the lost Q manuscript provided the basis for the sayings that are common to the Gospels of Luke and Matthew. Though it was written sometime later, many also accept the sayings found in the Gospel of Thomas that circulated in the East as late as the fourth century.

For the initial followers of Jesus, his sayings provide a continuation of his announcement of the world to come. These sayings are not only reassurance of the end-time, they are also the rule of life for the Christian community. Any emphasis upon Jesus' suffering, death, and resurrection would be meaningless in this context. Indeed, neither the Q manuscript nor the Gospel of Thomas considers Jesus' death a part of the Christian message.[31]

The conception of Jesus as a Jewish prophet is even reflected in the organization of Mark, which was probably written just after the Jewish rebellion had been suppressed in 70 CE. It has no mention of his birth and Jesus is selected as God's messenger only after his baptism. These may be some of the reasons why Mark, even though it is the first of the gospels written, is placed after Matthew in the New Testament. And most scholars believe that the resurrection ending in Mark 16:9-20, where Jesus is seen by his followers, was added in the second century.[32]

What was yet to be resolved was the position of Jesus: was he a prophet in the mold of Moses; was he a human Messiah; or was he part of the Godhead? One could certainly argue that in his lifetime, his followers thought

---

31. Koester, *Ancient Christian Gospels*, 150.
32. Tabor, "Strange Ending."

of him as a prophet akin to Moses; and after his death and resurrection as the fallen Messiah. However, though Mark generally placed Jesus in the prophetic tradition, he does become part of the Godhead, as the "Son of Man" found in the earlier apocalyptic writings of Daniel and in the book of Enoch.[33]

To explain why his early followers did not see Jesus as more than a messenger from God, Mark indicates that Jesus hid his true identity. Indeed, in what most scholars believe is the original text, Mark ends without Jesus ever revealing his true godly identity. Only later, in its revised form, Mark tells us, "Lord Jesus . . . was taken into heaven and sat down at the right hand of God" (Mark 16:19). By contrast, in John, Jesus was "in the beginning with God" (John 1:2). And when responding to a query, Jesus says, "Now glorify me, Father, with yourself with the glory that I had with you before the cosmos existed" (John 17:5).

THE JEWISH CHRISTIAN APPROACH

There can be no doubt that Jesus saw himself as part of the movement for Jewish renewal. Jesus did not preach among non-Jews and remained a practicing Jew throughout his ministry. He regularly entered synagogues and hemmed his garments so that the religiously-inspired tassels would show. He also paid the half-shekel tax the Romans required of all Jews. In his healing of the leper, he accepted the special priestly role to verify cleanliness. And according to the Q manuscript, faithfully transmitted in Luke (16:17) and Matthew (5:18), he says: "It is easier for heaven and earth to pass away than for one tittle of the law to drop."

While Jesus was a rigorous religious practitioner, he rejected the strict interpretations proposed by the Pharisees and others in the renewal movement. His devaluation of dietary laws and emphasis on more ethical requirements became a distinguishing feature. This distinction is captured in Mark:

> Whatever enters a man from outside cannot defile him, because it enters his stomach not his heart and is eliminated. . . . What comes out . . . of the heart of man, produce evil thoughts adulteries, fornications, murders. (Mark 7:18, 21)

---

33. Boyarin, *Jewish Gospels*.

At times, Jesus appears to be rejecting the Sabbath laws but only when he believed the sanctity of life was endangered. In particular, he is willing to break the Sabbath prohibitions when he heals a sick person or when his apostles are famished. And when the Pharisees criticized these actions, Jesus said, "The Sabbath was made for man, not man for the Sabbath" (Mark 2:27).

Indeed, this was the exact position taken by rabbinic sages to justify why Jews were allowed to cut wood to heat homes on the Sabbath and holy days. This belief is captured in a nineteenth century Yiddish tale.[34] The setting is a Jewish shtetl where a highly respected rabbi disappeared every Yom Kippur, the holiest day of the year. Finally, one year the congregation delegated a member to spy on the rabbi to see where he went.

The spy followed the rabbi to a cottage deep in the woods. In the cottage was an elderly infirm woman whom the rabbi cared for as her family was at Yom Kippur services. He cut wood to warm the cottage and prepared her food. When the spy relates this to the congregation, one member said that surely for his good deeds, the rabbi will have a place in heaven. Another congregant quickly added, "If not still higher." Like the rabbi, Jesus put love and kindness above ritual regulations.

Like Jesus, the first apostles were all practicing Jews who saw their movement as heralding a transformation of Judaism. As the Sermon on the Mount signaled, Jesus is the authoritative interpreter of the law, providing a fulfillment of the law that is better than that of the Pharisees. As the initial apostles did not envision abandoning the Mosaic laws, they had to contrast their approach to that of the Pharisees. This suggests that the Christian disputes with the Pharisees were not generally acrimonious, so that the polemics in Matthew 23 and John 8 do not represent the situation during the first few decades after Jesus' crucifixion.

WANDERING CHARISMATICS

The earnest efforts of the first followers to proselytize among Jews in the land of Israel seem to have been remarkably unsuccessful. Jesus' closest Galilean followers moved to Jerusalem to await the coming apocalypse. While they undoubtedly comprised a significant group, the Protestant theologian Gerd Theissen noted that when Paul comes to Jerusalem three years after his conversion, "Peter was the only member of this supposed

---

34. Peretz, "If Not Still Higher."

Jesus' Ministry

church leadership whom he found there (Gal 1:18). Fifteen years later, Paul met only 'three pillars in Jerusalem, among them Peter (Gal 2:9) who was often on journeys (Acts 8:14; 9:32ff; 10:1ff; 1 Cor 1:12).'"[35]

Writing near the end of the first century, Josephus has little to say about Jesus and nothing about Christian communities in Israel. Before becoming an historian, Josephus was Roman administrator in the Galilee at the time of the Jewish revolt in 66 CE and never indicated that there was a Christian community there. In Acts, there is no mention of a Galilean Christian community, and even though Peter was the apostle to the Jews and his family is settled in Galilee, his ministry is neither in Galilee nor in Judea. Instead, Peter's efforts bring him to the Greek coastal cities, to Antioch, and finally to Rome.

Galilean animosity towards the cities was deep-seated. To a considerable extent, this hostility must have been the result of Jerusalem's efforts to recast Jewish culture in the Galilee. At the same time, however, the peasantry had a deep emotional attachment to the Holy City (Luke 13:34; Matt 23:37). As long as Jesus' message was perceived as reformist, he might have garnered a Galilean following. However, once it included a call to destroy the Temple and questioned the Mosaic laws, the *ammei ha'aretz* moved away. The Galilee also seemed to have experienced relative prosperity in the decades after Jesus' crucifixion and, by and large, did not support the Jewish revolt against the Romans.[36] Thus, it is likely that after his crucifixion, the evangelists could not revive Jesus' Galilean movement and moved their proselytizing to the cities and eventually toward Gentiles.[37]

While groups of Christian converts did not exist in the Galilee, they could be found in some urban centers of Asia Minor. There are two sources for these communities. First, Sepphorus was on an important trade route, making it likely that merchants from Asia Minor might have come in contact with Jesus' ministry there. Second, they may also have been converted by the apostles during pilgrimages to Jerusalem.

Linking these isolated Christian followers to the Jerusalem leadership was a band of wandering charismatics: homeless, lacking family, and lacking possessions. According to Theissen, the sympathizers to whom the wandering charismatics gave counsel were too few to form organized communities so that they remained part of the larger Jewish community.

---

35. Theissen, *Early Palestinian Christianity*, 9.
36. Rappaport, "How Anti-Roman Was the Galilee?"
37. Freyne, "Urban-Rural Relations."

Jewish and Christian Views on Bodily Pleasure

The vivid apocalyptic expectations of the early Christian wandering charismatics went along with their role as outsiders; they lived as though they expected the end of the world. They appear in Antioch (Acts 13:1) and in communities where, as we shall see, they made life difficult for Paul.[38]

In the late first-century text, the *Didache*, these evangelists seem to be similar to the wandering Cynic philosophers, who also led a vagabond existence. The Cynics believed it possible to live a happy life without goods and possessions, naked, without hearth or home, without anyone to care, without a slave, without a homeland.[39] Theissen believes that the Christian charismatics led a similarly ascetic lifestyle with a graduated series of norms for themselves and local sympathizers. This seems to be reflected in Matthew's counsel to a disciple: "If you would be perfect, go, sell what you possess and give to the poor . " (Matt 19:21).

Theissen's claim that local sympathizers would remain members of existing Jewish communities makes sense, at least in the pre-Pauline stages of Christianity. After all, the first apostles were practicing Jews who expected the Christian community to be faithful to the Mosaic laws. Less credible are the behavioral characteristics Theissen attributed to them. While ascetic behavior was common to many in the Jewish renewal movement, there is no direct evidence for it among the apostles and no clear references to Jesus' ministry. Theissen, moreover, undermined his position by noting that economic circumstances played an important role in creating a norm of rootlessness among an oppressed peasantry that faced economic uncertainty.

There were also profound contrasts between Cynic vagabonds and itinerant Christian disciples. Luke (9:3 and 10:4) contrasts the two groups: Cynics beg while Christian evangelists don't. Most important, Cynics had no interest in developing local communities and instead sought individuals to emulate their virtues. By contrast, over time Christian disciples "were called as catalyst for a community-based movement."[40]

None of these criticisms, however, undermine the core Theissen thesis: traveling preachers played a central role in the development of Christianity and preceded the formation of communities with local leadership. Indeed, wandering prophets and teachers may have still been decisive authorities at the beginning of the second century. They travelled to Judea and Caesarea

---

38. Theissen, *Early Palestinian Christianity*, 15.

39. Ibid., 15.

40. Horsley, *Sociology and the Jesus Movement*, 47.

(Acts 21:10). Their superiors were still the "apostles" who lived "in accordance with the teachings of the gospel" and were allowed to stay no more than three days in one place (*Didache* 13.1f; 11.3). Finally, Theissen's claim that there were few Christians in the Galilee or Judea seems to be correct.

SUMMING UP

Jesus built his movement in the post-Maccabean tradition of Jewish renewal, preparing for the coming apocalypse. His end-time event, however, does not have the blood and gore found in the Old Testament tradition. For Jesus, there was no blueprint for how this messianic age would occur but mass deaths and destruction were not part of it. God will bring about the messianic banquet in a caring and loving manner.

There is some question as to the robustness of Jesus' following. His distinct views concerning grace for the wicked and his devaluation of dietary and purity laws certainly would have been strongly opposed by Jewish leaders. When Jesus publicly challenged the religious leadership that fateful Passover week, it may not have been displeased when the Romans got rid of such a troublesome foe.

Jesus may very well have been a woodworker in the urban construction projects in Sepphorus and Tiberias that preceded his ministry. Indeed, he may have worked on projects where he saw firsthand the gap between the wealthy and the displaced peasantry. This would be the basis of his Lazarus and day laborer parables. Once these projects were completed, he could have become despondent, returned to village life, and been attracted to John the Baptist, who purified him from his sinful behavior.

Jesus, however, understood the human spirit and the need to bring joy into the lives of the *ammei ha'aretz*. Neither the asceticism associated with John the Baptist nor the rigorous application of the Mosaic law stressed by the Pharisees and the haberim would bring joy into people's lives. Only faith and visions of another life outside their current earthly realm—the good news—would bring joyfulness to the people. Whereas much of the prophetic apocalyptic literature and many of the Jewish renewal movements believed that only a select few would receive the messianic banquet, Jesus opened the doors to all. His stress on the most sinful signaled that if even the most detested have a place in the world to come, surely the *ammei ha'aretz* would be included.

Jesus and later Christians also embraced Isaiah's vision of the messianic banquet as being open to all. By contrast, other Jewish renewal movements had a much more restrictive vision. Ezekiel repeats the messianic message found in Isaiah: Israel's external enemies will be destroyed and fed to predators. The unrighteous within Israel will be destroyed (Ezra 34:2-10) and the righteous remnant will return where they will be abundantly fed (Ezra 34:17-30). Unlike Isaiah, however, these blessing will be extended to the righteous from other nations only as long as they followed the Mosaic laws (Ezra 47:22-23). Indeed, in 1 Enoch 60-62 and 4 Ezra 56, the banquet and the general prosperity of the future age would be limited to only the faithful within Israel.[41]

The Essenes, the Qumran communities, and John the Baptist's followers had deep hostilities toward the religious hierarchy that common Jews faced. In response, they built apocalyptic communities separated from mainstream society. This is quite analogous to the utopian socialist communities that sprang up during the first half of the nineteenth century. By contrast, Jesus rejected the formation of such Christian communities and, instead, strove to present the good news as bringing a future egalitarianism to the people. While the Romans and Temple leadership might have considered his ideas threatening to the social order, Jesus was not a theocratic revolutionary; his vision was God's intervention, not secular efforts. Thus, those who cast Jesus as a social revolutionary seeking to organize the Galilean peasantry against their class enemies miss his real revolutionary vision.

The next chapter will discuss a key issue the evangelists faced, particularly after they began proselytizing among the Gentiles: the role of the Mosaic laws. Jesus' devaluing of the Mosaic laws opened the way to their complete abandonment by the Christian movement by the end of the first century. In the evolving Christian movement, faith in Christ became much more important than behavior. By contrast, when the Pharisees gained religious leadership after the second-century Bar Kochba revolt, they made obeying the Mosaic laws central to the Jewish religion.

This chapter highlighted the parables Jesus used to condemn social and economic inequality and previewed the shifting emphasis to the centrality of God's grace. This ideological transformation is important for a comprehensive understanding of the evolution of Christian thought in the first four centuries after Jesus' ministry. And certainly Paul's focus on Jesus'

---

41. Steffen, *Messianic Banquet*.

death and resurrection played a crucial role in this transformation, which will be discussed in the next chapter.

The next chapter, however, will primarily focus on how Christianity came to view bodily pleasure. Unlike other Jewish renewal movements, Jesus' ministry rejected ascetic behavior. Jesus was accused of promoting gluttony and wine drinking, and of not observing the periodic fasting that was customary among observant Jews. By the end of the first century, however, Christianity began to embrace anti-pleasure views. The next chapter will show how Paul centered his personal behavior and much of his writings on the dangers of bodily pleasures, and how this opened up Christianity to the asceticism found in Hellenistic philosophies and Jewish Gnosticism.

5

Paul: The Beginnings of Christian Anti-Pleasure Views

THIRTY YEARS AFTER JESUS' crucifixion, the Christian movement had been transformed. The original apostles thought of Christ as a Jewish Messiah and strove to reach the Jewish masses by spreading his prophetic exhortations. For some disciples, however, Jesus' message transcended the limitations of Israel and its religious tradition: the good news should be brought to everyone. Indeed, it took someone from outside the original group to envision the truly revolutionary nature of the Christ. This individual was Paul.

Paul was born Saul of Jewish parents in the Asia Minor city of Tarsus. What we know of his life before his conversion is told in Paul's epistles, written twenty years after Jesus' crucifixion, and in Luke's writings an additional thirty years later. Saul claimed to have been a Pharisee. In Acts, Luke describes him as coming to Jerusalem at a young age to gain religious training, culminating with his studying under Rabbi Gamaliel, the foremost Pharisee teacher. In his own writings, however, even when attempting to buttress his standing among Jewish Christians, Paul only mentions that he was a Pharisaic follower. He says nothing about coming to Jerusalem at a young age or about training with Rabbi Gamaliel.

Acts claims that Paul's Pharisee beliefs led him to engage in anti-Christian actions. He watched approvingly the killing of the Christian evangelist Stephen just three years after Jesus' crucifixion. And thereafter, we are told, Saul went throughout Judea persecuting Jesus' first followers:

PAUL: THE BEGINNINGS OF CHRISTIAN ANTI-PLEASURE VIEWS

> Then Saul, still breathing threats and murder against the disciples of the Lord, went to the high priest nd asked letters from him to the synagogues of Damascus, so that if he found any who were of the Way, whether men or women, he might bring them bound to Jerusalem. (Acts 9:1-2)

On the road to Damascus, however, Christ appears and the Pharisee Saul converts to the faithful Christian Paul.

Much of this story is problematic. Why did Paul not mention in his own writings that he was a Jerusalemite rather than emphasizing his birthplace Tarsus? Why didn't he announce that he was a student of Rabbi Gamaliel when he was trying to enhance his religious stature among Jewish Christians? Indeed, his Pharisaic training in Jerusalem is suspect since when he quotes from the Old Testament, the Greek Septuagint translation always took precedence over the Hebrew version. This is much more consistent with the Greek-speaking Saul being raised in Tarsus—with a Hellenistic Jewish training—and only coming to Jerusalem as an adult.

How could Pharisaic teachings so inflame him against Christians when the Pharisaic leadership was having amicable discourse with Jesus over interpretations of the Mosaic laws? While disagreements existed, Jesus faithfully followed the laws and there is no reason to believe that he or his first disciples were considered unbelievers by the Pharisees. Indeed, there is evidence that the Pharisees were protecting Christians from Sadducee attempts to exact retribution. In particular, when the high priest brought charges against the evangelist leader Peter, Pharisees on the high council, led by Rabbi Gamaliel, saved him (Acts 5:34-39). How was Saul in such close collusion with the Temple leadership, the Sadducees, with whom the Pharisees were in conflict? Saul's actions are much more consistent with his being a guard for the Temple leadership than a faithful Pharisee.[1] Sanders believes that the "persecution of the Christian movement . . . had to do with Paul's zeal, but not with his Pharisaism."[2]

THE ABANDONMENT OF THE MOSAIC LAWS

All of the first disciples considered their nascent movement an apocalyptic branch of Judaism. They were all practicing Jews and expected Jesus' followers to obey all of the Mosaic laws, as Jesus had done. This was not a

1. Maccoby, *Mythmaker*.
2. Sanders, *Paul*, 8.

problem when they were proselytizing among Jews in the land of Israel. However, once efforts to engage Gentiles in the Mediterranean basin began, it was not practical.

The Diaspora Jew Paul was in the forefront of those followers who wanted to convert non-Jews by eliminating at least some of the Mosaic laws requirement. Indeed, Paul used his (supposed) Pharisaic past to not only convince his audience that the Pharisees were the enemies of Christ but to question those who wished to uphold the Mosaic laws as part of the Christian belief system. Thus, unlike the first disciples, Paul has a fundamentally antagonistic relationship with the Pharisees and those Christians who wished to sustain the Mosaic laws.

As Paul began to proselytize in Asia Minor, he had conflicts with the Jewish communities he encountered. In response, he decided that he should be the apostle to the Gentiles. To clarify the situation, we are told, in around 49 CE, there was a meeting in Jerusalem with the Christian evangelists, led by Jesus' brother James. At this meeting, it was decided that Paul would take the lead in proselytizing among the uncircumcised while Peter would take the lead among the circumcised. Moreover, it was agreed that the Gentile converts would not have to be circumcised. They would only have to respect Mosaic laws sufficient to engage in table fellowship with the Jewish Christians who continued to follow *all* of the Mosaic laws.

Reflecting his understanding of the Jerusalem meeting, initially Paul was willing to argue that the Mosaic laws were a matter of tradition: Jewish converts were therefore expected to follow them, but as they were not part of the Gentile tradition, Gentile converts were not. For Paul, these were personal preferences and had nothing to do with one's faith in Christ and willingness to follow the proper ethical path: "For in Christ Jesus neither circumcision nor uncircumcision avails anything but faith working through love (Gal 5:6)." In many ways, this could reasonably be thought to be in the tradition of Jesus. He seemed to follow Mosaic laws out of respect for tradition but appeared to believe that dietary laws and circumcision had little to do with his ethical precepts.

These limited requirements, however, proved to be unworkable in Antioch. As the capital of the Seleucid kingdom, it became a center of commerce and culture. In 64 BCE, the Romans liberated Antioch and envisioned it replacing Alexandria as the empire's eastern capital. Over the next century, a series of building projects reflected this Roman vision. The city expanded along grand colonnades and a new aqueduct facilitated the building of numerous community baths. Reflecting Antioch's status, the Romans built a hippodrome—the Circus of Antioch—modeled on the Circus Maximus in Rome. Measuring five football fields in length, it could house up to 80,000 spectators.

When Paul came to the city, it numbered half a million. The spacious colonnades had private houses mingled with public buildings—temples and baths—with enough capacity to allow the nearby quarter of the city to make use of them. At the hippodrome, thousands in attendance could witness "the fastest horses . . . Theaters resounded with contests of flute, lyre, and voice and the manifold delights of the stage."[3]

The Jewish community comprised 10 to 15 percent of the city's population. Together with God-fearers, the Jewish presence was substantial. While the Kerateion district in the southern end of the city had the largest concentration, Jews lived throughout Antioch. Their Hellenized community ran the whole gamut of degrees of Jewishness and assimilation. The most "orthodox" would have been gathered closest to the synagogues and other community facilities while the most assimilated would have positioned themselves wherever their lifestyle, social status, business, or political activity led them. Some of the lavish villas in the Daphne district likely belonged to well-off assimilated families.[4]

In Antioch, as elsewhere throughout the Roman Empire, it is quite likely that a majority of Christian converts were God-fearers. Many of Paul's epistles were clearly written for an audience that was quite familiar with Judaism. His epistle to the Romans "could be understood only by people who were trained in Jewish culture [which strongly suggests] that most people in the Roman church . . . had lived as sympathizers on the margins of the synagogues before they became Christian."[5]

Peter's visit to Antioch exposed disagreements as to the degree Gentile converts must observe Jewish dietary laws in order to foster table fellowship. Peter had approved the compromise worked out at the Jerusalem meeting. He was a wandering charismatic directly involved in gaining converts. Proselytizing activities made him more flexible than the insulated Jerusalem church leaders. For the God-fearer converts, "it would have been very easy to make the relatively minor concessions that made

---

3. Libanius, *Antioch*, 51.
4. Antiochian, "Jewish Quarter(s)."
5. Lampe, "Roman Christians," 225; and Stark, *Rise of Christianity*.

table fellowship with their Jewish fellow believers possible."⁶ However, when Peter accepted table fellowship with these Gentile Christians, the Jerusalem leadership sent emissaries to make Peter conform to stricter Jewish norms and he recanted (Gal 2:11).

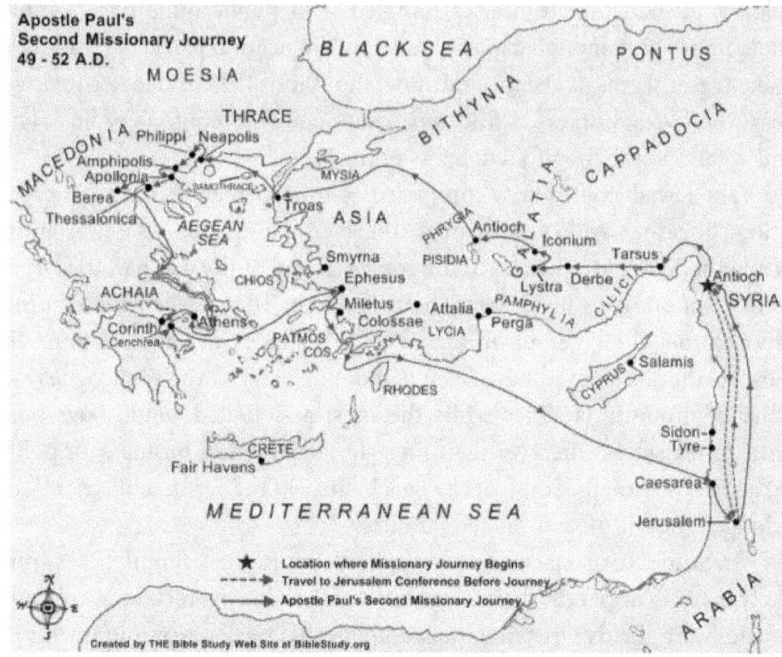

Figure 5.1: Paul's Second Journey

Paul was deeply troubled by Peter's about-face and in response he transformed his views on the Mosaic laws. Paul began arguing that *no* Christians should be required to follow them. Indeed, in retort to Peter, Paul exclaimed, "We have believed in Jesus Christ that we might be justified in faith in Christ and not by works of the law; for by works of the law no flesh shall be justified" (Gal 2:16). Paul now argued that you cannot have two paths to righteousness: giving your faith to Christ or obeying the Mosaic laws:

> Why then was the law given? It was added because of transgressions, until the arrival of the descendant to whom the promise had been made.... Thus the law had become our guardian until Christ,

---

6. Murphy-O'Connor, *Paul*, 43.

> so that we could be declared righteous by faith. But now that faith has come, we are no longer under a guardian. (Gal 3:19, 3:24-25)

Moreover, Paul claimed that with the death of Christ for man's sins, the former path to righteousness was no longer valid:

> Listen! I, Paul, tell you that if you let yourselves be circumcised, Christ will be of no benefit to you at all! . . . You who are trying to be declared righteous by the law have been alienated from Christ; you have fallen away from grace! For through the Spirit, by faith, we wait expectantly for the hope of righteousness. (Gal 5:2-5)

Though this was the message that Paul brought to the uncircumcised, in the Acts of the Apostles we repeatedly find Paul going into synagogues on the Jewish Sabbath: in Antioch (Acts 13:14), Iconium (Acts 14:1), Thessalonica (Acts 17:1), Beroea (Acts 17:10), Athens (Acts 17:17), Corinth (Acts 18:4), and Ephesus (Acts 18:19; 19:8). The Sabbath gathering was the only time large numbers of God-fearers congregated. This strongly suggests that Paul went into the synagogues not primarily to recruit Jews but to recruit the God-fearers there.[7]

PAUL AND DUALISTIC THOUGHT

Paul went beyond simply claiming that the law was no longer necessary. He now claimed that following the law was *responsible* for the sinfulness of man:

> I would not have known sin except through the law. For indeed I would not have known what it means to desire something belonging to someone else if the law had not said, "*Do not covet.*" But sin, seizing the opportunity through the commandment, produced in me all kinds of wrong desires. (Rom 7:5-8)

In his epistle to the Colossians, Paul counseled Timothy on how to proselytize in Colossae. He must remember that Christians are no longer governed by the Mosaic laws, for Christ "wiped out the requirements that were against us, which were contrary to us. And he has taken it out of the way, being nailed to the cross (Col 2:8-13)." As a result, Timothy can counter those who use the law to "cheat you through . . . deceit according to . . .

---

[7]. Crossan and Reed, *In Search of Paul,* xi.

the basic principles of the world, not according to Christ." By embracing the Spirit, Timothy will be immune to the dangers of the law.

Paul further counseled Timothy against compromising with the Law: "So let no one judge you in food or in drink, or regarding a festival or a new moon or sabbaths." Paul implored Timothy, "Do not subject yourself to regulations . . . These things have the appearance of wisdom in self-imposed religion . . . but are of no value against the indulgence of the flesh (Col 2:16-23)." Taken as a whole, Colossians is stating that following the Law will create temptations for indulgences of the flesh; only embracing the Spirit will free you from those temptations.

Paul's contrasting the Spirit and the flesh strongly suggested that he embraced Hellenistic dualism: the evil body houses the spiritual heart; and they are in mortal opposition. For those who are sympathetic to this dualistic interpretation of Paul's exhortations, one clear implication is that "to go back to the Law as a way of life puts one under the control of the flesh, it nullifies true spirituality by faith in the Holy Spirit. It results in domination by the sinful nature of the flesh."[8]

For many students of the New Testament, however, reading Hellenistic dualism into Paul's statements is wrongheaded. For example, Father John Echert wrote: "St. Paul does not share the wrong view of many ancient thinkers who viewed the material world as intrinsically evil, having proceeded from an evil source."[9] Others point out that nowhere in his epistles does Paul ever preach for Christians to reject material pleasures because they feed the sinful flesh. Indeed, as noted above, when counseling Timothy, he makes a point of saying, "Let no one judge you in food or in drink."

Paul did hold to a Jewish Diaspora view that was heavily influenced by the Hellenistic environment in which he lived.[10] Moreover, among Jews in the Diaspora, the idea developed that there were cosmic forces in the world; that God had a personal adversary, the Devil, who was responsible for suffering. God was still the creator of this world and would be the ultimate redeemer, but for now the forces of evil had the upper hand. This worldview gave rise to the Danielic apocalyptic literature.

---

8. https://bible.org/article/mosaic-law-its-function-and-purpose-new-testament

9. http://www.ewtn.com/vexperts/showmessage.asp?number=327311&Pg=&Pgnu=1&recnu=

10. Ralph Marcus, "Challenge of Greco-Roman Culture," 99. Finds strong parallels between Stoicism and the writings of the second-century BCE Jewish writer Ben Sira, especially in their concern for the less privileged.

Paul: The Beginnings of Christian Anti-Pleasure Views

Paul would very likely have been exposed to these writings, given his deep knowledge of the Septuagint. Cardinal Murphy-O'Connor believes that Paul also must have had a strong secular education in Taurus, given "his command of Greek and in the way in which he organized the content of his letters."[11] Indeed, he posits that Paul was likely to have been educated at the University of Taurus where, given that it was a "bastion of Stoicism ... Paul could hardly have escaped its influence even if he did not study it."[12] Indeed, Crossan and Reed contend, "What Paul did receive was a first-class education in the synagogue at Tarsus with a strong emphasis on apologetics for Judaism and polemics against paganism."[13]

The likelihood that Paul embraced Hellenistic philosophies is strengthened by the way he discussed sexual relations. He took an uncompromising position on sexual relations outside of marriage. He told his audience that they cannot give their bodies to both Christ and to sexual immorality:

> Now the body is not for sexual immorality but for the Lord, and the Lord for the body. . . . Do you not know that your bodies are members of Christ? Shall I then take the members of Christ and make *them* members of a harlot? Certainly not! Or do you not know that one who is joined to harlot is one body with her. "For the two," He says, "shall become one." But he who is joined to the Lord is one Spirit *with him*. (1 Cor 6:13-17)

Paul's vigorous condemnation undoubtedly was a response to sexual excesses in Hellenist society that went well beyond the degrading Roman brothels. In Egypt, such intemperance was embedded in the everyday life of upper-class Alexandrians. At the end of the second century CE, when Christianity was firmly rooted there, Clement of Alexandria railed against the pagan culture of sex. He condemned in the strongest terms possible the erotica disguised as mythology that adorned homes, stimulating passion and the rejection of modesty:

> Nowadays, nobody is ashamed to look quite openly at pictures which show sexual postures of utter abandon; what is more, they treat them like votive offerings, as if they were the images of their gods. . . . I denounce not only those who do all this, but also those

11. Murphy-O'Connor, *Paul*, 5.
12. Ibid., 6.
13. Crossan and Reed, *In Search of Paul*, 379.

who like looking at it and hearing about it. Your ears become whores, your eyes prostitutes, your perceptions become an adulterer at the sight of these [*symplegmata*] couplings [which show two or more people writhing around in the throes of passion.][14]

Figure 5.2: Erotic Scene from Tavern in Pompeii, 1st Century CE

Figure 5.3: Fresco from Pompeii

14. Montserrat, *Sex and Society*, 213.

PAUL: THE BEGINNINGS OF CHRISTIAN ANTI-PLEASURE VIEWS

Paul went further than rejecting sexual relations outside of marriage, already the norm within Jewish communities. He indicated that the *superior* way to respond was to reject *all* sexual relations, "for it is good for man to not touch a woman" (1 Cor 7:1). And he offered himself as that ideal: "For I wish that all men were even as I myself... [and] say to the unmarried and to the widows, it is good for them to remain as I am" (1 Cor 7:7-8). Paul, however, was realistic; he recognized that marriage was a bulwark against illicit sexual activities:

> Nevertheless, because of sexual immorality, let each man have his own wife, and let each woman have her own husband.... But if you cannot exercise self-control, let them marry. For it is better to marry than to burn with passion. (1 Cor 7:2-9)

Paul did counsel his audience to engage in sexual relations within marriage on a regular basis (1 Cor 7:3-4). The purpose was not, however, for procreation, since Paul has an apocalyptic vision that the end-time was near. For him, it was solely so that "Satan does not tempt you because of your lack of self-control" (1 Cor 7:5).

Even within marriage, Paul believed that sexual passion should be discouraged. To married couples, he preached, "That every one of you should know how to possess his vessel in sanctification and honor. Not in the passion of lust, even as the Gentiles which know not God" (1 Thes 4:4-5). Indeed, reflecting on the coming apocalypse, Paul counseled the Corinthians: "But this I say to you, brethren, the time is short so that from now on even those who have wives should behave as if they had none" (1 Cor 7:29).

Just as with his use of the spirit-flesh dichotomy, Paul's judgment on sexual behavior seems to go beyond what was necessary to win converts to Christ. Why did he do more than strongly condemn sexual relations outside of marriage? Once more this suggests that Hellenist philosophies, which place importance on control of one's sexual urges, must have played a role in Paul's thoughts.

EQUALITY WITHIN THE CHRISTIAN MOVEMENT

Paul was consumed by his need to convert as many people as possible before the Second Coming of Christ. He held the apocalyptic view found in Mark, where Jesus tells the disciples: "Truly I tell you, some of you standing here will not taste death till they see the kingdom of God present with power" (Mark 9:1). Paul told the Thessalonians:

> For this we say to you by the word of the Lord, that we who are alive and remain until the coming of the Lord will by no means precede those who are asleep . . . [for] the dead in Christ will rise first. (1 Thess 4:15-16)

His expectation that the end-time was near led Paul to ignore many issues that would stand in the way of individuals embracing Christ: "There was not time to remake society."[15] Some Christians, particularly in Jerusalem, were hostile to Rome. By contrast, Paul rejected opposition as it would conflict with attempts to win converts throughout the Roman Empire. He told Christian followers:

> Let every soul be subject to the government authorities. For there is no authority except from God, and the authorities that exist are appointed by God. Therefore whomever resists the authorities resists the ordinance of God, and those who resist will bring judgment on themselves. For rulers are not a terror to good works, but to evil. (Rom 13:1-3)

How different this is from the prophet Samuel's forewarning of the disastrous impact when the people demanded that he anoint Saul as the unified ruler of the twelve tribes.

More contentious, in some of New Testament epistles, Paul strongly supported the social institutions that maintained class and gender hierarchies. For Paul, there was no Lazarus fighting with wild animals for the scraps left over from the rich. Indeed, if all of the New Testament letters attributed to Paul are believed,[16] he held that slaves were to serve faithfully their masters:

> Bondservant, obey in all things your master according to the flesh . . . not with eyeservice as men-pleasures, but as bondservants of Christ, doing the will of God from the heart (Eph 6:5-6). Not pilfering but showing all good fidelity, that they may adorn the doctrine of God our Savior in all things. (Titus 2:10)

---

15. Sanders, *Paul*, 12.

16. In "Deutero Pauline Letters," Just contends that "80 percent of scholars believe that these letters were not written by Paul but by his followers after his death." For support for the authenticity of the Pastoral Letters, see Hawthorne and Merton, *Dictionary of Paul and His Letters*, cf. 659-665.

Paul: The Beginnings of Christian Anti-Pleasure Views

Paul does indicate his approval of the efforts of slaves (and supporters) to buy their freedom: "Were you called *while* a slave? Do not be concerned about it; but if you can be made free, rather use it" (1 Cor 7:21). In this regard, Paul focused, like many Stoics, on humanitarian concerns for slaves. These concerns led to Roman reforms of the slave system: prohibiting castration; masters from condemning their slaves to fight wild beasts in the arena; and the sale of individuals to pimps. It made owners liable if they killed their own slaves without cause and required them to sell slaves whom they treated cruelly. Like Paul and the Christian community, Stoics "did not turn their understanding of the humiliation of slavery into a call for manumission. Stoics advocated good treatment of slaves ... kind masterly behavior and restraint were urged to improve the spiritual state of the master, not the social life of the slave."[17]

While Paul did not openly support universal manumission, the treatment of enslaved people *within* the Christian movement was an important issue. Slaves were so inexpensive that ownership went far down the social scale. As a result, some estimate that a majority of the population in Roman society was comprised of either slaves or former slaves. This was particularly true of Corinth, since at its founding in 44 BCE, Julius Caesar populated it with ex-slaves.[18]

Many slaves and ex-slaves were converts, and Paul was adamant that they be treated equally within Christian communities. This position is reflected in Paul's letter to Philemon. It concerns Onesimus, a slave from Colossae who had run away from his master, perhaps committing theft in the process. Onesimus was converted to Christ by Paul. Paul sends him back to his master with this letter asking that he be welcomed back, not just as a slave but as a brother in Christ. In his touching appeal, Paul suggests that he would like to have Onesimus work for the gospel.

Paul does not attack the institution of slavery for this is something the Christian communities of the first century were in no position to do. Yet by presenting Onesimus as "brother, beloved to me, but even more so to you" (Phil 16), Paul voiced an idea central to his Christianity: equality within the community between slave and free.

This contrast between Paul's desires for the Christian community and his stance on societal institutions is also found in his writings on women. Paul may have supported patriarchal households: "But I want you to know

---

17. Joshel, *Slavery in the Roman World*, 73.
18. Pickett, "Conflict in Corinth," 123.

that the head of every man is Christ, the head of woman is man, and the head of Christ is God" (1 Cor 11:3). Or as he stated in Ephesians, "Just as the church is subject to Christ, so also wives ought to be, in everything, to their husbands" (Eph 5:24). And women were to serve their husbands: "To be discreet, chaste, homemakers, good, obedient to their own husbands, that word of God may not be blasphemed" (Titus 2:5). All of these supports for patriarchy are from letters where Paul's authorship is questionable.

Whether or not Paul confronted the societal legitimacy of patriarchal households, he strongly advocated equality between Christian men and women. Central to this goal was the undermining of the sexual exploitation most women had to endure, particularly those who were or had been enslaved or who came from families that had been enslaved. The mistreatment of brothel women was seared into their consciousness. It was these women, not those who lived in the gilded cages of the Hellenist aristocracy, who demanded a different Christian ethic; one that provided an alternative to not only licentious behavior but the sexual degradation of women.

This is why it was important for Paul to make clear that Christianity went beyond condemning sexual relationships outside of marriage. Paul sought to bring equality to those within the Christian community. He summed up this view:

> There is neither Jew nor Greek, neither slave nor free, there is neither male nor female; for you are all one in Christ Jesus." (Gal 3:27-28)

Paul's demands for gender equality within Christian communities extended to his own relationships. Paul often relied upon women in his proselytizing efforts. In Philippians, we are told that Lydia's house was the assembly center for the budding Christian movement there. Paul also mentions Euodia and Syntyche as having "striven side by side with me in the gospel, together with Clement and the rest of my co-workers, whose names are in the book of life" (Phil 4:3). Indeed, these two women must have been heads of their own house churches. As Murphy-O'Connor writes,

> This is why Paul, contrary to his normal practice, draws public attention to the need for reconciliation between these two women (Phil 4:2). The dispute must have gone beyond the personal, and polarized the community. Clearly the women were leaders with a significant number of followers.[19]

19. Murphy-O'Connor, *Paul*, 69.

Paul: The Beginnings of Christian Anti-Pleasure Views

Many scholars agree that a number of the women he singles out in Romans 16:7 had leadership roles within the Christian church. In particular, the carrier of the letter is Phoebe, who is identified as a leader from the church at Cenchreae, a port city near Corinth. Paul attaches to her the title *diakonos*, which most scholars translate as deacon rather than its more ambiguous meaning, servant. He also mentions Junia, who is "among the apostles," and a number of other women with whom he had done missionary work: Priscilla, Mary, Tryphena, Tryphosa, Julia, Nereus's sister, and Rufus's mother. Indeed, Priscilla must have been one of his more trusted leaders, as he brings her to Ephesus (Acts 18:18) and then on to Rome to prepare the groundwork for his letter (Rom 16:5).

Women, slaves, and ex-slaves comprised a significant share of Christian converts, but many free men joined as well. As Paul traversed the Christian communities from present-day Turkey to Rome, he was housed in private homes and was able to raise funds to carry on his proselytizing efforts. Since Christians did not beg for funds to survive, this strongly suggests that many evangelists were successful craftsmen who could practice their trades wherever they resided. Indeed, Paul was said to be a tentmaker who would work in the communities in which he traveled.

The structure of Roman society facilitated these efforts. A relatively small share of local citizens engaged in commerce or trade since these endeavors were associated with the work of slavers or provincials. This engendered an attitude among Roman citizens that work was beneath their dignity. As a result, outsiders dominated the crafts and commerce, including many Jews and God-fearers who became Christian converts. The more successful could live in comfort in roomy homes in good neighborhoods, exactly the places suitable for house churches.

Most of the residents of Rome, however, were not as fortunate. There was no public transportation. As a result, working men and women had to walk to work, so they lived in highly congested small quarters in three- and four-story apartment houses. These apartments lined narrow streets often no wider than twelve to sixteen feet; side streets were a mere six.

Since workingmen had to sardine themselves in waterless and airless apartments at night, they spent much of their free time on the crowded streets. During daylight, they were joined by peddlers, shoppers, schoolchildren, and other pedestrians. Given the foot traffic, Julius Caesar banned all wheeled vehicles other than those used for construction from travelling the streets from dawn to dusk.[20]

For some workingmen, houses of prostitution offered a bit of relief in an otherwise dreary existence. For others, it was the expansive and luxurious public baths open to all. The bathing area occupied the center of a complex that was surrounded by gardens and walking paths. One could buy snacks from vendors and watch games being played. However, workingmen were required to labor seven days each week, so they had little free time or spending money. Given such bleak lives, they, too, could be receptive to the good news offered by Christian evangelists.

CONCLUSIONS

Under Paul's leadership, Christianity shifted away from a movement that highlighted political and economic inequalities. Whereas the Jerusalem church continued to demand full conformity to the Mosaic laws, Paul did not. Whereas Jesus highlighted the deep gulf between the rich and the poor, Paul did not call for the manumission of slaves. Indeed, according to the Pastoral letters, Paul counseled them to be obedient to their masters. Similarly, in these letters, Paul seemed unwilling to overturn the patriarchal structure of the married household.

While Paul may have accommodated these societal inequalities, he consistently stressed equality *within* the Christian movement. His exposure to Hellenist philosophies led him to use dualist language in his condemnation of the Mosaic laws. Though he did not embrace dualism, Paul did shift Christianity away from Jesus the imbiber to concerns for sins of the flesh.

As the apocalyptic vision faded, the ascetic lifestyle that was read into Paul's writings was built upon in the next two centuries. Religious followers sought holiness in following the ascetic behavior of John the Baptist and the ascetic Therapeutae community identified by Philo. Indeed, in the first great compilation of Christian history, *Ecclesiastical History*, Eusebius claimed that this community housed the first Christian monks. Asceticism was carried forward by leading Christians who were trained in Hellenist philosophies, by the Desert Fathers who worked to discipline the flesh in order to attain the salvation of the soul, by the monastic communities that celebrated abstinence, and by the vestal virgins consecrated by Ambrose.

20. Casson, *Everyday Life*.

Paul: The Beginnings of Christian Anti-Pleasure Views

This growing privileging of ascetic behavior will be the subject of the next chapter.

While Paul may have been unwilling to confront the patriarchal family that dominated Roman society, just as Jesus, he seemed to make clear that gender inequality had no place within the Christian community. Jesus was reputed to have women followers who associated with him in public, ate with him, touched him, and supported him. So, too, Paul had women leaders in his churches and insisted that in Christ "there is not male and female."

Not everyone believes, however, that Paul championed the rights of women. In particular, historian Peter Brown is not willing to explain Paul's acceptance of patriarchal households as an expediency reflecting apocalyptic expectations. For Brown, Paul's thought was dominated by the notion that rich married adherents were central to the long-term growth of the Church. His letters to the Corinthians rejected the radical thoughts of some of the new Christians who would renounce marriage and commit to perpetual abstinence. Brown argued,

> A community rendered starkly separate from its neighbors by group celibacy would hardly have attracted many pagans into its midst. In coming down firmly on the side of allowing marriage to continue within the Church, Paul acted as he usually did whenever his converts were tempted to erect excessively rigid barriers between themselves and the outside world. As in his tolerant attitude to the eating of "polluted" pagan foods, so in his attitude to marriage, Paul sided with the well-to-do householders who had most to lose from total separation from the pagan world. For it was they who would support his ambitious mission to the gentiles most effectively.[21]

Whether or not Paul had these motivations, there is no question that determining the place of married households within Christian communities was an important consideration. In particular, as support for the ideals of male celibacy and female virginity grew, they threatened to make married households second-class Christians: individuals who could not attain the highest religious ideals. In subsequent chapters, we will see how Christian leaders dealt with this issue.

---

21. Brown, *Body & Society*, 54.

Jewish and Christian Views on Bodily Pleasure

In addition, one passage from Paul's authentic writings seems to support gender inequality *within* the Christian church. In First Corinthians 14:34-35, Paul wrote:

> Let your women remain silent in the churches. They are not allowed to speak, but must be in submission, as the Law says. If they want to inquire about something, they should ask their own husbands at home; for it is disgraceful for a woman to speak in the church.

This statement has been used by church leaders to justify exclusion of women from church leadership positions. It seems, however, to be in fundamental opposition to Paul's own behavior toward women since he took counsel from many and relied on them to accompany him as equals on his missionary work. Not surprisingly, there are many scholars who claim that this passage was included after Paul's death or a response to specific circumstances rather than a general statement of principle.[22]

In the next chapter, we will see that the struggle for gender equality continued. Paul's name is ascribed to later writings that might have been shaped to support a church leadership comprised solely of married men, a requirement that Paul would not have accepted. These Pastoral letters also strongly reject the ascetic tendencies found in his authentic writings.[23]

Finally, citing his authentic writings, many Christians believed that virginity was the only way men and women could have truly equal relationships. For others, virginity was also a means for women to become church leaders. During the second century, tales of ascetic women were prominent among Christian writings. Here were women who refused to participate in the constraints of patriarchal society. They remained unmarried, not under the control of a husband. And they were travelers, not staying at home under the authority of their fathers and brothers.[24] The next chapter will detail how the organized church was able to accept, if not promote, the value of female virginity while rejecting the ability of Christian women to attain leadership positions.

---

22. Crossan and Reed; and Joseph Tkach, "Women 'Should Remain Silent.'"
23. 1 Tim 4:3-5 and 1 Tim 5:23.
24. Bart Ehrman, *Lost Christianities*, 46.

6

The Triumph of Ascetic Values

Paul died on the eve of the Jewish rebellion in 66 CE. Over the next centuries, Christianity evolved from a small sect of Judaism that met in congregant homes to the major alternative to pagan rule. As the apocalyptic vision faded, Christianity had to develop an organizational structure that reflected a permanent earthly presence. It also had to determine its relationship to the Jewish scriptures and the Jewishness of its first evangelists. Most important for our purposes, however, is how the basic Christian tenets concerning ascetic behavior evolved so that by the middle of the third century, they formed one of the centerpieces of Christianity.

ORGANIZATIONAL STRUCTURE EVOLVES

During the last decades of the first century, the administrative structure of local Christian communities was loosely determined and spiritual leadership still resided with the itinerant holy men. They traveled between Christian communities, answering questions and recruiting new members through their preaching near synagogues and in the homes of the faithful. As the number of followers grew, a more permanent local structure was needed that included personnel responsible not only for administrative but also for spiritual communal needs. This is spelled out in the *Didache*, the earliest extant manuscript that sets out the governing principles of the Christian movement.

The *Didache* is divided into two parts. The first part describes the guidelines for Christian behavior: the dos and the don'ts. A Christian should be charitable: "Give to everyone that asks, without looking for any repayment, for it is the Father's pleasure that we share His gracious bounty with all men." A Christian should be meek: "The meek are to inherit the earth." Moreover, a Christian should have humility: "Do not parade your own merits . . . and do not make a point of associating with persons of eminence, but choose the companionship of honest and humble folks."[1]

The second part presents, for the first time, the desired church structure. The *Didache* encouraged Christian communities to appoint *episkopoi* and deacons for themselves. They are to be held in the same honor as the prophets and teachers who are visiting and sometimes taking up residence in the communities. *Episkopoi* is a general term that makes no distinction between priests (presbyters) and bishops. In mentioning deacons in the same breath as *episkopoi*, the *Didache* also draws attention to the administrative functions that both fulfilled. The spiritual and pastoral care of the congregation, by contrast, fell to the itinerant holy men.[2]

Fairly quickly thereafter, a new communal hierarchy is developed that shifts leadership to the office of a single bishop appointed to lead each local Christian community. The first recorded instance of the privileging of this organized church hierarchy is in Clement of Rome's letter to the Corinthians when a conflict over communal leadership arose. Clement forcefully argues that the first evangelists chose the local leadership:

> So preaching everywhere in country and town, they appointed their first fruits, when they had proved them by the Spirit, to be bishops and deacons unto them that should believe. (1 Clement 42:4)

Around 110 CE, Ignatius of Antioch, on his way to martyrdom in Rome, went further than Clement and championed the monarchic episcopate as a reflection of the One God and as a guarantor of the doctrinal unity of the church. Dissension can be avoided by uniting the faithful under the supreme local bishop. Nothing should be done without the bishop's consent. "One God, one bishop" became the orthodox slogan.[3]

---

1. http://www.instituteofcatholicculture.org/wp-content/uploads/2012/06/The_Didache_Handout.pdf

2. Rapp, *Holy Bishops*, 26.

3. Pagels, *Gnostic Paul*, 35.

The Triumph of Ascetic Values

Ignatius believed that a bishop's effective pastoral care was dependent on his personal conduct. He should be constant in his prayer, asking especially for the gift of understanding. He must oppose heterodox teaching and win over the unruly elements in the congregation through his gentleness. As the historian Claudia Rapp noted, "Bishops should constantly exercise his care for his congregation, he should look after the widows, and he should admonish the slaves and the married men and women to be content with their station in life."[4]

Ignatius identified the structure that became prevalent: the bishop's tasks were not only administrative, but also pastoral and liturgical; and in order to maintain the respect and cooperation of this flock, the bishop must be an exemplar of Christian conduct.[5] The guidelines for the behavior of bishops are spelled out in the Pastoral Letters. Indeed, one of the reasons for dating their authorship to the beginning of the second century is that this is when questions of church organization become prominent; and ascribing authorship to Paul gave them standing. In particular, 1 Tim 3:1-7 states:

> Whoever aspires to the office of bishop desires a noble task. Now a bishop must be above reproach, married only once, temperate, sensible, respectable, hospitable, an apt teacher, not a drunkard, not violent but gentle, not quarrelsome, and not a lover of money. He must manage his own household well, keeping his children submissive and respectful in every way—for if someone does not know how to manage his own household, how can he take care of God's church?

THE DECLINE OF JEWISH CHRISTIAN COMMUNITIES

The *Didache* demonstrated that the Jewish Christian community was still prominent at the end of the first century. It began as a Jewish catechetical work that was taken up and transformed by the Church into a manual of Church life and order.[6] It articulated the major elements of the emergent Christian faith in a more basic manner than the gospels. In keeping with

---

4. Rapp, *Holy Bishops*, 27.
5. Ibid., 28.
6. Draper, "Jesus Tradition in the *Didache*," 74-75.

a dominant theme of the first evangelists, Jesus' death plays no significant role.

In the *Didache*, the custom of drinking wine and breaking bread and saying thanks after the meal is firmly rooted in the tradition of Jewish prayer. There is a complete absence of any reference to a "mystical" bond between the body and blood of the "Son of God" who commands: "Do *this* in memory of Me." The rituals proposed in the *Didache* indicate that the language of the Eucharist had not yet been normalized.

This is also when the Gospel of Matthew was written. It was written from a Jewish viewpoint for an audience that had a working understanding of Jewish traditions. When Matthew tells the story of Jesus, he draws on Jewish symbols. Just as Moses, Jesus goes up on a mountain—the Mount—to teach and talk about the law. Just as there are the five books of Torah, Jesus delivers five different sermons. Matthew alone reports Jesus saying, "I am not sent but unto the lost sheep of the house of Israel," and instructing the disciples, "Go not into the way of the Gentiles, and into any city of the Samaritans enter ye not: But go rather to the lost sheep of the house of Israel." It uses the term "son of David" more times than the other Gospels combined.

In both Matthew and the *Didache*, we have a Jewish Christian perspective on obeying the Mosaic laws. The *Didache* commanded, "As regards diet, keep the rules so far as you are able, only be careful to refuse anything that has been offered to an idol, for that is worship of dead gods." In Matthew, Jesus says, "think not that I've come to destroy the law and the prophets—I've come not to destroy them but to fulfill them." Matthew's community subscribed to the law, but they saw apostles—not the Pharisees—as its rightful interpreters.[7]

Like the *Didache*, Matthew drew on the Jewish traditional obligation to the poor and needy. It quotes Jesus as saying, "If you would be perfect, go, sell what you possess and give to the poor [and] give to the one who begs from you, and do not refuse the one who would borrow from you" (Matt 19:21, 5:42). And Matthew preached humility in giving:

> When you give to the needy, sound no trumpets before you, as the hypocrites do in the synagogues and in the streets, that they may be praised by others. . . . When you give to the needy, do not let your left hand know what your right hand is doing, so that your giving may be in secret. (Matt 6:1-4)

---

7. http://www.pbs.org/wgbh/pages/frontline/shows/religion/story/matthew.html.

The Triumph of Ascetic Values

The preeminent position Matthew held across Christian communities demonstrated that at the beginning of the second century, Christianity continued to recruit heavily from among Diasporic Jews and God-fearers. This approach was undoubtedly accelerated by the growing realization that the Jerusalem Temple was never going to be rebuilt. In addition, after the murder of Roman Emperor Domitian in 96 CE, Nerva relaxed the rules for collection of the Jewish tax, limiting it to only those who openly practiced Judaism. Since Christians escaped the tax, this probably increased the success of Christian proselytizing efforts.[8] As the second century unfolded, Christianity began recruiting a significant number of pagans who had no relationships to the Jewish community. Many undoubtedly saw little reason to maintain Christian attachment to its Jewish past. This position was most forcefully articulated by Marcion, the son of a bishop and a wealthy ship-owner who converted to Christianity around 130 CE.

According to Marcion, the God of the Old Testament, whom he called the Demiurge, punishes mankind for its sins through suffering and death. By contrast, the gospel is given by Christ. It is the good news of deliverance; it involves love, mercy, grace, forgiveness, reconciliation, redemption, and life. The God of Jesus came into this world in order to save people from the vengeful God of the Jews.

For Marcion, as Jews who followed the law, Jesus' disciples never understood their master, wrongly thinking that he was the Jewish Messiah. As a result, Jesus had to start afresh and he called Paul to reveal "the truth of the gospel." Since Paul is credited with correctly transmitting the universality of Jesus' message, ten of his epistles were included in the Marcionite canon. It also included Marcion's edited version of the Gospel of Luke. None of the other gospels were included because Marcion believed that he was recovering the original message of Jesus; a message that was corrupted by Peter and the other apostles but recovered by Paul. Marcion's views were denounced as heresy by church leaders. After his excommunication by the Church of Rome, he returned to Asia Minor where he led many church congregations.

There is some disagreement as to why church leaders fought to maintain the Old Testament as the original message of the one true God. Some have argued that it reflected the remaining influence of Christian communities that still observed the Mosaic laws.[9] This seems unlikely, however, since after being forced to flee Jerusalem, Christian communities

---

8. Shaye J.D. Cohen, "Review."
9. Schoeps, *Jewish Christianity*.

that obeyed the Mosaic laws seemed to have been sustained only east of the Jordan River, in Pella and maybe some areas of Babylonia, not in the Mediterranean basin.

It is much more likely that Christian leaders had other reasons for maintaining ties to the religion's Jewish origins. There were still many in the pagan world who highly valorized aspects of Judaism and it would be hard to so harshly reject the original apostles as well-meaning dullards. In addition, the Gospel of Matthew had wide prominence in the Christian world and to condemn it as false would call into question those church leaders like Ignatius who had embraced it. Instead, Christianity took the position articulated by Justin Martyr that the error was the refusal of the Jewish community to accept Christ and the proper understanding of the Old Testament. In a hypothetical conversation with a rabbi, Justin used Isaiah to demonstrate that Christ brought forth the eternal law which is rejected by pious Jews:

> The Lawgiver is present, yet you do not see Him; to the poor the Gospel is preached, the blind see, yet you do not understand. . . . The new law requires you to keep perpetual sabbath, and you, because you are idle for one day, suppose you are pious, . . . and if you eat unleavened bread, you say the will of God has been fulfilled. The Lord our God does not take pleasure in such observances.[10]

Justin Martyr continued: "For other nations have not inflicted on us and on Christ this wrong to such an extent as you have, who in very deed are the authors of the wicked prejudice against the Just One, and us who hold by Him." This perspective signaled the end of the acceptance of practicing Jews within the Christian fold and provided the foundation of the evolving enmity toward Judaism.

THE STRUGGLE OVER ASCETICISM

The *Didache* and the Jewish Christian community rejected asceticism. This rejection was most explicit in the Pastoral Letters. First Timothy proclaimed that teachings which forbade marriage and demanded abstinence from certain foods came from "deceitful spirits and doctrines of demons." (1 Tim 4:1-3). It also instructed, "No longer drink only water, but take a little wine for the sake of your stomach and your frequent ailments" (1 Tim

---

10. Justin Martyr, "Dialogue with Trypho."

The Triumph of Ascetic Values

5:23). Though Paul did not insist, he preferred that Christians choose sexual continence. By contrast, the Pastoral Letters required bishops to be married and judged on the manner in which they governed their households.

As we have seen, Paul embraced women as equals in building the church. They led houses of assembly, they participated in his missionary activities, and he trusted them to be his envoy. In the letter Clement of Rome wrote to the Corinthians, however, the status of women within the organized church was not yet well formed. On the one hand, he began:

> Women ye exhorted to perform all things in a blameless and honorable and pure conscience, loving dutifully their own husbands; and ye taught them to manage the affairs of their houses with gravity, keeping in the rule of obedience, being temperate in all things. (1 Clem 1:3)[11]

On the other hand, Clement noted approvingly, "Many women being strengthened through the grace of God have performed many manly deeds"[12] (1 Clem 55:3). Clement then proceeded to describe the heroic efforts of Judith and Esther.

At the same time, we find in Luke that women's religious pursuits are legitimate. When Martha wants her sister to help with household chores instead of listening to Jesus, Jesus responds, "Mary has chosen the good portion which should not be taken away from her" (Luke 10:38-42). Thus, at the end of the first century, women had not yet been excluded from participating in public life, including church activities.

We now begin to have documents that link lifelong virginity with gender equality. The Gospel of the Egyptians endorses "sexual asceticism as the means of . . . overcoming the alleged sinful differences between male and female, enabling all persons to return to what was understood to be their primordial androgynous state."[13] By contrast, 1 Timothy 2:15 declared that women would not be saved by living chaste lives but rather through bearing children. Thus, the Pastoral Letters should also be understood as an attempt to limit the public and religious role of women in Christian communities.

By far the most important threat to the positions taken in the Pastoral Letters was the figure of Thecla. A strong tradition emerged that centered on this legendary companion of Paul. Penned during the second century,

---

11. Translation: http://www.earlychristianwritings.com/text/1clement-hoole.html
12. Ibid.
13. Cameron, *Other Gospel*, 49.

the Acts of Thecla circulated in several languages, and was included in the early biblical canon in Syrian and Armenian churches.

Thecla is a woman from an influential family who is converted after hearing Paul speak. As a result of Paul's exhortation to remain a virgin, she breaks her engagement, is persecuted, and is sentenced to face beasts in the arena and then to burn at the stake. But she is rescued from death, baptizes herself, and is commissioned as a teacher and evangelist by Paul. Her story reflects a Pauline tradition that provided apostolic blessing for women's leadership roles in the church.

Besides the Thecla narrative, a number of similar apocryphal Acts circulated widely in the East. They all exhorted Christians to abstain from the flesh, wine, meat, and marriage. Just as Thecla, they all highlighted ideal women. In Acts of Andrew, we have Maximilla. After being cured by Andrew, she removes herself from her husband. Her chastity and faith survive all attacks. Acts of Thomas gives us Mygdonia, a woman converted to a life of Christian continence; she renounces her husband, adopts a life of poverty, and converts the king's wife, Tertia, to Christianity. In Acts of John, it is Drusiana who is locked in a tomb when she rejects her husband. She weathers the ordeal and eventually convinces her husband to join her in a life of Christian continence. In Acts of Peter, we learn of the apostle's ability to convince many women to choose continence and leave their husbands.[14]

As wandering charismatics were being replaced by bishops, these apocryphal Acts may have sought to preserve in narrative form a "style of Christian ministry vanishing from the world."[15] They were not, however, intended for use by missionaries in their proselytizing efforts. Instead, they were written for an audience already converted and ready to accept these women as role models. Except for the apostles themselves, in the Acts of Andrew, Thomas, John, and Peter, no male Christians are as favored or as highly praised as the women. Thus, it is likely that the apocryphal Acts were popular among communities of continent Christian women, the widows of the church, who were participants in stable church structures.

This perspective was an important component of Marcion's beliefs:

> Only by demanding that . . . men and women renounce the marriages that had previously held them together, and even by dissolving the ties that bound children to their parents, could true

---

14. Davies, *Revolt of the Widows*, 55.
15. Ibid., 30

The Triumph of Ascetic Values

> Christians come together in a freely chosen communion, not undermined by preexisting family bonds, loyalties, and habits.[16]

Indeed, followers would pull individuals out of their family settings to join small churches scattered throughout Asia Minor and Syria.

A similar movement, labeled Encratism, developed; it forbade marriage and counseled abstinence from meat. Its leader, Tatian, believed that bonding to Christ required sexual abstinence. Like Marcion, Tatian had been a Christian teacher in Rome at mid-century and was a disciple of Justin Martyr. Upon Justin's death, he left the city and eventually established a school in Mesopotamia. In a lost writing, *On Perfection,* Tatian considered matrimony a symbol of the tying of the flesh to the perishable world and an invention of the devil. "To gain the Spirit of God humans must... abandon married intercourse, the most decisive obstacle to the indwelling of the Spirit."[17]

Both Marcion and Tatian led movements in the hinterlands of the East, where apocalyptic visions continued. More so than in urban areas, there was a firm belief in magic and demons. When the apocryphal Acts report exorcisms of demons, they reflected widely held views. Indeed, Justin believed that Christianity could most effectively combat them: "For every demon, when exorcised in the name of this very Son of God... is overcome and subdued."[18]

In these small-town settings, many young Christians sought purity and redemption through ascetic behavior. Some prominent Christian men and women believed that time was running short and rejected the unbroken flow of a human sexual nature that caused life to continue from generation to generation.[19] This milieu is captured in the Acts of Judas Thomas. Written at the beginning of the third century, it describes the impact of Encratite traditions on society. Christ has reached down into the abyss of a world dominated by demonic powers.

Building on the Lazarus imagery, Judas Thomas condemns a world where "the poor went hungry in winter while kings planned huge palaces, where servants carried great ladies in towering palanquins, trampling their fellow-creatures underfoot to make way for their mistresses."[20] Just as with

16. Brown, *Body & Society,* 89.
17. Ibid., 92.
18. Davies, *Revolt of the Widows,* 20.
19. Brown, *Body & Society,* 64.
20. Ibid., 98.

Thecla, Judas Thomas recounts sexual renunciation on the wedding night: "And the young people were persuaded by our Lord, and gave up themselves to Him, and were preserved from filthy lust, and passed the night in their places."[21]

While Tatian and Marcion preached in the rural East, Valentinus spread ascetic ideals in the urban West. Trained in Alexandria, he became a widely recognized Christian teacher in Rome and, owing to his brilliance and eloquence, was a candidate for bishop of Rome. However, when he was not selected, Valentinus went to Cyprus to teach until his death in 161. He had many students who spread his views throughout the Christian world.

Unlike Tatian or Marcion, Valentinus embraced aspects of Gnosticism. In Gnosticism, the world of the Demiurge is represented by the lower world, which is associated with matter, flesh, and time. The world of God is represented by the upper world and is associated with the soul and perfection. Most important, the true knowledge of the world—*gnosis*—is only known to a select few individuals. In the case of Valentinus, he claimed that he learned it from an alleged disciple of Paul, Teudas.

Valentinus's followers attended established churches but sustained the tradition of spiritual leadership in the hands of holy men; those who had absorbed the *gnosis* that was hidden from others. As a result, they did not believe that the monarchal bishops understood the true wisdom of Christ. Indeed, Bishop Irenaeus of Lyons feared that while Valentinians attended the organized church, they met separately to critique the bishops' pronouncements. He was outraged at their claim that they, being spiritual, were released from the ethical restraints that he, as a mere servant of the Demiurge, ignorantly sought to foist upon them.[22] Thus, variants of Gnosticism were a major obstacle to the bishop assuming the uncontested authority that Ignatius of Antioch and subsequent church leaders desired.

Just as important, all these variants followed Paul's seeming acceptance of women as equals within the Christian fold. Valentinian churches were run on the principle of equal access, equal participation, and equal claims to knowledge. This was particularly upsetting to Tertullian, a Christian convert who lived in Carthage in the late second century and wrote influential books against the Christian gnostics. He protested the participation of "those women among the heretics" who share with men positions of authority: "They teach, they engage in discussion; they exorcise, they

---

21. William Wright, *Apocryphal Acts*, 156.
22. Pagels, *Gnostic Paul*, 44.

The Triumph of Ascetic Values

cure." Tertullian also complained that some Christians were using the example of Thecla to legitimize women's roles of teaching and baptizing in the church.[23] He was particularly outraged by Marcion, who had the audacity to appoint men and women on an equal basis as priests and bishops.

Tertullian vehemently rejected any role for women in the church. He believed that virgins should conform to Paul's precepts and keep themselves strictly veiled. Like Clement of Alexandria, he practiced a strict personal code and later in life joined the Montanists, a movement that practiced asceticism in preparation for the final judgment.

Tertullian believed that continence brought down the gift of the Spirit: "By continence you will buy up a great stock of sanctity, by making savings on the flesh, you will be able to invest in the Spirit."[24] Moreover, he claimed that children distracted parents from preparing for martyrdom and the kingdom to come.[25]

Another church leader, Bishop Irenaeus, was appalled that the local Valentinian priest allowed women to prophesize. Still worse, he allowed them to act as priests in celebrating the Eucharist with him. More generally, Irenaeus wrote, "The so-called Encratites preach abstinence from marriage and so made void God's pristine creation, and indirectly reprove him who made male and female for generation of the human race."[26]

The efforts of Tertullian, Irenaeus, and other church leaders proved successful. The challenges to the spiritual primacy of the bishop were turned back and the ability of women to participate in religious leadership was restricted. At this point, the organization of the New Testament began to be formalized. In particular, Irenaeus criticized the heretics for selecting only one of the gospels: the Jewish Christian Ebionites selected only Matthew; the Marcionites used only Luke; those who separated Jesus from the Christ (most Gnostics) used only Mark; the Valentinian Gnostics used only John. Irenaeus continued:

> For, since there are four zones of the world in which we live, and four principal winds . . . and the pillar and ground of the Church is the Gospel and the spirit of life, it is fitting that she should have four pillars, breathing out immorality on every side.[27]

23. Tertullian, *On Baptism*, Chapter 17.
24. Brown, *Body & Society*, 77.
25. Hunter. *Marriage, Celibacy, and Heresy*, 118.
26. Ibid., 101.
27. Bart Ehrman, *Lost Christianities*, 239-40.

The canon eventually comprised twenty-seven writings: the four Gospels; thirteen letters ascribed to Paul, including the Pastoral Letters; and ten other texts. None of the apocryphal Acts were included, though many continued to circulate in individual Christian communities, particularly in the East.

Now the *Apostolic Tradition* articulated the position espoused by these church leaders: The bishop is a successor of the apostles and partakes of the same Spirit as they do. It is the apostolic succession of the bishop that bestows on him the Holy Spirit. As a consequence, spiritual authority resides not just in the person of the bishop but also in the episcopal office per se. It comes from the other bishops thorough the imposition of hands and the prayer of ordination.[28]

ASCETICISM TRIUMPHS

The defeated movements combined their attack on the primacy of the bishop with the role of women and ascetic practices. For their attack on the bishops' position, Clement of Alexandria condemned them as heretic Gnostics. Unlike Tertullian and Irenaeus, however, he was open to the religious involvement of women and saw gender equality before God:

> Let us ... give ourselves to the Lord; clinging to what is surest, the cable of faith in Him, and understanding that the virtue of man and woman is the same. For if the God of both is one, the master of both is also one; one church, one temperance, one modesty; their food is common, marriage an equal yoke; respiration, sight, hearing, knowledge, hope, obedience, love all alike.[29]

Clement also offered a list of women whose achievements he admired: Judith; Queen Esther; Arignote, the writer; Themista, the Epicurean philosopher; and many other women philosophers, including two who studied with Plato and one trained by Socrates.[30] Indeed, his views on the position of women were strikingly similar to those of Clement of Rome a century earlier. They represented a moderate interpretation of Paul's authentic writings and a rejection of the views found in the Pastoral Letters.

---

28. Rapp, *Holy Bishops*, 29.
29. Schaff, *Sacred Writings*, Book I, Chapter 4.
30. Pagels, *Gnostic Paul*, 68.

The Triumph of Ascetic Values

Clement drew on Stoicism. His portrait of the perfect individual closely resembles that of the wise man as drawn by the Stoics. Hence, Clement counseled his readers to shake off the chains of the flesh as far as possible, to live already as if out of the body, and thus to rise above earthly things. Stoics favored a marriage devoid of pleasure. The Stoic Seneca commented,

> It is also shameful to love one's wife immoderately. In loving his wife the wise man takes reason for his guide, not emotion. He resists the assault of passions, and does not allow himself to be impetuously swept away the marital act. Nothing is more depraved than to love one's spouse as if she was an adulteress.[31]

Similarly, Clement's defense of marriage was "totally caught up in the Stoic ideal of *apathia*—no feeling—and the Stoic idea that marriage is exclusively at the service of procreation."[32] In agreement with Seneca, Clement wrote: "One commits adultery with one's own wife if one has commerce with her in marriage as if she were a harlot."[33] Extending this viewpoint, Clement rejected intercourse with pregnant spouses or between older partners as counter to the Christian ideal and embraced a Christian tradition of speaking of pleasure as a source of pollution.[34]

Clement's negation of pleasure reflected his attitude toward the decadence he observed among well-to-do Alexandrians. He was repulsed by their sexual indulgence and opulent lifestyles. This affected not only his views on marital sex but also on the consumption choices made by good Christians. Whereas the Pastoral Letters encouraged the drinking of wine, Clement preached total abstinence:

> I admire those who have adopted an austere life ... and flee as far as possible from wine ... It is proper, therefore, that boys and girls should keep as much as possible away from this medicine ... Wild impulses and burning lusts and fiery habits are kindled; and young men inflamed from within become prone to the indulgence of vicious propensities ... An intoxicated woman ... is quickly drawn down to licentiousness, if she only set her choice on pleasures.[35]

---

31. Ranke-Heinemann, *Eunuchs*, 11.
32. Ibid., 49.
33. Ibid., 50.
34. Ibid., 50.
35. Schaff, *Sacred Writings*, Book 2, Chapter II: On Drinking.

Jewish and Christian Views on Bodily Pleasure

Continuing his criticism, Clement condemned in no uncertain terms the decadent wealthy: "The vulgar rabble, attached to ephemeral pleasure, flourishing for a little, loving ornament, loving praise, and being everything but truth-loving, good for nothing but to be burned with fire."[36] Clement also took to task their excessive use of servants:

> Avoiding working with their own hands and serving themselves, men have recourse to servants, purchasing a great crowd of fine cooks, and of people to lay out the table, and of others to divide the meat skillfully into pieces.... The Word, testifying by the prophet Samuel to the Jews, who had transgressed when the people asked for a king, promised not a loving lord, but threatened to give them a self-willed and voluptuous tyrant, "who shall," He says, "take your daughters to be perfumers, and cooks, and bakers."[37]

Many second-century Christian women believed that sexual abstinence could enable them to gain reputations equal to those achieved by any cultivated male. They embraced the Thecla narratives. In response, the church leadership after Clement sought to separate the ideal of chastity from the ability of women to provide religious leadership. They began to alter their texts so that in the Acts of Paul, the emphasis is on his missionary message that all should lead a life of celibacy in Christ:

> Blessed are the pure in heart, for they shall see God.
> Blessed are those who keep the flesh pure, for they shall become the temple of God.
> Blessed are those who remain continent, for to them shall God speak.
> Blessed are those who have wives as if they had them not, for they shall inherit God.
> Blessed are the bodies of virgins, for they shall be well-pleasing to God and shall not lose the reward of their purity.[38]

Now thoroughly sanitized, these narratives could be embraced as stories of the Christian ideal of virginity without any reference to the role of women within the established church. Their heroines are paragons of Christian virtue. Indeed, Methodius, the late third-century bishop of Olympus, has Thecla as the centerpiece of his Symposium in which ten

---

36. Schaff, *Sacred Writings*, Book 2, Chapter XI: On Clothes
37. Schaff, *Sacred Writings*, Book 2: Chapter IV: With Whom We Are to Associate.
38. Clark, *Reading Renunciation*, 25.

The Triumph of Ascetic Values

virgins discuss the unsurpassed merits of celibacy, "something that is great, marvelous, wondrous, and exceedingly honorable."[39]

The ideal of virginity unrelated to gender equality is also found in the writings of Vibia Perpetua as she awaited martyrdom. A well-educated woman from a prosperous family, she became the spokesperson of the martyrs in prison in Carthage in 203. Attesting to the Pauline notion of true equality, the well-bred Perpetua addressed her companions—including the former slaves Revocatus and Felicitas—as "brothers and sisters."[40] When these martyrs were put to death for being Christians, they went joyfully.

Ascetic behavior also gained adherents who believed that the crucifixion and ongoing martyrdom indicated that physical suffering was a gateway to the next world. For these Christians, ascetic behavior to resist the temptations of the body was not enough. Steeped in a primary narrative of suffering, they came to perceive the "good news" of Christ's message was precisely his promise of redemption *through* suffering.[41] Whereas earlier sages, both Israelite and Greek, had counseled the avoidance of suffering as a condition of happiness, for these Christians, Christ recommended suffering's active embrace.[42] They followed the prescription found in all three of the Synoptic Gospels: "If anyone desires to come after me, let them deny himself and take up his cross daily and follow Me" (Luke 9:23).

The Stoics had suggested that man could be happy even on the rack, happy *in spite of* suffering. These Christians took it a step further, proposing that happiness was not just impervious to pain, but its direct outcome and consequence.[43] While this was a comforting thought to those who became martyrs, it led some Christians who were not in danger of persecution to inflict pain on themselves through various forms of self-mortification. For these zealots, pain brought them closer to Christ and the next world.

ASCETICISM AND CHURCH LEADERSHIP

While the established church had successfully beaten back the second-century challenges it faced, there still remained the widespread belief that the Spirit was possessed by holy men. The *Apostolic Tradition* claimed that

39. Harper, *From Shame to Sin*, 80.
40. McMahon, *Happiness*, 90.
41. Ibid., 76.
42. Ibid., 83.
43. Ibid., 95.

through apostolic succession, spiritual authority resided with the bishops. For many of the faithful, however, personal qualities were crucial. For them, spiritual authority required that the bishop possess the same traits they associated with holy men. As a result, though bishops certainly controlled the administrative functions within Christian communities, their ability to sustain spiritual leadership could be challenged.

One example of this challenge came to the fore with the persecutions in 248-249. Emperor Decius ordered that those who did not give sacrifices to pagan gods would be executed. Some Christians chose martyrdom; not surprisingly, others performed pagan sacrifices under these Roman threats.

It was a long-standing tradition that penance for capital sins—apostasy, murder, and adultery—would not be possible. While awaiting their execution, however, the martyrs prayed for those Christians who had given pagan sacrifices and suggested that they should be reintegrated into Christian communities. Since martyrs were considered on par with bishops in terms of moral authority, their ability to offer forgiveness to apostates was a threat to the bishop's spiritual authority.

The conflict was resolved by Bishop Cyprian of Carthage. Born a pagan, Cyprian converted as an adult, chose a life of celibacy, and disposed of most of his estate. Cyprian accepted the moral authority of martyrs. However, it was the bishops who had responsibility for the spiritual welfare of the *entire* Christian community. As a result, the martyrs could make recommendations but it was the bishops' prerogative to readmit sinners into the community.[44]

One of the reasons Cyprian was able to assert the primacy of the bishops' spiritual authority was that his personal behavior in giving away his personal wealth and living an ascetic life mirrored that of the holy men. Increasingly, ascetic behavior became a linchpin that linked spiritual and administrative authority. Ascetic behavior was simultaneously the humanly and freely accessible precondition for spiritual authority and its openly visible confirmation.

Like Cyprian, bishops were judged increasingly by their ascetic behavior because many of the faithful believed that nobody can sustain such demanding practices unless he or she receives the help of God. This was particularly important when penitential judgments must be made, as

---

44. Rapp, *Holy Bishops*, 90.

The Triumph of Ascetic Values

during the Decius persecutions. As Gregory of Nazianzus wrote, "A man must himself be cleansed, before cleansing others."[45]

The ability to embrace ascetic behavior was most fully met by Origen. Born in 184, he grew up in Alexandria, devoting himself to a study of the philosophers, particularly Plato and the Stoics. At seventeen, his father was martyred. This quickened Origen's resolve to dedicate his life to Christ. At eighteen, in his quest for perfection, Origen castrated himself, invoking Jesus' counsel:

> For there are eunuchs who were born that way; others were made that way by men; and still others live like eunuchs for the sake of the kingdom of heaven. The one who can accept this should accept it. (Matt 19:12)

Origen soon became a spiritual guide to a nucleus of committed young Christians and recent converts. Cloistering himself, first in Alexandria and then in Palestine, Origen wrote extensively and his work circulated widely. He believed that free will allowed each individual to choose between invisible helpers and invisible seducers. Through piety and firm resolve, however, the individual could bring healthful properties to the fore and allow for the healing of the Spirit.

It was the same with temptation. Consent to evil thoughts could occur when the needs of the body—for food or sex—led the individual to collaborate with demonic spirits. Origen, however, believed that the body could be transformed; that it was a "vessel of clay" that could be remolded into containers of ever wider capacity.[46] Physical indulgence, undue eating, undue enjoyment of sight and sound, the joy of sexual bonding in marriage: these became subjects of his vigilance.

Later in life, Origen recognized his error in taking Matthew's passage literally, but he still saw celibacy as higher in the eyes of God.[47] Virginity was not simply a youthful transitory phase nor should it be an anomaly practiced by a few prophetesses and priests.[48] For Origen, virginity was the joining of an immaculate spirit with its well-tempered, material frame: "the

---

45. Ibid., 44.
46. Brown, *Body & Society*, 166-168.
47. Ranke-Heineman, *Eunuchs*, 51.
48. Brown, *Body & Society*, 169.

Jewish and Christian Views on Bodily Pleasure

continent body was a waxen seal that bore the exact 'imprint' of the untarnished soul."[49]

Similar to the Gnostics, Origen made clear the large schism between marital sex and "true" spiritual joining. Married love could never be a stepping stone by which the soul might rise to a higher spiritual sense of partnership with God. Rather, the experience of sexuality, even in marriage, was the darkened antithesis to the blazing, light-filled embrace of Christ in the Spirit.[50]

> If you wish to understand . . . for what reason the body was made, then listen: it was made that it should be a *temple to the Lord*; that the soul, being holy and blessed, should act in it as if it were a priest serving before the Holy Spirit that dwells in you.[51]

In 250, Origen was imprisoned. He died a few years later as a result of the sufferings he endured.[52]

The persecution unleashed by Decius abated but did not end until 260, when Gallienus's reign began, ushering in forty years of freedom from official sanctions. With the ending of persecutions, the Christian community grew substantially, by some estimates from a population of 1.1 million in 250 to a population of 6 million by 300, about 10 percent of the empire's total population.[53] Churches were no longer as inconspicuous as they had been in the first and second centuries. Now large churches were prominent in major cities throughout the empire. These reflected not only growing affluence but also church influence. Many Christians were appointed to high military ranks and government positions.

These advancements troubled important Greek philosophers and pagan priests. Seizing on an incident in the army in 299, these anti-Christian forces began purging Christians. At the time, the Roman Empire was organized as a tetrarchy: four areas, each with its own emperor. One emperor, Diocletian, argued that banning Christians from the bureaucracy and military would be sufficient to appease the gods, while another, Galerius, pushed for their extermination. At the behest of his court, in 302 Diocletian acceded to demands for a universal persecution. The persecutions

---

49. Ibid., 170.
50. Ibid., 174.
51. Ibid., 175.
52. Catholic Encyclopedia, "Origen and Origenism."
53. Hopkins, "Christian Number."

The Triumph of Ascetic Values

lasted almost a decade and were most intense in areas controlled by Galerius (Greece and the Balkans) and Deocletian's successor, Maximian (Asia Minor).

The full freedom of religion would have to wait for Constantine, son of the tetrarch emperor Constantius. Upon taking over when his father died in 306, Constantine immediately ended Christian persecutions in his domain. As the instability of the tetrach grew, a civil war ensued. In a decisive 311 battle, a Christian vision came to Constantine that enabled him to be victorious. This cemented his sympathies toward Christianity. Along with a recently appointed tetrach emperor, Licinius, he agreed on the so-called Edict of Milan. It officially repudiated past methods of religious coercion and extended full tolerance to all religions in the Empire. The document had special benefits for Christians, legalizing their religion and granting them restoration for all property seized during Diocletian's persecution.

CONCLUDING REMARKS

At first glance, it might seem surprising that Origen became so revered by the Christian leadership. After all, he rejected marital sex even when motivated by procreation. When this was raised a generation earlier, Clement of Alexandria, Tertullian, and Irenaeus fought a determined battle, sometimes relying on Stoic notions of the ideal of marriage. However, Stoicism made no distinctions between the behavior of leaders and that of common followers. This was not the best foundation for a religion that had developed a hierarchy that was distancing the lives and behavior of Christian leaders from their congregants.

Origen's reasoning rested instead on Neo-Platonist views of the cosmos that were quite compatible with Christian thought: an unseen, immaterial world in which "the Good," or God, could be described as absolute. In contrast to Stoicism, Neo-Platonism argued that only a few could glimpse the reality of the immaterial world, including the true nature of "the Good"/God. This could be used to support the rationale of church authority, if the "few" were equated with the Christian hierarchy. Indeed, Origen put the matter succinctly when he showed how the concept of faith could be used to keep the "multitude" in line:

> As the matter of faith is so much talked of, I have to reply that we accept it as useful for the multitude, and that we admittedly

teach those who cannot abandon everything and pursue a study of rational argument to believe without thinking out their reasons.[54]

In this way, church leaders like Origen could uphold belief in the superiority of lifelong continence because it would only be expected of the chosen few.

The triumph of Origen's ideas completed the radical transformation of Christianity. It began as a movement of rural Jews seeking a Judaism that offered redemption for the common farmer, not mediated through Pharisee leadership. When Christianity initially grew, it was among God-fearers who looked positively on Judaism but were unwilling to embrace all of its formalism and the privileging of Israel. It accepted marriage and the dictum to be fruitful and multiply.

The first-century Pastoral Letters privileged men, and remain the most prominent justification for why women were excluded from church leadership. Christianity's behavioral requirements for church officials, however, were not very demanding. They did not include abstinence from alcoholic consumption nor from human passions. As John Chrysostom concluded, they only required men of moderate but not "highly exalted virtue; for to be sober, of good behavior and temperate, were qualities common to many."[55]

While these requirements were quite compatible with the ethics expected of married householders, they proved insufficient to justify the demands that bishops have *spiritual* authority. Their desire to replace the itinerant holy men created a dynamic that brought ascetic behavior to the forefront of Christian practices.

The door to privileging ascetic behavior was opened by Paul. His attempt to negate fully the Mosaic dietary laws led him to adopt dualistic language that separated the good soul from the evil body. His revulsion at the sexual excesses of pagan society and desire to bring equality to women led him to question sexual passion among married couples. And for many, Paul's chosen lifestyle signaled that ascetic practices were necessary for the faithful.

During the second century, elite converts entered the Christian fold and brought with them the Hellenistic philosophies that were part of their training. Whether wedded to Stoicism, Platonism, or Gnosticism, these converts amplified Paul's ascetic views so that the rejection of bodily

---

54. Freeman, *Closing of Western Mnd*, 144.
55. Rapp, *Holy Bishops*, 39.

The Triumph of Ascetic Values

pleasures, especially sexual relations, became associated with holiness. Increasingly, Hellenistic ideas clothed the body of Christianity.

Paul left a fatal legacy to future ages. An argument against abandoning sexual intercourse within marriage slid imperceptibly into an attitude that viewed marriage itself as no more than a defense against desire. In the future, a sense of the presence of "Satan," in the form of a constant and ill-defined risk of lust, lay like a heavy shadow in the corner of every Christian church.[56]

The influence of Greek philosophies was substantial; and Hellenists certainly had evidence in Paul to support their asceticism. But ultimately asceticism's real staying power came from the role of personal behavior in the merging of administrative and spiritual roles of the clergy, especially the bishops. Asceticism became the yardstick by which holiness was measured.

Origen's Platonic solution set the holiness of the bishops apart from the expected behavior of the faithful masses. While this cemented the spiritual prominence of the church leadership, it did not stem the desires of many individual Christians to demonstrate their devotion to Christ by rejecting bodily pleasures. For other individuals, ascetic behavior had a penitential role, as well as a basis for asking for godly intervention for others. As a result, during the fourth century, the church had to deal not so much with organized rebellions but rather containing and channeling the ascetic impulses of individuals.

As ascetic behavior was undertaken not only by the church leadership but also by many of the faithful, the status of the married householders, the backbone of the church, came into question. As ordinary individuals who engaged in ascetic behavior, particularly lifelong virginity, began to be privileged by the church hierarchy, married householders began to be seen by some as lesser Christians—not simply lesser than church leaders, but also lesser than their ascetic fellow congregants. The way these views on the status of married householders evolved in Christian thought is the subject of a subsequent chapter.

---

56. Brown, *Body & Society*, 55.

7

The Emergence of Rabbinic Judaism

THE GREAT REVOLT WAS caused by the Roman authorities' decision to no longer respect the integrity of the Second Temple. This infringement on religious autonomy grew until there was a revolt led by the Zealots, another of the politico-religious factions of that era. Along with a majority of the priestly class, most of the patrician segment of the Pharisees, including Simeon ben Gamaliel, supported the armed rebellion.

By contrast, most of the plebeian wing, led by Johanan ben Zakkai, opposed it. Beyond the expectation that military efforts would fail, Ben Zakkai believed that religious study, not the Temple rituals, was central to Judaism. The Pharisees had already formed study groups led by the most learned, and Ben Zakkai saw this arrangement providing the future foundation of religious practices.

As the military situation grew more desperate, the Zealots considered martyrdom superior to surrender and refused to allow Jews to flee Jerusalem. At that point, Ben Zakkai carried out a successful escape plan. He feigned death and had his casket transported outside the city walls for burial. When safely outside Jerusalem, Ben Zakkai immediately contacted the Roman military leader, Vespasian, and proposed that Rome should subsidize a scholarly academy. There, the Pharisee scholars would study Torah and determine how the Mosaic laws should be interpreted. The Roman ruler Titus agreed as he hoped not simply to defeat the rebellion but also to foster reconciliation with his Jewish subjects. As a result, Ben Zakkai was able to build an academy in the coastal town of Yavneh.

The Emergence of Rabbinic Judaism
YAVNEH BEGINNINGS

At Yavneh, Ben Zakkai strove to fill the administrative, as well as the religious, vacuum left by the elimination of the two major sources of leadership: Jewish rulers and the Temple priestly class. Like Paul, Ben Zakkai was questioned by traditionalists who believed that neither he nor his academy had a legitimate claim to leadership of the Jewish people. Undeterred by the magnitude of his task, he set a course to reinvigorate Judaism.

Ben Zakkai exhorted Jews to reject past practices. When one of his students, Joshua ben Hananiah, lamented the ruins of the Second Temple "where the iniquities of Israel were atoned for," Ben Zakkai said to him, "Be not grieved. We have another means of atonement as effective as that; and what is it? It is acts of loving-kindness, as it is said, 'For I desire mercy and not sacrifice.'"[1]

More importantly, the Yavneh rabbis claimed that Torah study is more beloved by God than burnt offerings, for one who studies Torah comes to know the will of God. The Judaic scholar Jacob Neusner stated:

> The study of Torah substitutes for the ancient cult and does for Israel what sacrifice did then: reconcile Israel to its father in heaven, wipe away sin, secure atonement, so save Israel.... The Torah not only sanctifies, but saves.[2]

Whereas many religious leaders saw Roman persecution as signaling the approach of messianic times, Ben Zakkai looked to the long-term future of the Jewish people.[3] This point was reflected in a saying attributed to him: "If you are holding a sapling in your hand and someone tells you, 'Come quickly, the Messiah is coming here!' finish planting the tree before going to greet him."[4]

The problem that Ben Zakkai faced, however, was that the Yavneh academy had neither the necessary prestige nor an infrastructure to bring its message to the Jewish populace in dispersed towns and villages. Indeed, Ben Zakkai had not even convinced all of those in the academy of a larger goal for Jewish practice beyond providing a place for those who wished to give their lives to Torah study.

---

1. Stuart Cohen, *Three Crowns*, 137.
2. Ibid., 170.
3. Meyers, "Jewish Culture," 164.
4. *Avot de-Rabbi Nathan*, 31b. https://www.sefaria.org/Avot_D'Rabbi_Natan?lang=bi

This lack of authority within the nascent rabbinic movement meant that Ben Zakkai's desire for the Beit Din at Yavneh to replace the Sanhedrin did not materialize. Indeed, during the first few decades of the second century, a situation arose whereby any number of independent, local Beit Din simultaneously dispensed parallel forms of rabbinic justice; and many of the outstanding scholars of the time continued to hold individual court for their own disciples—Rabbis Tarfon and Akiba at Lod and still others in Sepphorus.[5]

After Ben Zakkai, leadership at Yavneh was passed onto Gamaliel II, son of Simeon ben Gamaliel. To strengthen the role of prayer, he instituted the practice of reciting the nineteen blessings that comprise the Amidah three times daily. He also instituted the practice of burying the dead in the simplest possible shroud to counter the extravagance that was becoming commonplace. These religious practices, which are still followed today by Orthodox Judaism, began to broaden the influence of the rabbis beyond their academies.

Gamaliel II also struggled to eliminate the divisions between the followers of Shammai and those of Hillel. Indeed, when his stifling of disagreements went too far—as with his humiliation of Rabbi Joshua ben Hananiah—he was replaced as leader and became an ordinary student at the Yavneh academy. However, his personal modesty and commitment to learning led to his eventual reinstatement.

During the first two decades of the second century, Rabbi Akiba rose to prominence. His life mirrored that of the other legendary leader of the plebeians, Hillel. Both men came from poor backgrounds that required them to perform physical labor for much of their young adulthood. Both men came to Torah as mature adults. Both men stressed the humanity of Judaism over religious rigor. The next generation of rabbinic leaders would be dominated by Akiba's students, including Rabbi Meir, Rabbi Eleazar ben Shammai, and Jose ben Halafta.

When the Roman governor began to restrict Jewish practices, Akiba was part of a delegation to Rome that pleaded for more religious autonomy. The first important restriction was the outlawing of the religious ritual performed when the rabbis determined the new Jewish calendar. A twelve-month lunar calendar, as the Jews used, encompasses only about 354 days. If unadjusted, after a few years the season in which festivals occur will shift.

---

5. Stuart Cohen, *Three Crowns*, 152.

In recent times, with more precise understanding of the relationship between a lunar cycle and the effects of Earth's rotation around the sun, the rabbis have instituted a nineteen-year cycle in which seven of the years have a "leap" month. In addition, ten or eleven dates must be placed so that certain holidays do not fall on the Sabbath.

During the Second Temple period, the priestly class set the calendar each year following a necessary ritual, and this task was subsequently delegated to the Yavneh leadership. While some of the rabbis wanted to disobey the Roman restriction and suffer the consequences, Akiba convinced them it was better to circumvent it. Akiba was sent to Babylon to observe the establishment of the calendar and the necessary ritual by the religious leadership there.

In an attempt to forestall further restrictions, Akiba developed a dialogue with Rufus, the Roman governor. Despite his efforts, Rome continued to further restrict religious practices. When circumcision and celebrating certain Jewish festivals that were deemed too nationalistic were outlawed, rebellious voices within the Jewish community grew. Having lived through the disastrous revolt, and having seen how Rome had brutally suppressed Jewish resistance in North Africa in 115-117 CE, Akiba strongly opposed these militant nationalists.

Akiba argued that study was more important than any Jewish ritual so that the Jewish community should not enter into another disastrous war to protect even most requirements. Martyrdom was acceptable only to avoid three practices: idol worship, murder, and prohibited sexual relations. Other practices could be sacrificed in the short run, enabling Judaism to survive in the long run.

Unfortunately, Akiba's accommodationist position did not win out, and a large share of the rabbis supported the Bar Kochba revolt in 135 CE; a revolt that was met with a brutal Roman response. Indeed, the response was so brutal that Akiba felt it necessary to disobey Roman restrictions. For his actions, Akiba was executed and became a Jewish martyr.

THE MOVE TO THE GALILEE

After the disastrous Bar Kochba revolt, the remaining Jews were dispersed from the Jerusalem environs. When most moved to the Galilee, that region became home to the largest concentration of Jews in the land of Israel, known then by its Roman-designated name, Palestine. Responding to these demographic changes and postwar turmoil, the academy was moved from Yavneh to successive Galilee towns, beginning with Usha. By the middle of the second century, the rabbinic community was concentrated in Galilean religious academies.

The movement to the Galilee solidified rabbinic unity. The new leader, Simeon ben Gamliel II, ended much of the personal conflicts by reaching an accord with Rabbi Meir, even dispatching his own son Judah to the Akiban schools. This strategy neutralized much of the opposition among the rabbis. Unity was also reinforced because, once again, respect for minority positions was maintained. Thus, disputes over interpretations and applications of religious principles could be handled constructively.

This rabbinic unity, however, came at a time when rabbinic influence over the populace was waning. Many rabbis had been killed during the Bar Kochba revolt, and none among the next generation of scholars rose to the prestige and prominence of their former teachers. Rome's prohibition against new ordinations also weakened the ability of the various academies to replenish their membership. Dislocated by war, many rabbis were reduced to the status of penniless refugees, eking out an existence by manual labor or as self-employed craftsmen. Their poverty made it impossible for the rabbis to use school buildings for teaching purposes. Instead, instruction took place in vineyards, marketplaces, and private homes.[6] Their lowly status as immigrants and manual laborers further weakened the rabbis' ability to gain the allegiance of Jewish communities.[7]

In addition, the number of rabbis from the wealth-owning class declined substantially, as Ben Zakkai and most of the first generation at Yavneh had come from the plebeian wing of the Pharisees. As a result, wealthy families that constituted the administrative leadership of Galilean communities rarely had familial ties or other allegiances to the rabbinical academies. In addition, the rabbis imposed heavy economic demands on farmers. Purity laws required checking foodstuffs in storage, and tithing sacrificed a sizeable portion of agricultural produce. The sabbatical year, when fields were left fallow, cut a farmer's income by a seventh, and other religious restrictions prevented the most efficient use of precious land. Rabbinical decrees also forbade the export of grain, wine, and oil surpluses from Palestine.

---

6. Goodman, *State and Society*, 76.

7. Stuart Cohen, *Three Crowns*, 151; and Goodman, *State and Society*, 111.

Just as importantly, there remained a strong distrust between the rabbis and the *ammei ha'aretz*. The *ammei ha'aretz* consistently tried to observe many basic religious precepts: circumcision, ritual bathing, kosher slaughter, and sexual purity. However, they were unable to follow some of the laws rigorously enough to satisfy the rabbinical community. For example, maintaining the necessary purity of their household utensils and of meat and vegetables bought in the marketplace always proved problematic.

Besides thrice-annual pilgrimages, the Pharisees had been strongly discouraged from entering the homes of the *ammei ha'aretz* or sharing meals with them. This attitude instilled hostility among Galilean Jews toward the Pharisees. Indeed, Akiba described the indignation that he felt in his youth as an unschooled *ammei ha'aretz*: he could wish for no greater pleasure than sinking his teeth into the neck of a rabbi.[8]

IMPROVING RELIGIOUS AUTHORITY

After the two defeats, Galileans came to desire a religious system that conferred holiness on the individual and their families. By the mid-second century, the vast majority of Galilean communities had their own synagogue, which became the central institution to maintain religious solidarity. The synagogues were characterized by their monumental blocks of hewn stone, particularly in the southern façade facing Jerusalem. The town's relative prosperity was often reflected in the size and quality of its construction; some had façades richly decorated with elaborate stone carvings while others had no decoration. Most typical were carvings of eagles and lions.

Whereas the entrance to pagan temples generally faced east, the source of light and life, almost all Galilean synagogue entrances faced south, in the direction of Jerusalem. Synagogues had a prayer room from 600 to 1500 square feet depending upon the size of the community. In the most prosperous communities, synagogues contained elaborate mosaics. Next to the prayer room was a separate structure that housed the Torah scroll that was often flanked by statues.

In the Galilee, Jewish communities gathered in synagogues for the Sabbath, religious festivals, and familial events. Since the rabbis stressed study in their academies, they had little presence in synagogues, which functioned independent of rabbinic oversight, and inscriptions of donations

---

8. Shaye J.D. Cohen, "Place of the Rabbi," 166.

rarely listed them.⁹ Indeed, artwork was incorporated into synagogues that would never have been approved by rabbinic authorities.

Toward the end of the second century, however, a few of the wealthier rabbis seemed to have understood the obstacles their behavior had created. As a result, the restrictions on the sabbatical year were eased, and the places in which they were completely eliminated were expanded. So, too, the restriction on exporting of grain and wine was relaxed. Most importantly, there was no longer an expectation that ordinary Jews would strictly follow the laws of purity and tithing. In addition, a good number of the students were by then Galileans from landowning families.

During the third century, if not earlier, the rabbis came to temper their hostility toward the *ammei ha'aretz* "for the sake of peace." They even allowed their daughters to marry an *ammei ha'aretz* as long as it was stipulated in advance that the wife would adhere to the rabbinic laws of purity. The evidence for continued rabbinic hatred derives exclusively from the Babylonian Talmud, which was compiled in the fifth century CE.¹⁰

The more inclusive attitude that was becoming dominant is captured in the saying attributed to the mid-third century Palestinian Resh Lakish:

> The people of Israel is like a vine: its branches are the aristocracy, its clusters the *Talmidei hakhamin*, its leaves the *ammei ha'aretz*, and its twigs those in Israel who are empty of learning. Let the clusters pray for the leaves, for were it not for the leaves, the clusters could not exist.¹¹

This rabbinic accommodation is most associated with Rabbi Judah ha Nasi, the son of Simeon ben Gamaliel II. Legend has it that he was born on the same day as Rabbi Akiba's execution. His family lineage and wealth rendered him the ideal person to complete the compilation of the Oral Torah in the form of the Mishnah. Known simply as Rabi, Rabbi Judah ha Nasi stood in a class by himself after the destruction of the Second Temple and not simply for his personal contribution to the final redaction of the Mishnah and its presentation as the authoritative basis of all subsequent *halakic* rulings. Rather, it was his selective emendations and presentations designed to serve pedagogic purposes that ultimately ensured that his code

---

9. Shaye J.D. Cohen, *Maccabees to the Mishnah*, 210.

10. Shaye J.D. Cohen, "Place of the Rabbi," 166. He noted that there is an entire folio page documenting this hatred even including a statement equating sexual relations with an *am ha'aretz* to sexual relations with a donkey.

11. Oppenheimer, *Am Ha-aretz*, 189.

would become far more than a mere summary of previously scattered rulings.

For Rabi's anthology to win acceptance, the standard of its scholarship had to be buttressed by the author's administrative skills and political clout. As it was, some of his younger colleagues were so dissatisfied with his compilation that they thought it necessary after his death to compile a more comprehensive Tosefta to supplement the Mishnah. Their criticisms would have been more severe had Rabi not had ties to the Akiban school. Thus, his substantial political credentials outweighed any presumably marginal scholastic shortcomings.

Rabi's rise was also aided by the decision of the Romans to provide Jewish courts with imperial backing and to allow them to adjudicate a much wider range of cases. The scope of rabbinic jurisdiction increased, as did the power of the central rabbinic office. Rabi also assumed the responsibilities of a communal functionary by appointing and deposing local leaders and by checking the lineal integrity of Jews in distant locales.

Similarly, he invested unprecedented efforts in creating a more popular *halakic* system. In this vein, he permitted the use of produce immediately following the end of the sabbatical year, and the import of produce into the Holy Land. He also exempted some towns from tithing requirements. His lessening of religious requirements broadened the base of his power, enabling him to become a widely revered leader.

ASCETIC TENDENCIES

After the destruction of the Second Temple, excessive joyfulness was discouraged. It was said, "It is forbidden for a person to fill his mouth with levity in this world."[12] This reflected the practice of Rabbi Ben Zakkai's contemporary, Rabbi Eliezer ben Hyrcanus, who believed sex was only for procreation. He was said to have made love to his wife "as if being forced to by a demon, uncovering an inch of her body and immediately covering it again."[13]

Rabbi Akiba also believed that personal joyfulness should be tempered: "Jesting and light-headedness lead a person to immorality."[14] Though he desired to constrain pleasure activities, unlike his mentor Rabbi Eliezer,

---

12. Friedman and Friedman, *God Laughed*, 108.
13. Boyarin, *Carnal Israel*, 47.
14. Friedman and Friedman, *God Laughed*, 111.

he did not include sensual relations with one's wife. Akiba's positive attitude toward sexual relations was reflected in his view of the Song of Songs, a sensual poem included in the sacred body of Jewish writings.

Written sometime before the Common Era, the Song of Songs describes the passionate desires of a young girl and her lover as they are about to be wed. It begins with her dreaming of him: "Let him kiss me with kisses of his mouth, for your love is better than wine, better than the fragrance of your perfumes."

She has remained virginal by the "high fortresses" she had erected but she is now eager to passionately embrace her betrothed. He commends her for having been "a garden locked, a fountain sealed" (Song 4:12), but now they are looking forward to lustful lovemaking:

> How beautiful you are, how charming, my love, my delight!
> In stature like the palm tree, its fruit-clusters your breasts.
> I have decided, I shall climb the palm tree, I shall seize its clusters of dates!
> May your breasts be clusters of grapes, your breath sweet-scented as apples,
> and your palate like sweet wine.
> Beloved: Flowing down the throat of my love, as it runs on the lips of those who sleep.
> I belong to my love, and his desire is for me.
> Come, my love, let us go to the fields. We will spend the night in the villages,
> and in the early morning we will go to the vineyards. We will see if the vines are budding, if their blossoms are opening, if the pomegranate trees are in flower. Then I shall give you the gift of my love. (Song 7:1-13)

Rabbi Akiba felt passionately about the Song of Songs and its importance to Jewish couples. He and other rabbis thought of marriage as a *kiddushin*, or sanctification, so nuptial songs like the Song of Songs should not blaspheme the holy consummation. For this reason, Akiba said, "He who sings the Song of Songs in wine taverns, treating it as if it were a vulgar song, forfeit their share in the world to come" (Taanith 4:8), Far from being a bawdy song, it was the "holy of holies" of the sacred writings, according to Akiba. Indeed, he claimed that the Song had long been treasured by most members of the Jewish community.[15]

15. Phipps, "Song of Songs."

The Emergence of Rabbinic Judaism

It should be noted that the Song of Songs' encouragement of newlyweds to engage in passionate, lustful sex was not unique. It is echoed in a poem from Proverbs:

> Be grateful for your own fountain,
> And have your pleasure with the wife of your youth;
> A loving doe and a graceful deer.
> Always let her breasts satisfy you.
> Always be intoxicated with her love. (Prov 5:18-19)

The disastrous Bar Kochba rebellion caused some rabbis to mourn the loss by abstaining from wine, meat, and joyful wedding festivities.[16] One example was Akiba's student Rabbi Meir, whose "advocacy of abstinence and purity led to his being given the title 'kadosh' (saint), a title granted to but few sages."[17] Unlike the growing Christian embrace of ascetic practices, however, Jewish abstention was not a means of self-improvement. In particular, it was unlike Christians "who make a point of extreme self-denial . . . through which control is imposed over one's senses, actions and thoughts in order to achieve a goal higher than those provided by natural impulses."[18] Indeed, rabbinic Judaism fundamentally rejected the three distinguishing characteristics of Christian asceticism: self-inflicted physical injury (except for fasting), celibacy, and the establishment of separate ascetic societies or orders.[19]

The only form of extended abstinence that had significant adherence among Jews was the taking of the Nazirite vows: pledging to abstain from drinking wine, let one's hair grow, and avoid defilement by contact with corpses. The vow was for a determinate period of time, usually thirty days. This vow involves neither poverty nor pain, and has nothing to do with "cleansing the body." Indeed, the motivation for this symbolic sacrifice was often the hopes of gaining favor for an upcoming event. As a result, it was discouraged, if not condemned by the sages.[20]

Some scholars contend that ascetic behavior should be defined more broadly to include any proscribed religious restrictions on pleasure that is

---

16. Schiffman, *From Text to Tradition*, 163-4.
17. Oppenheimer, *Am Ha-aretz*, 145.
18. Ibid., 150-51.
19. Fraade, "Ascetical Aspects of Ancient Judaism," 259.
20. Ibid., 261.

otherwise permitted.[21] They point to Mishnah Avot 6:4 which states most dramatically:

> Thus is the way of Torah: Bread with salt you shall eat, and a measure of water you shall drink, and on the earth you shall sleep, and a life of sorrow you will live, and in the Torah you will labor. And if you do so, "You will be happy and good [will be] with you. You will be happy—in this world; and 'good [will be] to you'"—in the world to come.[22]

This exhortation did not mean, however, that religious study *required* deprivation—neither poverty nor pain had any positive value and were firmly discouraged. The saying meant simply that the student should be *unconcerned* with material wellbeing. Religious study provides the fundamental sustaining nourishment. Similarly, the sages stressed that one studied for the love of God and not in the hopes of receiving personal rewards; for only by having the proper attitude can one expect to be rewarded in the world to come:

> Antigonus of Sokho used to say: Be not like slaves that serve their master for the sake of compensation; be rather like slaves who serve their master with no thought of compensation, and let the fear of heaven be upon you, so that your reward may be doubled in the age to come.[23]

In addition, this broader definition ignores a crucial issue: For the reduction in consumption to be truly ascetic, it must in some intrinsic way enhance the attainment of spiritual perfection. Such was certainly the view of the many Christians who embraced a dualism that posited a soul being housed in a sinful body. Only by clearing the mind and body of the desire for personal pleasures could the individual attain moral perfection. In fundamentally rejecting such dualism, Judaism could never approach the essential characteristic of asceticism.

Supporters of this broader definition try to paper over this difference and claim that Judaism's constraint on material pleasures was qualitatively similar to Greek-inspired asceticism.

---

21. Ibid., 256; Michael Satlow, "And on the Earth," 205.

22. Diamond, *Holy Men*, 156n.

23. Fraade, "Ascetical Aspects," 271. Using this and a subsequent passage, Fraade asserts: "According to one later rabbinic tradition (*Avot de-Rabbi Nathan* 5), [the Pharisees] expected their self-denial in this world to be rewarded in the future world."

The Emergence of Rabbinic Judaism

Talmud Torah required the same mental and physical discipline demanded by the non-Jewish study of philosophy. Body and soul, working together in a disciplined (i.e. ascetic) fashion, can help a man overcome his evil inclination.[24]

There is no evidence, however, that the sages believed that ascetic behavior would improve religious study other than by providing more time. Indeed, in one clear instance involving a Talmudic discussion of ascetic behavior, its proponent, Ben Azzai, makes no reference to disciplining his body: it simply freed up his time for study.[25]

Rabbinic Judaism was guided by biblical passages where the Israelites thank God for the bountiful sustenance provided: Israel was the land of milk and honey. Moreover, the Bible's interest is in life upon earth, and this earth is the land of the living; there is no romantic nostalgia for the wilderness. On the contrary, the desert is an accursed place, and if the period of the wandering in the wilderness is mentioned, it is only as a preparation for entrance into the Promised Land.[26] Indeed, the Mishnah condemns ascetic tendencies by stating: "Were not enough things forbidden to you by the Torah that you should want to add to them?"[27]

CONTRASTING JEWISH AND CHRISTIAN VIEWS

The new Christianity and the new Judaism both had important leaders who placed significant boundaries on bodily pleasures. However, it would be a mistake to overstate these similarities. While Rabbi Meir and Ben Azzai can be highlighted for their sexual restraint, their behavior actually points to the large gulf between rabbinic and priestly practices.

Ben Azzai was not a role model. His decision to abstain from sexual intercourse is ridiculed and totally rejected by the rabbinic sages. He agreed that the choice not to have children is like the shedding of blood and the diminution of the Divine image. This admission caused Abba Hanan to proclaim that one who chooses not to have children "deserves the penalty of death."[28]

---

24. Satlow, "Earth You Should Sleep," 213, 215; and Fraade, "Ascetical Aspects," 257.
25. Safrai and Stern, 748 footnote 5.
26. Urbach, *Sages*, 216.
27. Kolatch, *Second Jewish Book*, 86.
28. Sweeney, *Form and Intertextuality*, 278.

Jewish and Christian Views on Bodily Pleasure

As for Rabbi Meir, it is true that his views on marital relations are similar to those of Clement of Alexandria. There is one crucial difference, however. Whereas Clement desired that all Christian married householders embrace passionless sex, Rabbi Meir never suggested that his behavior should be emulated, even by the other sages.

Rabbi Meir witnessed massive death and destruction during the Bar Kochba revolt. Before his very eyes, the Romans murdered his illustrious teacher, Rabbi Akiba. Rabbi Meir's father-in-law, Rabbi Hanina ben Teradyon, met a similar fate, being burnt alive. Thus, Rabbi Meir's actions were motivated by a desire to honor these deaths, not by some deeper religious calling to improve his ethical behavior.

In Judaism, deaths require family mourners to abstain from pleasurable activities for a length of time. For example, it is against Jewish custom to send or bring flowers to a funeral or cemetery since flowers are associated with joyous celebrations. During the first thirty days of mourning, mourners are not allowed to go to parties or celebrations, including family religious occasions like a bar mitzvah or bris (the celebration of the circumcision of newborn male child). These restrictions are extended to one year in the case of the death of a parent. Given the enormity of the tragedies he witnessed, Rabbi Meir chose to extend restrictions on personal pleasures over his lifetime. It is also why he never considered it appropriate to exhort others to emulate his behavior.

Our analysis has also identified important factors that explain the divergent religious attitudes toward bodily pleasures. Most important are biblical exhortations to "be fertile and increase." Christian leaders who were committed to privileging celibacy struggled to reconcile their ascetic agenda with the Old Testament's many passages that seemed to champion marriage and reproduction. In the fourth century, Manichean critics who, like Marcion, rejected the Old Testament cited passages as being in conflict with Matthew's recommendation to "become a eunuch for the kingdom of heaven" (Matt 19:12).

These Christian leaders had to walk a fine line to uphold their own values yet distinguish themselves from their "heretical" opponents. As Jerome put it, Catholics must keep to the king's highway, not turning to the left (i.e., to the lust of the Jews and the Gentiles) or to the right (i.e., to the errors of the Manicheans); although aspiring to virginity, they should nonetheless not condemn marriage.[29]

---

29. Clark, *Origenist Controversy*, 42.

The Emergence of Rabbinic Judaism

According to the church fathers, "literal" readings were set forth by "heretics" to mock the Christian retention of the Old Testament. Origen claimed that Gnostics, in their polemics against Catholics, derive much mileage from "fleshly" interpretations of Scripture. Augustine countered Manichean critiques of scriptural "carnality" via spiritualizing interpretations. He claimed that "be fertile and increase" should be read figuratively as referring to a spiritual, rather than a physical, union.[30]

The efforts to replace the literal meaning of the Song of Songs with a figurative one were paramount. Origen goes to great lengths to bleach away any carnal interpretations. He pleaded, "We earnestly beg the hearers of these things to mortify their carnal senses. They must not take anything of what has been said with reference to bodily functions but rather employ them for grasping those divine senses of the inner man."[31]

A century later, Jerome viewed the poem as an allegory praising virgins who mortify the flesh. For Gregory of Nyssa, it provided a message that only when the soul becomes passionless can it be fully united with God. Thus, Christian leaders were able to convince the faithful that marriage and reproduction, though acceptable, was not the only or even God's desired behaviors.

Religious divergence also reflected the contrasting Jewish and Christian experiences with Hellenism. The licentiousness and degradation of Hellenistic culture were seared into the minds of early Christians proselytizing in the Mediterranean basin. In reaction to the *porneia* Paul witnessed, he formulated a harsh view of the sexual act. By contrast, until the third century, the land of Israel was substantially free of Hellenist penetration so Hellenism had no influence on the formative beliefs of rabbinic Judaism.

Furthermore, Christian recruitment necessarily included many individuals who had absorbed Hellenistic philosophies which they grafted onto Pauline Christianity. While some, like Marcion, were rejected, others came to wield substantial influence over the direction of their new faith. Indeed, the two most important third-century religious leaders, Clement of Alexandria and Origen, both based their ascetic views on the Hellenistic philosophies they brought with them into Christianity.

By contrast, rabbinic Judaism firmly rejected Hellenistic philosophies even when articulated by Jewish philosophers like Ben Sira or Philo of Alexandria. For Rabbi Akiba, these extra-canonical writings should never be

---

30. Ibid., 80.
31. Phipps, "Song of Songs."

read, as they have "no share in the world to come."[32] One rabbi who was deeply influenced by Hellenism, Elisha ben Abuyah, is roundly condemned by the other Talmudic rabbis. When some rabbis asked why the study of Torah did not save him from eternal condemnation, the answer was that "Greek song did not cease from his mouth."[33]

The divergent roles of Jewish and Christian religious leaders also help explain the contrasting approaches to ascetic behavior. The sages were respected foremost for their scholarly knowledge. By contrast, bishops gained legitimacy through their ascetic behavior. This behavior was increasingly important as bishops, unlike rabbis, had to regulate the penance required by congregants who had engaged in sinful behavior.

CONCLUDING REMARKS

The Old Testament highlights the forty years that Jews wandered between exodus from Egypt and entrance into Canaan. The Jewish holiday of Sukkot memorializes this experience by requiring Jews to take their meals outdoors to symbolically experience living in the wilderness. The forty-odd years that the sages lived in Yavneh and began the formulation of the Oral Torah were a similar wilderness. When the sages finally entered the Galilee, they eventually won the masses to the principles of rabbinic Judaism, just as the Jewish prophets eventually won biblical Jews away from idol worship.

The Yavneh rabbis had a revolutionary impact on Judaism similar to Paul's impact on Christianity. Indeed, the Yavneh rabbis' first compilation of the oral tradition, the Mishnah, heralded their triumph in the same way that the inclusion of Paul's epistles in the New Testament signaled the triumph of Pauline Christianity. Thus, by the early third century, both religions were on a new arc that differed fundamentally from what existed at the time of Jesus' ministry.

We have begun to see the cleavage between the two religions as the reasons for the modest ascetic practices among Galilean Jews differed dramatically from the more severe Christian practices in the Mediterranean basin. The next two chapters will detail how these divergent attitudes toward ascetic behavior only increased. While there were still examples of ascetically inclined sages, they were an increasing anomaly to normative religious behavior. Generations born after the Bar Kochba revolt did not

---

32. Lieberman, *Hellenism*, 108-109.
33. Feldman, *Jews and Gentiles*, 37-38.

experience the same personal tragedies that Rabbi Meir's generation experienced, and as rabbinic study expanded, the destruction of the Second Temple had less of a pull on the religious community. Not surprisingly, there was no longer a need to restrict pleasurable activities. A more joyous attitude came to dominate, especially as more prosperous Jews, typified by Rabi, came to influence rabbinic beliefs.

We will find that this trend toward pleasure increases as Jewish religious leadership shifts from the land of Israel to Babylonia. By contrast, Christian asceticism becomes more institutionalized until, for the first time, leadership is restricted to only those men who have *always* been celibate. This further evolution will be told through the lives of the most important Church fathers: Ambrose, Jerome, and Augustine.

8

Ascetic Values Confront Roman Society

WHILE THE EDICT OF Milan legalized Christianity, the full benefits of Constantine's support had to wait until he became the ruler of a reunified Roman Empire in 324. The next year, Eastern Church leaders met at the Council of Nicea and attempted to reach a consensus on important religious dogma. Through a series of fortuitous events, a radical sexual ideology, possessed by a small committed group on the periphery for two centuries, was thrust into the forefront of Roman society. Surely second-century Christians would have been astounded that Christian leaders would now have the opportunity to shape Roman sexual morays away from the repugnant behaviors that they so openly condemned. We will trace how this project progressed over the next century.

CHRISTIANITY AND MARRIED HOUSEHOLDERS

Christianity had to struggle to transform attitudes toward married life. Roman men took for granted their ability to have sex outside of marriage as long as it was not with married women. Sexual relations with slaves, prostitutes, and courtesans were quite acceptable. A fourth-century catalog of the urban amenities of Rome still included some forty-five public brothels.

These conflicts formed the battleground within Roman society more than any attempts to promote celibacy or passionless sex among married couples. Throughout the fourth century, Christian leaders sought to change pagan attitudes that viewed lust as natural. In the East, John Chrysostom railed against the typical pagan wedding ceremony that encouraged lustful behavior, condemning the "whorish songs," "shameful speeches," and "unrestrained laughter." Consistent with such ceremonies, archaeological excavations demonstrate the continued widespread presence of lamps decorated with erotic images and other sexual objects throughout the homes of the Roman populace. Only by the sixth century did the central role of ministers at wedding ceremonies become commonplace among Christian couples and homes become completely purged of erotic artifacts.[1]

While attitudes toward male sexual prerogatives did change, the late fourth-century bishop of Milan, Ambrose, still despaired that Christians could visit the brothel "as though it were a law of nature."[2] While in no way condoning their presence, his contemporary, Augustine, understood that given current Roman attitudes, brothels were a necessary evil. He noted,

> What could claim to be more filthy and more worthless, more full of shame and defilement, than prostitutes and pimps and other infections of this kind? But take whores out of human affairs, and you will overturn everything because of lusts. Put them in the place of matrons, and you will ruin honor with fallenness and disgrace.[3]

One area in which church sexual beliefs triumphed was its uncompromising attitude toward homosexual sinfulness. Christian leaders took to heart Paul's warning that the "wrath of God" would befall "men [who] burned with the lust for one and other, men with men committing what is shameful" (Rom 1:18-27). In the early fourth-century canons of Elvira, pederasty, unlike other forms of sexual deviance, "is placed explicitly beyond the possibility of return to communion."[4]

Though Roman laws did penalize homosexual behavior severely, they were not strongly enforced. Nothing was done about homosexual acts in brothels until the end of the fourth century, when the Theodosian Code came down harshly against male prostitutes. It stated, "We cannot allow the city of Rome, the mother of all virtues, any longer to be polluted by the contaminating emasculation of men's sexual honor." To end this obscenity, male prostitutes were dragged out of brothels "so everyone will know that the soul of a man is to be treated by all as an inviolable precinct."[5] By the

1. Harper, *From Shame to Sin*, 167.
2. Ibid., 165.
3. Ibid., 166.
4. Ibid., 143.
5. Ibid., 141-42.

mid-fifth century, the adoption of a thoroughly Christian attitude toward homosexuality was completed.

To help facilitate this transformation, the Church had to develop a practical system of penance for those who strayed from acceptable sexual behavior. For Paul, the issue was simple: they were cast out of the Christian community. By contrast, fourth-century Christianity had to moderate penalties if it was going to win over Roman pagans. Finally, the more extensive role of penance once again increased the need for bishops to be model citizens as measured by their ascetic behavior. The Council of Elvira, in southern Spain, declared that "bishops, priests, deacons and all member of the clergy connected with the liturgy must abstain from their wives and must not beget sons." Married clergy may have raised families but the Council made clear that they could no longer have intercourse with their wives.[6]

This resulted in the two-tiered approach Origen favored. For most married householders, there was a set of regulations that did not include ascetic behavior. By contrast, church leaders were expected to pursue higher ideals. This dualism is found in early fourth-century church historian Eusebius's writings:

> Two ways of life were thus given by the Lord to His Church. The one is above nature, and beyond common human living; it admits not marriage, childbearing, property nor the possession of wealth. Like some celestial beings, these gaze down upon human life, performing the duty of priesthood to Almighty God for the whole race.
>
> And the more humble, more human way prompts men to join in pure nuptials, and to produce children, to undertake government, to give orders to soldiers fighting for right; it allows them to have minds for farming, for trade, and for the other more secular interests as well as for religion.[7]

ASCETIC BEHAVIOR IN THE EAST

At the same time that Christian leaders sought to transform Roman pagans into God-fearing Christians, they also had to contend with the yearnings among idealistic Christians for an ascetic lifestyle. Martyrdom had

---

6. Peter Brown, *Body & Society*, 202-203.
7. Ibid., 205.

enshrined a tradition of suffering at the heart of Christian history. Once persecution and martyrdom abated, self-mortification had an even stronger presence among idealistic young men and women.[8]

In the third century, some Christians had fled to the Egyptian desert to escape persecution. Even after the legalization of Christianity, a few young men continued to seek a desert life that would allow them to follow God's call in a more deliberate and individual way. The privations of the desert were a means of learning stoic self-discipline. These young men saw Jesus' fasting on the mountain and John the Baptist as two models for such self-discipline. Many may have heeded the exhortations in the apocryphal acts to give up homes, possessions, fathers, mothers, bodily consorts, and children (Thomas 6:61). While the apostles and their followers renounced fine clothing and fasted frequently, the renunciations that are stressed in the apocryphal Acts are social, familial, and marital.

In 270, a young Christian named Anthony sold off his belongings, moved to the edge of his village, and began leading a solitary ascetic existence. Fifteen years later, he moved to a desert fortress across the Nile, and then in 313 moved even further into the eastern desert, where he lived until his death in 356. In this way, Anthony was following earlier ascetics who considered the desert an ideal place to strengthen the body in order to conquer its demons that held back the soul from union with the divine.[9]

Anthony inspired others who were searching for a way to come closer to the Holy Spirit. During his lifetime, little colonies of renouncers first settled on the edges of the desert. They burrowed into the depressions among the dunes, to form a series of tiny man-made oases. Each oasis had its own well, dug into the brackish water that seeped beneath the sands from Lake Mareotis, the home three centuries earlier of the Therapeutae community.[10] These renouncers were not true anchorites like Anthony since they consistently interacted with one another, being unable to sustain an extremely isolated existence.

Many of these men had moved past sexual temptations and were challenged to purify their bodies through extreme diets. Self-mortification, however, was only a preliminary. It was to the heart that the Desert Fathers

---

8. Freeman, *Closing of the Western Mind*, 236.
9. Ibid., 238.
10. Brown, *Body & Society*, 213.

Jewish and Christian Views on Bodily Pleasure

directed their most searching attention. Only when the heart had become dead to the self would they find peace.[11]

One of these men was Pachomius. Born in 292, he converted to Christianity in 314. Three years later, he set out for the desert to lead the life of an anchorite. Observing the cells of those unable to achieve the rigors of Anthony's solitary life, Pachomius consolidated them. By doing so, he created the first Christian monastic or *cenobitic* organizations.

Possessions were held in common under the leadership of an abbot. Pachomius himself was hailed as "Abba" (father), which is where we get the word Abbot from. After the establishment of the first monastery around 320, the demand grew rapidly. By 400, nearly five thousand monks were settled on the periphery of the desert, and thousands of anchorites were scattered up and down the length of the Nile and in the bleak, waterless mountains beside the Red Sea.[12]

At first these monasteries did not separate completely from Christian communities. However, the Pachomians began to emphasize the boundaries that demarcated their "desert" from "the world," increasingly cloistering themselves behind high monastery walls. Pachomius discouraged his monks from seeking or accepting clerical positions within established Christian communities. Clerical life was presented as a temptation to be resisted by those in search of holiness.[13]

Not only did the monks have to more clearly cordon themselves off from the Christian villages, they had to maintain separation from each other. Shorn of the normal affective bonds of the family, the young monks longed to re-create, within the monastery, a world of "easy laughing and playing with the boys." All of this had to end. The young monks had to learn to maintain a distance of one cubit between each other's bodies, and use robes and well-tied belts to stop wandering hands at night. Young monks corseted their bodies to muzzle any sexual urgings.[14]

Pious practices linked the settled world to the desert. In the season of Lent, the laity also would undergo, through fasting, a measure of self-mortification. By periods of sexual abstinence, by vigils, by small repeated vows of renunciation, they breathed a little of the free air of the desert.[15] By

---

11. Ibid., 225-226.
12. Ibid., 215.
13. Hunter, *Marriage, Celibacy*, 55.
14. Brown, *Body & Society*, 246-247.
15. Ibid., 255.

Ascetic Values Confront Roman Society

the end of the fourth century, however, the separation was complete and the truce between the married householders and the Desert Fathers was well established in Egypt. The deeper strivings for ascetic perfection were tacitly declared to be for only anchorites and monks.

Origen's optimistic view that the body could be perfected seemed to be realized in the lives of the Desert Fathers. Through their personal stories, they became role models for many young idealistic men and women, especially in the East where the apocryphal gospels were widely circulated. There, clergy had reputations for extreme asceticism: Procopius of Eleutheropolis, for instance, "from a child had embraced chastity and a more rigorous mode of living . . . His meat was bread and his drink was water, and these would be his only food every two or three days while from his meditation on the divine words he ceased not day or night."[16]

The East had been the home to Tatian's Encratite communities in the second century and an even more robust Gnostic Christian sect, the Manichean movement, a century later. The idea of the wandering stranger, his continent body charged with the power to shake the kingdoms of the earth, had lost none of its appeal in the Christian Near East.[17] Many young men from prosperous families heard the ascetic calling and joined the hermits in the forest-clad mountains of the Black Sea or vanished among the caves in the tufa-rock gulleys that lay at a temptingly short distance from the tranquil cities of Cappadocia. Unlike the Egyptian deserts, however, these sites were not permanent, so that these influential men often brought their values back home.[18]

Despite the frequently expressed disapproval of the clergy, they were joined by little bands of women who continued to live the life of Paul's wandering companion Saint Thecla: they covered huge distances along the roads that led to the pilgrimage-shrines of the Christian East. In cities, virgins often coalesced in small groups, forming intense friendships.[19] Many of these women sought out platonic relationships with religious males. They chose common dress to expunge all gender and social distinctions. Some even shaved their heads as a symbol of casting off their perceived role in traditional society.

16. Ibid., 204.
17. Ibid., 197.
18. Ibid., 286.
19. Ibid., 265, 272.

REINING IN ASCETIC BEHAVIOR

Bishops feared the mingling of virgins with male compatriots. A persistent campaign of preaching and canonical legislation came to be directed against members of the clergy who sought female spiritual companions of this kind. Bishops cautioned that these relationships underestimated the innate sex drives in all individuals where even a mere touch can spark uncontrolled sexual urges.

Church leaders desired to direct the religious strivings of women and the charitable imperatives of the righteous so that the institution of married households was not weakened. Brothers Basil and Gregory signaled one approach. Christian families such as theirs had dominated the small cities of the region, as lawyers, *rhetors*, great landowners, and bishops. Theirs was a stern, ceremonious Christianity, firmly rooted in the continued life of great households.[20]

When Basil became bishop at Caesarea, he developed urban brotherhoods where voluntary poverty and almsgiving would predominate. And when Gregory became bishop in Nyssa, he followed suit. In these Christian "households," hard-working celibates would take any surplus wealth and immediately hand it over as alms to the poor.[21]

Both brothers believed that these monastic brotherhoods could create communities that would shape the behavior of ordinary Christians. Brotherhoods would be less about taming sexuality in the few than about creating an example for married householders to emulate in the husbanding of resources for the needs of the poor.[22] Instead, a deep admiration for the life of these monks provided many married householders with an alibi for abandoning their own quest for Christian perfection.

Just as important, Gregory wrote a lengthy treatise defending the role of sex within marriage. Gregory wished to convey to married householders that they should not feel less righteous because they engaged in sexual relations. He rejected Clement's claim that sex was a concession to man's weakness. Sexuality was a privileged sign of God's abiding care, designed for marriage and childbirth: it enabled humankind to continue to stem the tide of death by producing progeny.[23]

---

20. Ibid., 285.
21. Ibid., 290.
22. Ibid., 303.
23. Ibid., 294-295.

Ascetic Values Confront Roman Society

Weakening the pull of virginity and strengthening the traditional family were central components of John Chrysostom's spellbinding preaching in Antioch and then in Constantinople at the close of the fourth century. In his youth, Chrysostom received the calling and went to live an austere life among monks in the Syrian hills. After two years, his gastric system was permanently impaired by long fasts, forcing him to return to town. In 381, he was ordained deacon in the Great Church of Antioch and began his acclaimed sermons.

The city's large number of virgins was undermining the centrality of marriage. John Chrysostom, like Paul before him, believed that marriage would bring down the high temperature of sexual needs of young men. He counseled that marriage should be at an early age. Husbands and wives should protect each other from the dangerous tides of lust by engaging in sufficiently regular intercourse. Since it led to the lasting joys of legitimate children, married intercourse was what young men needed: it kept them away from the transient pleasures of the brothel.

Chrysostom reinforced traditional patriarchy whereby husbands ruled over their wives and parents over their children. He rejected the desire of women to have independent civic lives and instead preached that they should be cloistered in their homes as nuns should be cloistered in their monasteries. Reflecting his concern for the poor, Chrysostom condemned the opulent lifestyle of wealthy women. He exhorted them to cut back on jewelry and dress, for they must not walk past the poor with the price of many dinners hanging from their ears.[24] Nor should the household spend lavishly:

> Do you wish to honor the body of Christ? . . . Do not pay him homage in the temple clad in silk, only then to neglect him outside where he is cold and ill-clad. . . . What good is it if the Eucharistic table is overloaded with golden chalices when your brother is dying of hunger? Start by satisfying his hunger and then with what is left you may adorn the altar as well.[25]

What would sanctify married householders was their almsgiving:

> For the greatest of things is charity, an austere lifestyle and the giving of alms, which hits a higher peak of virtue than does virginity.

---

24. Ibid., 312.

25. John Chrysostom, *In Evangelium S. Matthaei*, hom. https://contemplativeinthemud.wordpress.com/2012/06/03/john-chrysostom-satisfy-jesus-hunger/

For without virginity, indeed, it is possible to see the Kingdom, but without almsgiving this cannot be.[26]

Like other church leaders before him, Chrysostom made no secret that he wished the theater and the hippodrome to fall silent forever. He was outraged by easy-going nudity in the great public baths and frank eroticism in the public spectacles. To him, the public life of Antioch was a "Devil's garbage tip," piled high outside the simple walls of Christian houses.[27] Only in individual Christian families would a touch of the holiness survive.[28]

John Chrysostom was a widely popular orator because his congregants could choose to follow what they liked and reject what they did not. The well-to-do heads of households rejoiced in his defense of marriage but rejected his call for more than symbolic almsgiving. Ordinary Christians enjoyed his criticism of the privileged but ignored his condemnation of public events and behavior. They could do this since as a church deacon, he did not have the power to force his views on a resistant public.

In 398, Chrysostom was selected as the new bishop of Constantinople. There, he soon gained the admiration of the people by his eloquence, his ascetic life, and his charity. Chrysostom's railing against civic life and the solemnity of married life he promoted reflected the anti-pleasure pronouncements that had come to dominate the church. However, his exhortations against the luxuriant lifestyle of church leaders were unacceptable. They feared that the ascetic movement would become a threat to their own status and authority.[29] Chrysostom's incessant criticisms led Emperor Arcadius to exile him to Armenia in 404, where he died a few years later.

AMBROSE AND JEROME

At the middle of the fourth century, Italy was an intensely conservative, under-Christianized region. Many men continued to follow their fathers into paganism even after their mothers had brought Christianity into the homes. Since it went against pagan tradition, young girls often became consecrated virgins only after their fathers were deceased.

---

26. Brown, *Body & Society*, 311.
27. Ibid., 312-313.
28. Ibid., 313-314.
29. Hunter, *Marriage, Celibacy*, 58.

Ascetic Values Confront Roman Society

The deep religiosity of many upper-class Christian women led them to form an assertive alliance with the clergy. As patrons of individual writers, aristocratic Latin women acted as arbiters of intellectual life to a degree unparalleled in the Greek East.[30] This undoubtedly strongly influenced the thinking of Ambrose when he became bishop of Milan in 374.

Ambrose strove to make Milan, the capital of the Western Roman Empire, into a Christian stronghold. He did this through both preaching and construction. He built three churches around the city with names that highlighted his religious priorities: Basilica Apostolorum, Basilica Virginum, and Basilica Martyrum.

Ambrose desired to increase the influence of Christianity over the daily lives of Roman citizens. He believed that to curry favor with the Roman rulers, previous church leaders had been too compromising on the role that Christianity should play in the empire. Throughout the 380s, Ambrose threatened to bar the doors of his church to emperors polluted with the dark "admixture" of tolerance for pagans, heretics, and Jews.

Ambrose had read the sermons of his Cappadocian counterparts, and may even have aided in the development of brotherhoods in Italy that were similar in structure to those initiated by Basil. Charity, however, was not his objective. Ambrose did not counsel his wealthy patrons to increase their almsgiving to the poor as John Chrysostom had preached. Instead, he desired that they maintain their patronage of the Church whose influence he wished to expand.

Ambrose was very sensitive to the weakness of the flesh that could at any moment lead to the slip and tumble of the soul's resolve.[31] He rejected Origen's hopefulness that human perfection was attainable. The bloody stains of human birth could be mitigated but not completely overcome.[32] Ambrose stressed that an unbreakable "invisible frontier" lay between a virgin's body and the polluting "admixture" of the outside world.

Mary's virginity became central to Ambrose's theology. Many church leaders had believed her virginity ended with her conception of Jesus. After her miraculous role was completed, Mary became an ordinary married woman, the wife of Joseph and the mother of his children begotten by ordinary intercourse. This life story was easily embraced by married

---

30. Brown, *Body & Society*, 345.
31. Ibid., 349-350.
32. Ibid., 353.

householders because it fit with their desire for their daughters to remain virgins only until their betrothal.[33]

Ambrose argued that Mary had remained a virgin for her entire life. Mary was a "royal hall of undamaged chastity."[34] In arguing that Mary was even a virgin *during* conception, Ambrose was unique. Others, like Origen, were unwilling to make this claim. They feared that it suggested that since Jesus was not from human intercourse, his body was not really corporeal so that his appearance of suffering was an illusion: a claim of docetism associated with the heretical Manicheans.

His emphasis on continence led Ambrose to embrace a hierarchal view of his Christian congregants: virgins, widows, and married householders. He preached, "Every day, in the readings of the Scriptures, and in the preaching of the bishops, the Church proclaims praise for marital morality, but the glory goes to virginal integrity."[35] Under his leadership, the celebration of the veiling of consecrated virgins took on a more public role. For Ambrose, married sexuality lay in the shadow of the bright peak of the virginal state.

Ambrose's focus on virginity caused him to take a more aggressive stance on the continence of the priesthood. Throughout the fourth century, the Latin clergy was dominated by married men who had fathered children before assuming their religious posts. In many regions, there were clerical dynasties as sons followed fathers and nephews followed uncles. By contrast, Ambrose believed that church leaders should only come from among men who had lived lives of perpetual celibacy.[36] When a growing number of young celibates joined brotherhoods and desired a more central place in the church, Ambrose urged churches to appoint only them to the clergy.

In 396, the town of Vercelli chose a wealthy landowner to lead its congregants instead of a lifelong celibate. Ambrose led a successful effort to reverse this decision. In a long letter, Ambrose claimed that society's hardest battle was an unremitting fight against sensuality. To prefer non-ascetic leaders was to maintain that this struggle was unnecessary; to deny the whole trajectory of man's painful return to paradise through sexual abstinence and fasting.[37]

33. Ibid., 355-56.
34. Ibid., 354.
35. Ibid., 361.
36. Ibid., 357.
37. Ibid., 361.

Ascetic Values Confront Roman Society

In the heat of the battle, Ambrose went even further. He advocated anew, but in a much more public way, that married householders must maintain more stringent standards of sexual conduct than had become the accepted norm in Christian families. The legal husband must not allow himself to be tempted, through love of sensuous delight, to play the adulterer to his own wife. More than ever, lustful intentions and the desire for pleasure should be eliminated from the marriage bed.[38]

In his advocacy of lifelong virginity and passionless sex, Ambrose found an ally in Jerome. No church father wrote more offensively about marriage or more contemptuously about sex than Jerome.[39] Though both men were united in their defense of continence, they had little else in common. Unlike the urbanized Ambrose, Jerome had lived two years as a Syrian anchorite, embracing Origen's belief that a sustained ascetic life would bleach the body of its birth stains.

Jerome had little sympathy for the prosperous church he encountered upon moving to Rome in 382. Indeed, he did not conceal his derogatory attitude toward church leaders and became an outcast. Unlike the activist Ambrose, the contemplative Jerome accepted the traditional civic norm that pagans, Jews, and Christians could live peacefully together. After he moved to Jerusalem in 386, Jerome would converse with Jews to better learn Hebrew so that he would not have to rely completely on the Greek Septuagint in his thirty-year project to create a Latin Bible.

Like Ambrose, Jerome relied on financial support from wealthy widows. But there is where the comparison ends. For Ambrose, these patrons were a means to support the church. He never thought of them as equals, never engaged in intellectual or social relations with them. Indeed, much of his fear of the contaminant of sensuality was based on the belief that women were inherently temptresses.

By contrast, Jerome had absorbed Origen's vision that continent men and women could sustain healthy intellectual and social relations. He saw no reason why Origen's ideal of an ascetic labor of the mind, associated with the Christian's daily meditation, should not be extended in its full rigors to these mature and well-educated women. In the Holy Land, streams of women on pilgrimage offered opportunities for the flowering of spiritual

---

38. Ibid., 362.
39. Ranke-Heinemann, *Eunuchs*, 60.

companionship between male and female ascetics that were unique in the Mediterranean world.[40]

When Roman society became increasingly threatened from the North, the church sought to unite with the Roman pagan aristocracy and softened the behavior expected. At most, the pagans were required to confess their sins, increase their almsgiving, and engage in short periods of fasting. In this compromised environment, Origen had to be rejected because, as John Chrysostom, Evagrius Ponticus, and Jerome clearly demonstrated, he provided a language that expected the clergy and its wealthy patrons to maintain much more rigorous standards.

The first sustained attack on Origen was initiated by Epiphanius, bishop of Cyprus and a founder of Palestinian monasticism. He condemned Origen's speculation that the Son and Holy Spirit were subordinate to the Father was considered heretical.[41] Central to the attack, however, was Origen's linking salvation with sexual purity, thus denying the central role of God's grace. The attack on Origen's ideals was part of the process of rooting out the more radical ideas of the Desert Fathers as then reflected by the writings and preaching of the Egyptian monk Evagrius Ponticus.[42]

Jerome reluctantly joined the attack on Origen, whose ideas had provided a guidepost for his attitudes and writings. Jerome undoubtedly feared that going against the rising orthodoxy would jeopardize acceptance of his Latin Bible project. He no doubt anticipated that those in the East, like John Chrysostom, who remained advocates of Origen's views on human nature would be marginalized.

SAINT AUGUSTINE

In condemning Origen, Christian leaders turned away from the prospect of a limitless fluidity of the human person. No longer would continence and self-mortification be a means of perfecting the body; they would become increasingly associated with penance for sinful behavior and sinful thoughts. It would be Augustine of Hippo who would complete this reversal.

Born in 354, Augustine arrived in Carthage at eighteen to further his studies. Soon thereafter, he began a thirteen-year relationship with

---

40. Brown, *Body & Society*, 372.

41. The subordination of the Son and the Holy Spirit to the Father is most associated with Arianism; see http://www.arian-catholic.org/arian/arius.html

42. For a discussion of the views of Evagrius Ponticus, see Clark, *Origenist Controversy*.

Ascetic Values Confront Roman Society

a woman that produced a child in 373. Augustine became an *auditor*, a "hearer" of the Gnostic-inspired Manicheans. He would bring them the special foods necessary for their ritual meals. He fasted on Sunday, when he would have attended solemn readings of the great cosmic myths that explained the destiny of his soul.[43]

From their Syrian origins, the ideas of Mani had spread throughout the North African coast. Manicheans absorbed contempt for the body from Gnostic thought. The physical world was deeply polluted, but it was not irrevocably fallen. Just beneath its surface there shimmered the hope of a great deliverance.[44] The total cessation of desire, however, was possible for only a few—the Elect. They abstained as much as was humanly possible from the processes of eating, of producing and preparing food, and of begetting. Their emaciated bodies spoke of the spirits already liberated from the kingdom of darkness.[45]

The Manicheans maintained that all sexual activity, in whatever circumstances, aided the powers of the kingdom of darkness. Marriage was no less regrettable than a more frankly sexual relationship with a concubine. Augustine's relationship was the best he could do. He was still enslaved to the tyranny of the world. Augustine, as a mere *auditor*, was no more expected to abandon sex than he could be expected to imitate the Elect in abstaining from meat or abandoning the pursuit of wealth. His salvation depended on their mysterious prayers that flowed from the seven books of Mani.[46]

When Augustine came to Milan in 384, his mother began to arrange his marriage to a much younger woman. In response, Augustine sent his concubine and son back to Carthage, never to see them again. When he impulsively took a stopgap mistress, Augustine understood that marriage would just be a means for him to satisfy his sexual desires. Realizing that his life was driven by an unfulfilling sense of pride and lustfulness, he had an epiphany:

> I noticed a poor beggar who must, I suppose, have had his fill of food and drink, since he was laughing and joking. . . . My ambitions had placed a load of misery on my shoulders and the further I carried it the heavier it became, but the only purpose of all the

---

43. Brown, *Body & Society*, 391.
44. Ibid., 198.
45. Ibid., 392.
46. Ibid., 391-392.

efforts we make was to reach the goal of peaceful happiness. This beggar had already reached it ahead of us, and perhaps we should never reach it at all. For by all my laborious contriving and intricate maneuvers I was hoping to win the joy of worldly happiness, the very thing which this man had already secured at the cost of the few pence which he had begged.[47]

As a result, Augustine began to study Greek philosophy and, moved by Ambrose's sermons, considered joining the church. Augustine contended, "While Platonism might represent the highest intellectual and spiritual point of the pagan world, Christianity went beyond it and provided an everlasting haven."[48] He formed intellectual relations with other young men and they collectively undertook the conversion to Christianity.

When he became a priest in Hippo five years later, Augustine founded a monastery. The interpersonal bonds fostered within it, by continence and poverty, remained the calm eye of the storm for the remaining forty years of Augustine's life. It provided the ideal against which he would henceforth judge the society around him.[49]

Augustine believed that good Christians needed to be reassured that the marriage on which their whole society was based was not merely the result of regrettable accident; that instead, God had created humanity for marriage and childbirth. Augustine interpreted Paul to indicate that marriage was not evil but a lesser good compared to virginity (1 Cor 7:38). As did Paul, he rejected the possibility that sexual pleasure might in itself enrich the relations between husband and wife. Thus, he was pleased by the continent relationship of Paulinus of Nola with his wife Therasia.[50]

While he now abandoned sexual relations to cast out his demons, Augustine never believed that virginity alone would make one a better Christian. He was upset by the smug superiority that many rich ascetic patrons exuded. He hoped that they would recognize the fragility of their virtue and adopt a genuine attitude of humility. Augustine also beseeched nuns to never look down on married women.[51]

Augustine's defense of married householders led him to reject Ambrose's hierarchy. He noted that martyrdom was a superior virtue to

47. McMahon, *Happiness*, 99.
48. Freeman, *Closing of Western Mind*, 281.
49. Brown, *Body & Society*, 395.
50. Ibid., 403.
51. Ibid., 397.

Ascetic Values Confront Roman Society

celibacy. As a result, he argued: "No one, in my opinion, should dare to consider virginity superior to martyrdom, and no one should doubt that martyrdom is a gift that remains hidden if there is no test to bring it to light."[52] Thus, he believed it would be wrong to consider celibates morally superior to married householders, many of whom would be willing to suffer martyrdom.

Like Origen, Ambrose contended that sexuality and marriage arose when Adam and Eve lapsed from an "angelic" state into physicality. For Augustine, sexual desire introduced no disruptive element into the clear serenity of their marriage. Only when lustfulness—concupiscence—became the consuming objective of the sexual relationship, did Adam sin.

If these were the final views of Augustine, he would not have gained the stature accorded him within Christianity. He would have been known for his distinctive views on the nature of Adam and Eve in paradise—just as Ambrose was known for his distinctive views on Mary's virginity. Augustine would have been just one more defender of the central role of marriage in Christian life. Events, unfolded, however, that led him to embrace much harsher, more pessimistic attitudes—the nature of *original sin*—when the followers of Origen made one last attempt to shape Christian thought.

This conflict arose around the teachings of Pelagius. An Irish ascetic he had gained widespread respect and many followers after arriving in Rome at the end of the fourth century.[53] Just as Jerome, Pelagius was appalled by the laxity of Roman society. He argued that this situation was the result of predestination which freed individuals from taking responsibility for their actions. Pelagius believed that man had free will to choose between good and evil. Like the Desert Fathers, he taught that through personal discipline, man could attain sinless behavior.

When Rome was sacked in 410, Pelagius fled to North Africa, where Augustine condemned his views. In doing so, Augustine was forced to look more closely at the nature of the downfall of Adam. For Augustine, Adam's original sin now reflected sexual shame. The stirring of an erection—over which he had no control—captured the sinfulness that could not be escaped.[54] God inflicted more than death on human beings: He condemned

---

52. Hunter, *Marriage, Celibacy*, 282.

53. Peter Brown, *Religion &Society*, 185.

54. Brown, *Body & Society*, 416-417; Lancel, *Saint Augustine*, 424; and Schroeder, *Vestal and the Fasces*, 90.

Adam and all his descendants to the burden of concupiscence transmitted from generation to generation through the sexual act.

Concupiscence was a dark drive that turned one's private desires against all the good things that had been created by God. "It lay at the root of the inescapable misery that afflicted mankind."[55] The sexual act submerged the soul and obliterated everything.[56] This original sin made it impossible for man to be pure without God's grace, no matter how he might engage in ascetic behavior. Indeed, Augustine went so far as to claim that newborns dying without baptism are excluded from both the kingdom of heaven and eternal life.

Pelagius defended his position against this conception of original sin. He claimed that with the coming of Christ, "men and women did not carry sin in their bones, were not irreparably, congenitally marred. On the contrary, they were fully capable of perfection, and it was their duty to realize this end."[57] One of Pelagius's defenders, Julian of Eclanum, castigated Augustine for "delivering children to the flames before they are capable of choosing good or evil."[58] In 418, Pelagius was condemned as a heretic by the Council of Carthage.

The last of Pelagius's defenders was an authentic representative of the desert tradition, John Cassian. He had been a disciple of Evagrius in Egypt and, later, of John Chrysostom in Constantinople. At the beginning of the fifth century, he became a member of the monastic diaspora that had been scattered from Egypt and Constantinople as a result of the Origenist controversy. Settled in Lérins, a deserted island opposite Cannes, Cassian wrote against Augustine.[59]

For Cassian and the Desert Fathers, sexual dreams and sexual temptations betrayed the tread of a far heavier beast within the soul—anger, greed, avarice, and vanity. By contrast, Augustine placed sexuality irremovably at the center of the human person. Cassian was no more successful than Pelagius. By the time he wrote, sexuality was held inflexibly in the grip of Augustine's notion of a human race condemned to endure, in their bodies and their minds, lustfulness as a permanent symptom of Adam's fall.[60]

55. Brown, *Body & Society*, 418.
56. Lancel, *Saint Augustine*, 423.
57. McMahon, *Happiness*, 103.
58. Clark, *Holy Bishops*, 220.
59. Brown, *Body &Society*, 420.
60. Ibid., 422.

CONCLUDING REMARKS

The condemnation of both Origenism and Pelagianism signaled the flourishing of a "Christian theology whose central concerns were human sinfulness, not human potential; divine determination, not human freedom and responsibility; God's mystery, not God's justice."[61] Augustine let in the hard male puritanism that Romans relished, with its harsh distrust of sensual delight and fear of the body's pleasures.

Augustine persistently emphasized the impotence of human will to counter concupiscence. He presented earthly existence as unremittingly steeped in suffering and pain.[62] His writings have been used to justify extreme piety and self-mortification as penance without any belief in their transformative abilities. Whether or not Augustine ultimately embraced the Gnostic contempt for the body, this became his legacy.

---

61. Clark, *Origenist Controversy*, 254.
62. Hunter, *Marriage, Celibacy*, 286; and McMahon, *Happiness*, 106.

9

Bodily Pleasures: Foundational Jewish Values

WITH THE TRANSCRIPTION OF the Oral Torah into the Mishnah, and the astute strategies of Rabi, the rabbinic sages attained undisputed leadership of the Palestinian Jewish community. Rabbinic scholars then began the task of analyzing the text in more detail to understand the application of the laws to different situations. Over the next three centuries, scholars worked in both Palestine and Babylonia to complete this project.

Over that period, however, there was a profound change in the composition and location of the Jewish people. On the eve of the first century rebellion, there were more than five million Jews worldwide, with half living in the land of Israel. When the Babylonian Talmud was completed during the fifth century, the worldwide Jewish population numbered about one million, with only about 100,000 living in Palestine. The first part of this chapter will describe the impact of this profound transformation on Judaism and on the task of rabbinic scholars.

The second half of this chapter will detail how bodily pleasure is treated in both the Jerusalem Talmud and the Babylonian Talmud, highlighting the contrasting commentaries by biblical scholars David Biale and Daniel Boyarin. We will find that the constraints on pleasure recommended by some of the Palestinian sages are rejected decisively as religious leadership shifts to Babylonia. Finally, it will describe the link between literacy requirements of rabbinic Judaism with the movement of Jews to urban areas and their specialization in commercial activities.

BODILY PLEASURES: FOUNDATIONAL JEWISH VALUES

ADAPTING TO THE HELLENISTIC ENVIRONMENT

When the Mishnah was completed at the beginning of the third century, the sharp decline of the Jewish population in Palestine was matched by similar declines throughout the Mediterranean basin. Viable Jewish communities remained in only a few cities in Asia Minor and North Africa. These communities regained their stability when Roman authorities reverted to a willingness to tolerate non-proselytizing, non-pagan religions. In order to avoid conflict, Jewish leadership made clear that their adherents would be good citizens of whatever city in which they resided. They stressed that the law of the land is the law they would follow and willingly participated in city governance.

Jewish communities in Asia Minor did not desire to flaunt their religion, so the sages condemned those who wished to study Torah in public.[1] Rabbis tried to accommodate to local norms by, for example, issuing edicts calling for extreme modesty in women to conform to Christian sensibilities: "It is forbidden for a woman to adorn her daughter and take her out to the marketplace because she is risking her life, and a woman who has perfumed herself and goes to [houses] of idol worship is to be flogged and her hair to be shaved off."[2]

These efforts allowed for meaningful contact with paganism beyond condemning idolatry.[3] As a result, the vitality and influence of these Jewish communities was substantial. During the third century, Sardi, an important Roman community, had numerous Jewish city council members and functionaries in the provincial government.[4] In Antioch, Jews were employed by the Greek theater and the communal leader, Rabbi Abbahu, sent his daughters to Greek schools and frequently visited the home of the Roman governor.[5]

In second-century Galilee, Hellenist influences were minimal. Though Greek theaters were present in major cities, Jews refused to attend events there because of their use of pagan symbols and rituals. While many of the cities had schools to train students in Greek rhetoric, few Galilean Jews participated as there continued to be a discouragement of eloquence and

---

1. Meyers, "Jewish Culture," 165.
2. Irshai, "Confronting," 193.
3. Kaufman, *Christianity and Judaism*, 200.
4. Feldman, *Jews and Gentiles*, 364.
5. Irshai, "Confronting," 186.

distrust of its use in practice. Indeed, the learning of Greek was not a part of male education in Galilean towns and villages.[6]

As rabbinic academies moved to more urbanized areas, however, they were increasingly exposed to the Greek language. As a result, more than two thousand Greek words had been incorporated into the Hebrew and Aramaic languages. Synagogues of that era were styled after Greek buildings, and inscriptions of dedication were sometimes written in Greek.[7]

To the extent possible, Jews embraced the dress, food, artifacts, utensils, art, or forms of domicile of Hellenistic culture. As *halakah* favors the use of stoneware since it is more resistant to ritual impurity, Jews preferred such utensils and eschewed the pottery found in Greek homes. Otherwise, however, Jews and Gentiles dressed, to a large degree, in similar fashion, and they lived in similarly designed homes. The *Sifre*, a third-century Palestinian text, makes clear that in matters that have no religious or moral significance, the Jew should not be expected to behave differently from his Gentile neighbor.[8]

The rabbinic sages viewed Greco-Roman culture and its art, including mythological scenes, as a means of participating in the larger cultural identity. Far from attempting to preserve the purity of traditional biblical culture in the face of foreign temptations, the sages grafted their own innovations onto old traditions, incorporating the language, art, and law of the Greco-Roman world of which they were an active and integral part.[9]

Synagogue preachers provided entertainment and aesthetic pleasure. They believed that "humorous parables, anecdotes, or riddles" would inspire the public.[10] Allegories, tales, expositions, and narratives became an integral part of their talks. Rabbis compared these sermons to the Roman theater or circus, praising Jews who attended the former and avoided the latter.[11] Indeed, a third-century sage, Resh Lakish, said, "We should be grateful to the nations of the world who bring their mimes into their theaters and circuses and are entertained by them."[12]

---

6. Goodman, *State and Society*, 73.
7. Ralph Marcus, "Challenge of Greco-Roman Culture," 108.
8. Blidstein, "Rabbinic Judaism," 48, 52.
9. Meyers, "Jewish Culture," 174.
10. Friedman and Friedman, *God Laughed*, 112.
11. Irshai, "Confronting," 200.
12. Weiss, *Public Spectacles*, 128.

The effectiveness of these sermons reflected the willingness of Jews to respect the sound contribution of the Greeks to learning, including insights into the human world and its workings. Non-Jewish aphorisms and anecdotes pepper religious texts, and there was a willingness to retell stories using universal folk motifs, Greek puns, and proverbs.[13] Preachers and the sages would use these references for the clarification and definition of their own teachings.[14]

This behavior of the sages reflected a strong distinction between secular and philosophical material. In the domain of facts, truth was to be accepted, whatever its source. As a result, the sages respected the secular material that Hellenism provided, in particular with respect to language, architecture, and science. The sages drew the line, however, at Hellenistic philosophy; the study of Greek wisdom was forbidden. Greek philosophical terms are absent from the entire ancient rabbinic literature.[15]

THE ASCENDENCY OF THE BABYLONIAN COMMUNITY

At the beginning of the third century, a succession of Roman rulers was supportive of Rabi and his religious project. The Palestinian religious academies grew and attracted scholars from Babylonia. While many of these students remained in Palestine, some returned. The leading figure in the development of religious academies in Babylonia was Abba Arikha, simply called Rav. He came to Israel to study with Rabbi Judah, but then returned to Babylonia and established his own academy in Sura. His cousin Shmuel set up an academy in Nehardea and became the head of the Babylonian Beit Din.

Rabbi Yochanan was the major religious force in Israel after Rabi's death. He lived to almost one hundred years and guided the first three generations of compilers of the Jerusalem Talmud. His academy in Tiberias became the most widely respected place of study, attracting students from Babylonia. Indeed, many of the most important Babylonian scholars were Rabbi Yochanan's students. To strengthen ties between the two communities, Rabbi Yochanan would periodically send his best students to Babylonia to deliver news from the Tiberias academy. These exchanges explain

---

13. Blidstein, "Rabbinic Judaism," 20, 39.
14. Lieberman, *Hellenism*, 64.
15. Blidstein, "Rabbinic Judaism," 31.

why, though Rabbi Yochanan never left Palestine, his role in the Babylonian Talmud is prominent.

Many of the Palestinian sages and their Babylonian counterparts, however, did not subscribe to the mutual respect that Rabbi Yochanan promoted. They worried that the centrality of the land of Israel might be lost. The third-century religious text, Tosefta, states, "He who leaves the country in a time of peace and goes abroad is akin to an idolater." This attitude led many of the Palestinian sages to be unwilling to consider Babylonian scholars as their equals. Indeed, many would not ordain the Babylonian students who attended their academies for fear that they would return to their homeland. This lack of formal ordination explains why much of the Babylonian religious leadership assumed the title Rav rather than Rabbi.

By the same token, many of the leading Babylonian scholars considered Palestinian Jewry to be of inferior lineage. It was widely thought that only Jews of inferior stock had returned to Canaan after the Babylonian captivity. Indeed, even some of the Palestinian sages believe that in the time of Ezra, "he brought with him to Israel all the disqualified Jews, thus leaving Babylon pure semolina, a place for an elite society."[16] This elitism explained the contempt that the Babylonian leadership had for the *ammei ha'aretz*, comparing sexual relations with them to sexual relations with a donkey.

Further complicating the relationship were the dramatic changes in the economic situation in Palestine. When Alexander Severus died in 235, a succession of short-reigning military emperors created civil wars and great economic disruption. Taxes to finance these wars of succession became unbearable. The resulting deteriorating economic conditions devastated the Galilean communities. By contrast, the semi-independent Jewish communities in Babylonia maintained their prosperity.

The temptation to emigrate was enormous. Babylonia promised sources of livelihood, economic prosperity, and, above all, a full Jewish life—the opposite of the poverty and emptiness that characterized the Palestinian spiritual realm. As a result, many left the Galilee for Babylonia. By the beginning of the fourth century, only one-half million Jews remained in Palestine.

Predictably, this emigration adversely affected the Palestinian academies. By the end of the third century, they had to rely increasingly on donations from the Babylonian community. As their future began to seem bleak, the leading Palestinian rabbis– Rabbi Yochanan, Resh Lakish, and

16. Charney and Mayzlish, *Battle of the Two Talmuds*, 57.

Bodily Pleasures: Foundational Jewish Values

Rabbi Eleazar—believed that only migration from the Babylonian exile to Palestine had the potential to rescue Jewish life in the Holy Land. However, given the stark contrast in economic opportunities, none of the Babylonian students chose to remain in Palestine, while many of the Palestinian-born students migrated to Babylonian academies.

Despite these setbacks, the Palestinian scholars pushed forward. With fewer students, fewer resources, and increasing hostility from the growing Christian communities, they rushed to complete the Jerusalem Talmud. Due to the extremely harsh conditions that the Palestinian rabbis faced, the Jerusalem Talmud was poorly edited, and when completed around 400, the few copies that were made enjoyed but limited circulation. Soon thereafter, the Palestinian academies were closed. As a result, the Palestinian Talmud was practically unknown to religious scholars for hundreds of years. Indeed, only one copy of the entire manuscript, the Leiden Jerusalem Talmud of 1289, survived.

By contrast, the Babylonian academies were well funded and their leaders were generally quite wealthy. Arriving in Babylonia empty-handed, Rav lived there in poverty during his first years but eventually gained wealth and accumulated property, houses, and fields. The same was true of most of the other leading rabbinate there. These favorable economic and political circumstances permitted the Babylonian scholars to work without impediment. Completed 140 years after the Jerusalem Talmud, the Babylonian Talmud is more thorough, better edited, and four times larger. It was also more widely circulated and became the authoritative text for judging behaviors consistent with the Mosaic laws.

ASCETIC TENDENCIES FIRMLY REJECTED

Leaders of the Babylonian academies lived sumptuous lifestyles. Rav and Shmuel encouraged people to enjoy material pleasures. Shmuel told his pupil Rav Huna: "If you have good food, enjoy it because there is no pleasure in Hell, and Death does not loiter." Rashi interpreted Shmuel's "seize the day" attitude as: "If you have money to please yourself, don't wait for tomorrow, because you may die and miss the pleasure."[17] The historian Heinrich Graetz noted:

---

17. Charney and Mayzlish, *Battle of the Two Talmuds*, 91-92.

> The wealthy and luxurious lifestyle the Babylonian scholars had created for themselves set them apart as a snobbish class... Rabbis would go out dressed in silk and carried in golden seats by their slaves... They also had special privileges to buy and to sell..."[18]

Not surprisingly, these practices drew scorn from Palestinian counterparts who were imbued with the Pharisaic contempt for the lifestyles of the wealthy. Rabbi Ami stated,

> How they adorn themselves there in Babylonia, the sons of the Torah, in pleasant garments and luxurious raiment. It appears that they are not sons of the Torah.[19]

The more prosperous Jewish communities of Asia Minor also embraced bodily pleasure. This positive view was reflected in the numerous festivals that so enraged the church fathers. Jerome complained that Jewish preachers, in a theatrical manner, roused up applause and shouting.[20] As described earlier, the church leader John Chrysostom accused Jews of bringing troupes of actors and dancers into the synagogue. He railed against their use of drums, lyres, harps, and other musical instruments, probably at weddings or Purim celebrations.

Let us now move on to the central ascetic value: abstinence from sexual relations. The sages rejected celibacy, and, indeed, they sometimes projected a demeaning attitude toward Christianity for this behavior. For example, in 344 CE, not far from Babylon, the Christian sage Aphrahat reported: "A Jewish man insulted one of the brothers, members of our congregation, by saying to him: 'You are impure, you who do not marry women; but we are holy and better, we who procreate and increase progeny in the world.'"[21]

As discussed earlier, Moses abstained from sexual relations while he was in communication with God. This behavior of Moses fitted prominently into the writings of the Alexandrian Jew, Philo. In his *Life of Moses*, Philo contrasts the corporeal and passionate life with spiritual pursuits, concluding the one to be necessarily incompatible with the other.[22] Passionless sex was practiced by Rabbi Meir and Rabbi Eliezer ben Hyrcanus. In addition,

18. Ibid., 84.
19. Ibid., 4.
20. Feldman, *Jews and Gentiles*, 378.
21. Koltun-Fromm, "Sexuality and Holiness," 375.
22. Koltun-Fromm, *Hermeneutics of Holiness*, 177.

Meir's contemporary Rabbi Nehemiah appeared to teach that there is a higher level of holiness that requires abstinence, such as that practiced by Moses.

In striking opposition, the *Sifre* fiercely combats the notion that Moses's behavior should be emulated. It makes clear why Moses abstained from sexual relations while the prophets did not: Whereas God comes to the prophets in dreams or visions, He spoke to Moses directly. Thus, the text explains the uniqueness of Moses's situation and why his behavior should not inspire others to choose celibacy.

By postulating that Jewish prophets were expected to marry and procreate, the *Sifre* also rejects the notion that religious pursuits are in conflict with familial responsibilities. The text points to the suffering of wives caused by their husbands' neglect. In particular, Moses's sister, Miriam, comes upon a bedraggled, despondent Zipporah wandering around the camp and asks her why she has not taken care of herself. Zipporah lets Miriam know that Moses has been neglecting his conjugal duties. When Zipporah learns that two men, Medad and Eldad, have been drawn into prophecy, she becomes dispirited and exclaims, "Woe to the wives of those men."[23] This statement strengthens the reader's understanding of the anguish of her situation.

This narrative is also responding to the conflict among scholars between family and the pursuit of religious studies. Legend has it that Rabbi Akiba went thirteen years between visits to his wife so that he could pursue religious studies, behavior consistent with Philo's views. However, the *Sifre* rejects such behavior, emphasizing the suffering that it causes to wives. The text promotes the idea that "a balance must be struck" between family and study.[24]

Despite this evidence, the noted scholar David Biale contends that "an ideal of sexual abstinence had penetrated rabbinic culture to the point that it became a bone of contention." He states,

> The very insistence on a divine commandment to procreate and the drastic punishment threatened for those who fail to obey attest to a significant cultural conflict. Perhaps Ben Azzai, the one avowedly celibate rabbi, represented the tip of an ascetic iceberg. Where no one in the Bible entertained the possibility of celibacy, perhaps the fact that the rabbis turned the biblical fertility blessing

23. Ibid., 182.
24. Ibid., 185.

into a commandment suggests that some of their contemporaries were attracted by sexual renunciation ... Ben Azzai may have represented a real threat, a temptation that few followed but that had to be actively resisted.[25]

Steven Fraade wrote, "Although it affirms the ideal of sexual abstinence as a way to spiritual perfection, [the Talmud] recommends moderate sexual activity, especially for the sage."[26]

Biale then proceeds to explain why there is not more documentary evidence of sympathy for celibacy among the religious elite. Seizing on an isolated Talmudic reference, Biale suggests that there was an alliance between the sages and wealthy Jews. He contended that the leading rabbinic students were "deeply entangled in this upper class [and] celibacy would have meant forfeiting the considerable benefits that marriage conferred upon them."[27]

Here, Biale ignores core rabbinic beliefs. In particular, a celibate and hence unmarried religious elite would be in direct conflict with the importance of marriage in Jewish thought that went well beyond the issue of procreation. For the sages, "any man who has no wife lives without joy, without blessing, and without goodness."[28] The sages highlighted the importance of the interpersonal element in marriage: "Whoever loves his wife as himself and honors her more than himself—of him the Scripture says, 'And you will know that your tent shall be in peace and you will visit your habitation, and not sin'" (Job 5:24).[29]

This stress on the centrality of the marital relationship flows from the Torah when God speaks: "It is not good for man to be alone, I shall make him a fitting helper" (Gen 2:18). That passage has generally been interpreted as follows: "a lonely human existence is not good because it lacks God's action and exposes an imperfect form of being."[30]

Biale does note the strong belief in the goodness of sexual relations reflected in the Talmudic saying: "Three things are a taste of the world to come: the Sabbath, sunshine, and *tashmish*" (a term generally used in rabbinic language as a euphemism for sexual intercourse). He chooses,

---

25. Biale, *Eros*, 35-36, 49.
26. Fraade, "Ascetical Aspects," 275
27. Biale, *Eros*, 36.
28. Lichtenstein, "Of Marriage," 12.
29. Ibid., 12.
30. Joseph Soloveitchik, *Family Redeemed*, 17.

however, to focus on a dissenter who believed that there would be no sex in the world to come or in messianic times. Biale then infers, without any documentary evidence, "[B]y engaging in the sexual act of procreation in the *properly chaste manner* [emphasis added], one prepares the way for the asexual world to come."[31]

To make clear his goal of emphasizing the similarities between the views of the sages on sexuality and those of ascetic Christians, Biale ends his discourse as follows:

> The rabbis thus shared with Hellenistic culture the attention to the needs and passions of the individual, but they also agreed with the prevailing opinion in late antiquity that sexuality could not remain a private matter.... Although early Christianity took a much more radical course than did rabbinic Judaism, sexuality was deeply troubling for both and had to be subordinated to loftier goals.[32]

The sages quoted by Biale are those with the most negative attitudes toward sexual relations within marriage. These include Ben Azzai and Rabbi Eliezer, whom the Talmud presents as extreme figures whose practices were sharply rejected.[33] Furthermore, the sages firmly rejected dualism by using the parable of a blind man and a lame man. Each alone, they are limited, but working together—as the body and the soul—they are complete and able to attain lofty goals. Many observers see this rejection of dualism as an important distinction between Judaism and the neo-Platonism that came to dominate the early church. The historian Daniel Boyarin states:

> For rabbinic Jews, the human being was defined as a body—animated, to be sure, by a soul—while for Hellenistic Jews (such as Philo) and (at least many Greek-speaking) Christians (such as Paul), the essence of a human being is a soul housed in a body. For most of the Greco-Roman world an ontological dualism became as natural a way of thinking as the conscious and unconscious is for us, but the proto-rabbinate Jews of Palestine seem to have strongly resisted such dualist notions.[34]

---

31. Biale, *Eros*, 42-43.
32. Ibid., 57-58.
33. Boyarin, *Carnal Israel*, 47.
34. Boyarin, *Carnal Israel*, 5-6. In opposition, Biale, *Eros*, Boyarin (45) stated, "[For the sages,] the struggle for control of sexuality is therefore not primarily a war between body and soul, but a struggle within the realm of the will, a position similar to those of both Hellenistic writers and some of the early church fathers."

Rabbis saw intercourse and eating in similar ways. The primary purpose of each was utilitarian: procreation on the one hand and having a healthy existence on the other. But the rabbis understood pleasure as serving these utilitarian ends: by making sexual relations pleasurable, it is more likely that married couples would have intercourse, increasing the likelihood of children; and making food pleasurable makes it more likely that one will eat—think of ways we try to get our children to eat.[35]

Most importantly, the sages did not discourage lustful enthusiasm during love-making with one's wife. The Jewish marriage contract encourages lustful lovemaking by requiring that partners be unclothed: "One who says I do not desire it unless she is in her clothing, I in mine, must divorce his wife and pay her the marriage settlement."[36] Indeed, there was no revulsion from concupiscent pleasure or recoil from romantic passion:

> One was wont to say: "When our love was intense, a bed the width of a blade was room enough for both of us to lie upon. Now that our love is less intense, a [king-size] bed the width of sixty cubits does not suffice."[37]

There is a Talmudic passage where a student spied on the lovemaking of his mentor, Rav Kahana, and said to him, "You appear to me to be like a hungry man who has never had sex before, for you act with frivolity in your lust." In response, the Rav indignantly responded, "Get out! It is improper for you to lie under my bed!" To which the student retorted, "This is a matter of Torah and I must study." With no further Talmudic comment, this seems to indicate that the sages were unwilling to condemn such lustful behavior.[38]

Indeed, the sages were unwilling to discourage any efforts to make lovemaking more pleasurable. For example, there is a Talmudic passage where a wife complained to Rabi that her husband desired to have sex with her on top rather than in the traditional position. To this, Rabi responded, "My daughter, the Torah has permitted you to him, and I, what can I do for you?"

---

35. Ibid., 75.
36. Boyarin, *Carnal Israel*, 48.
37. Lichtenstein, "Of Marriage," 14.
38. Biale, *Eros*, 53. He situated this story in the context of discussions of other bodily functions that immediately follow it and concluded, "By placing sexual behavior in the same category as defecation, the text covertly undermines any affirmation of Rav's."

BODILY PLEASURES: FOUNDATIONAL JEWISH VALUES

Biale agrees that this and other Talmudic rulings allow "a man may do whatever he pleases with his wife."[39] He claims, however, that though Rabi did not agree, he was unable to overrule "the sexual privileges of men." In this way, Biale minimizes the sexually liberating aspect of the sage's ruling and instead associates it with the protection of patriarchal privilege.[40]

Biale's interpretation is not sustainable, however, because as he noted, "It is forbidden for a man to force his wife in a holy deed for it says One who presses the legs is a sinner [Prov 19:2]".[41] Indeed, far from treating a wife as a piece of property or mere object for the satisfaction of the husband's sexual desire, Talmudic law may be the first legal or moral system to recognize that when a husband forces his wife to engage in a sexual act, he commits rape, pure and simple, as condemnable as any other rape. Even if she has agreed to a first act of intercourse, he may not presume her agreement to a repeated act on the same occasion but must know explicitly that she wishes it.[42]

The sages understood that sexual relations were an integral part of strengthening the relationship between spouses in a number of ways. They considered it sinful for a husband, when having intercourse with his wife, to think of another woman, because doing so would undermine marital intimacy. The Talmud encourages the creation of conditions for mutual arousal, intimacy, and mutual satisfaction. The Laws of Onah guarantee every married woman the right to regular sexual relations and the purpose of such relations is explicitly to give pleasure.[43]

Couples were encouraged to have sexual relations on the Sabbath, for "marital relatons are part of the Sabbath delight."[44] The sumptuous Sabbath dinner was to be followed by a sumptuous night of lovemaking! To make clear that lovemaking was not solely for procreative purposes, it was expected at times when procreation was not possible: during pregnancies and

---

39. "The Torah disqualifies itself from any interference in the private sexual practices of married couples, who may behave sexually as they please with each other." Boyarin, *Carnal Israel*, 112.

40. Biale, *Eros*, 36. He quotes a statement by Rabbi Meir condemning the lovemaking of the *am ha'aretz* who "engages in intercourse and has no shame" as evidence that the sages rejected lustful lovemaking.

41. Ibid., 249 (footnote 108).

42. Boyarin, *Carnal Israel*, 114.

43. Biale, *Eros*, 54. He rationalizes this by claiming that pleasure increased the likelihood of procreation.

44. Lichtenstein, "Of Marriage," 16; and Boyarin, *Carnal Israel*, 52.

after menopause. The Talmud enjoined widowers to remarry even when they had fulfilled the obligation of procreation; and widowers may even marry women proven to be infertile. Indeed, there is even one Talmudic tale in which the pleasures received from sexual union keep a couple together.[45]

These more positive views of sexual relations between husbands and wives held by the sages are not completely absent from Christian thought. Though John Chrysostom privileged virginity, some of his later writings on sexual desire and marriage are indistinguishable from those of the sages: "There is never such intimacy between a man and a man as there is between husband and wife if they are united as they ought to be." And perhaps even more movingly, "But suppose there is no child; do they then remain two and not one? No; their intercourse effects the joining of their bodies, and they are made one, just as when perfume is mixed with ointment."[46]

These views of Chrysostom are, however, in no way reflective of the dominant Christian thought. As Peter Brown noted,

> For the rabbis, sexuality was an enduring adjunct of the personality. Though potentially unruly, it was amenable to restraint . . . Among Christians the exact opposite occurred. Sexuality became a highly charged symbolic marker precisely because its disappearance in the committed individual was considered possible, and because this disappearance was thought to register, more significantly than any other human transformation, the qualities necessary for leadership in the religious community.[47]

Indeed, Chrysostom captured this distinction when he said: "The Jews disdain the beauty of virginity. . . . The Greeks admired and revered the virgin but only the Church of God adores her with zeal."[48]

This gap grew over time. Boyarin claims that the *earlier* Palestinian discourse on sexuality, which Biale emphasizes, was closest in spirit to that of the Stoics, who indeed considered sexuality to be an irritating and necessary part of human existence but also an "enduring aspect of personality." Rabbi Eliezer personifies, perhaps, an extreme representation of this discourse.

The subsequent rabbinic movement was, in large part, a rejectionist movement against the increasing Hellenist and then Christian threat to

---

45. Boyarin, *Carnal Israel*, 54.
46. Ibid., 41.
47. Brown, "Late Antiquity," 266.
48. Boyarin, *Carnal Israel*, 46.

BODILY PLEASURES: FOUNDATIONAL JEWISH VALUES

Palestinian Jewry. In response, the sages increasingly dismissed dualistic understandings of the relation of body to soul. Such denials—which the church fathers characterized as carnality—became the very marker of the rabbinic formation. Increasing distance from both Platonic dualism and Stoicism carried with it a logic that affirmed sexuality per se. By the time the Talmuds were completed, sexuality was regarded as a beneficence of God for the pleasure and well-being of humans.[49]

Tikva Frymer-Kensky, feminist and professor of Near Eastern religion, also pointed to this evolution of religious perspectives:

> The Hellenic complex of ideas about women also had a major impact on Judaism . These ideas entered Rabbinic Judaism in its formative years . . The wave of sexual phobia and outright misogyny disappeared rather early and was replaced by a positive valuation of sexuality in marriage (beyond its importance to procreation) and an honoring of domesticated women as value-keepers, family preservers, and queens of the home.[50]

THE DEMOGRAPHIC IMPACT OF TALMUDIC LITERACY

The decimation of the Palestinian community certainly reflected the disastrous rebellions and also the economic decline and continued discriminatory actions in the following centuries. The increasing emphasis on Talmudic study in order to follow correctly the Mosaic laws may also have led many rural Jews to leave the religion. Even when the negative attitude toward the *ammei ha'aretz* was softened during the reign of Rabi, their status of second-class Jews remained, probably causing still more to abandon Judaism.

By the sixth century, three-quarters of world Jewry lived in Babylonia, with a majority still engaged in agricultural enterprises. In this prosperous environment, the ideal of a literate male population could be realized. With steady growth of literacy, Jewish men left their agricultural communities, moving to Babylonian cities where they could start commercial enterprises. By contrast, those who refused to educate their sons were treated more harshly and driven out of Judaism. This switch increased the similarities

---

49. Ibid., 56, 77.
50. Frymer-Kensky, *Wake of the Goddesses*, 214.

between the occupational distribution of Babylonian Jews with the remaining small urbanized Jewish communities in Asia Minor and the Mediterranean basin.

This transformation reflected the opportunities available to a literate population who engaged in Talmudic study. These studies heightened rational thinking and analytical skills which were valuable for commercial activities. Babylonian Jews became wine sellers, corn and cattle dealers, builders, agents and brokers, shopkeepers, ship owners, money changers, court bankers, pharmacists, physicians, merchants, and long-distance traders. Moreover, as economists Botticini and Eckstein note:

> The cannon of Talmudic laws, their adaption and application through response written by the heads of the academies, who adapted Jewish law to new and unforeseen contingencies, and the rabbinic courts, which ensured that contracts were enforced—all of these institutions represented invaluable assets for Jews engaged in occupations that benefit from contract enforcement.[51]

The urbanization of Babylonian Jewry was accelerated by the Muslim caliphates that conquered the Near East and then the Mediterranean basin, reaching southern Spain by the eighth century. In Mesopotamia, the cities of Baghdad, Samarra, Basra, and Kufa each grew to more than 400,000 inhabitants. Beginning in the mid-eighth century, Babylonian Jews moved to these burgeoning metropolises so that by the end of the ninth century, virtually their entire population had been urbanized.

By the ninth century, Bagdad was the center of the Muslim empire and the province of Ahwaz, southeast of Bagdad, became "the center of the imperial economy." Jewish merchants controlled the Ahwaz economy and initiated "early capitalist reforms, affecting the leading industry, that of fabrics."[52] The Ahwaz merchants set up bazaars in not only Bagdad, but also modern-day Mosul and Basra to sell their fabrics and other products. Jews also comprised a significant position in the Bagdad banking community.

The Muslim caliphs created a vast kingdom with common institutions, laws, and language, making migration within its territories relatively easy. As semi-autonomous provinces around the Mediterranean basin expanded, economic activities expanded. This was particularly the case when the Bagdad economy began to decline. With their international networks, held together by religious enforcement of informal contracts, Jews were

---

51. Botticini and Eckstein, *Chosen Few*, 128.

52. Massignon, *Hallaj*, 124, 127.

Bodily Pleasures: Foundational Jewish Values

best suited for the commercial environment set in motion by Muslim conquests. They moved freely throughout their empire, most notably to Spain, Tunisia, and Egypt.

At the beginning of the tenth century, Tunisia became the hub of economic activity as it was halfway between the Spain-to-Egypt trade route. Jewish merchants prospered as the ruling Fatima branch of Islam was more tolerate of their activities than elsewhere in the Islamic Empire. The reach of Tunisian Jewish merchants increased when the Fatimids gained control of Egypt. Yaquib ben Killis, a Bagdadi Jew who had recently converted to Islam "brilliantly revamped the financial structure of the country and instituted a significant reform of the currency."[53] Many Tunisian Jews moved to Egypt and remained in close contact with their relatives who stayed behind. Thus, Jewish family ties cemented increased trade relations between Tunisia and Egypt.

The Spanish situation was somewhat different. While Jewish merchants were present, the community primarily gained economic prosperity and influence through their positions as physicians and courtiers. The most influential Spanish Jew was Hasday ben Shaprut who on "several occasions was charged with delicate diplomatic negotiations with the Christian kingdoms of the North and with the Byzantine Empire."[54] Instead of commercial enterprises, Spanish Jewry was noted for its cultural activities and bringing about Jewish religious autonomy: no longer being bound by the rulings of the Babylonian academies.

At the same time, some Jews living in the Christian Byzantine communities of Asia Minor moved to the Christian communities of Central and Western Europe. This migration often reflected invitations extended to Jews by Christian rulers who believed that the Jewish skill set would help their kingdoms grow and prosper; as in, for example, Jewish emigration to Poland in the twelfth century. By the medieval period, there were substantial Jewish communities throughout Europe, concentrated in urban areas and solely engaged in commercial activities.

This narrative is at odds with those who minimize or reject notions of Jewish cultural uniqueness. They contend that the entire decimation of the Jewish population of Israel was due to its expulsion as Christianity began to dominate Palestine. Their late emigration into already-consolidated societies prevented Jews from owning land and excluded them from membership

---

53. Norman Stillman, *Jews of Arab Lands*, chapter 3.
54. Ibid., 55.

in craft and merchant guilds. As late arrivals, Jews were considered outsiders and vulnerable to further expulsions and forced migrations. As a consequence of these uncertain and restrictive conditions, Jews invested in human capital which was highly portable and not subject to the risk of expropriation, unlike land and other forms of physical capital. Thus, this thesis stresses that structural factors, not cultural uniqueness, led Jews to invest in education.[55]

By contrast, the narrative presented here puts the cultural uniqueness of Jewish society at the center of explanations for their urban occupations. Unlike Christianity and Islam, Judaism stressed universal male literacy. It was this educational requirement, not land ownership restrictions that caused the dramatic occupational shift. As will be documented in the next chapter, Jewish migration reflected the pull of occupational choice, not the push of economic restrictions.

---

55. Della Pergola, "Review of *The Chosen Few*."

10

Forward through the Nineteenth Century

THIS BOOK HAS DETAILED the evolution of first-century Jewish renewal movements. Starting from strikingly similar positions, Jesus' ministry and the Pharisees initiated the formation of two lasting religions: Christianity and rabbinic Judaism. Both groups rejected sumptuous lifestyles and absorbed the messianic fervor that grew as the economic and spiritual crises in the land of Israel deepened.

Both movements experienced the long-standing tension in Judaism between maintaining religious faith in one God and combatting economic inequality. Contempt for the wealthy was a central aspect of Jesus' ministry and Pharisaic thought. However, as both movements were transformed over the next centuries, concern for inequality weakened.

In Christianity, the Pauline shift away from the life of Jesus to his death weakened any emphasis on his struggle against inequality as found in the Lazarus parable. Within Judaism, it was the ascendency of the Babylonian religious leadership, which embraced economic inequality and the sumptuous living it afforded the wealthy. In both religions, a firm commitment to charity replaced opposing the wealthy and this perspective increased during the medieval period. Only with the rise of industrial capitalism did a focus on economic inequality reemerge.

THE MEDIEVAL PERIOD

Within Christianity, the fourth-century focus on the Old Testament to find justifications for celibacy led Christians to take more seriously the prophetic exhortations to seek social justice for the poor. The Church had always frowned upon sumptuous living and denunciations centered on "the luxury, pretentiousness, and avarice of the evil rich."[1] However, it did not promote shifting the power balance between wealthy and poor families. Instead, these inequalities were acceptable as long as the wealthy showed kindness and provided charity to the poor. Following the Old Testament, however, changed the perspective of some Church leaders on inequality. Now they believed that "the poor did not come to the rich as beggars [but] came to the powerful in search of justice."[2]

This more positive attitude toward social justice slowly changed. Thanks in no small part to the Church's appeals to widows and virgins, it became the largest landowner in Europe by the seventh century. This economic transformation forced bishops to become estate managers rather than solely religious leaders of Christian communities. Many bishops tried to manage estates in a way that was faithful to Christian principles: to use Church wealth in service of the poor. The unevenness among the bishops, however, often led to severe criticism:

> Nowadays because avarice has grown in the Church as it has done in the Roman empire, individuals who take advantage of the power and influence associated with the name of bishop ... reduce the entire order of deacons to their own use ... while the unhappy clergyman goes begging in the streets.[3]

1. Brown, *Through the Eye of a Needle*, 58.
2. Ibid., 79.
3. Ibid., 488.

Figure 10.1: Triumphrant Christ, 8th Century

Figure 10.2: Emaciated Christ, 12th Century

Concern for the protection of Church wealth increasingly stifled prophetic concerns for social justice. Indeed, instead of "denouncing the evil origins of wealth and insisting on its total renunciation," some writers came back to a traditional position that "wealth could consolidate the Christian community."[4] As a result, now the Church in major cities began to use its wealth, as the Roman aristocracy had historically done, on public expenditures designed to help the average citizen rather than focus on the poor.

As bishops became more distant from the faithful, monks became the most important representatives of Christian beliefs. Their ascetic ideals and emphasis on personal piety transformed the image of Christ on the cross. In particular, in the seventh through the ninth century, there was a triumphant Christ. As historian Sara Lipton noted:

> In keeping with contemporary religious texts that extol the glory of the Savior, this Christ, although suspended on the Cross that was the instrument of his death, is more Lordly Redeemer than Suffering Servant. His body is strong and whole, his posture is erect and alert, his eyes are preternaturally large and conspicuously open, his mustache and beard are smooth and well groomed, his expression is proud and composed.[5]

By the thirteenth century, however, the triumphant Christ had been replaced by one that emphasized his pain and suffering. His shoulders slumped, his eyes were closed, and blood gushed from his emaciated body.

To emphasize the suffering of Christ, medieval texts went well beyond the narratives in the Gospels. Widely circulated texts heightened Christ's pain and the torments he experienced. For example, while John states that the Jews took Jesus and bound him, medieval treaties elaborated with additional details: Christ's hands were tied so tightly that blood burst from his fingernails.[6] Writings related Psalm 21:18 to a "description of Christ being stretched so tightly on the cross that all his bones were clearly visible and therefore numerable."[7]

The medieval Franciscan Saint Bonaventure (d. 1274) asked the faithful to conform to the Passion of Christ, participating in his suffering so that they may regain the image of his divinity. Bonaventure forced "our attention again and again on the deformed body of Christ, which is repeatedly

---

4. Ibid., 529-30.
5. Lipton, "Images in the World," 176.
6. Bestul, *Texts of the Passion*, 23.
7. Ibid., 28. Psalm 21:18 includes the phrase "they have numbered all my bones."

seen as torn, disfigured, ravaged, covered with gore, and made ugly through pain."[8]

These images and exhortations led a modest share of pious Catholics to engage in self-mortification. Following the example of the Benedictine monk Peter Damian in the eleventh century, flagellation became a form of penance in the Catholic Church and its monastic orders. Its followers were noted for taking this self-mortification into the cities and other public spaces as a demonstration of piety. Public rituals were built around processions, hymns, distinct gestures, uniforms, and discipline. When singing a hymn, upon reaching the part about the passion of the Christ, one must drop to the ground, no matter how painful or how dirty the area.

The heightened devotion to the Passion with its greater attention to the physical suffering of Christ inevitably shifted attention to the perpetrators of the torments—the Jews—showing them to be exceptionally cruel and depraved as a means of increasing the emotional response of readers.[9] Anti-Semitism was also ignited by the economic instability and dislocation that was occurring where some feared that Jews would gain economic hegemony. Moreover, in many Christian urban areas, Jews had attained economic success in endeavors that many considered to be unethical, most prominently moneylending.

It is sometimes claimed that Jews were pushed by legal restrictions and impediments into despised and risky professions, namely to the performance of what were considered "polluted activities." Botticini and Eckstein contend that it had little to do with Jewish occupational choices in late antiquity and the medieval period. In particular, they claim that Jewish moneylending became widespread during the tenth and eleventh centuries, a time when Christian involvement was discouraged but not banned. They argue that Jewish success reflected "their comparative advantage in the four assets that were and still are the pillars of financial intermediation: capital, networking, literacy and numeracy, and contract enforcement institutions."[10] The anti-usury movement gained momentum only after 1311 when Pope Clement V enacted a ban on Christian involvement.

Christian anti-Semitic exhortations began much earlier. By the twelfth-century, leading Church leaders began to place Jews in the category of beasts and encourage their degradation and abuse. After the pogroms

---

8. Ibid., 46.
9. Ibid., 71.
10. Botticini and Eckstein, *Chosen Few*, 241.

inspired by the Second Crusade, Peter the Venerable asserted that the Jews should not be killed, but rather they should be subjected to even greater torments and ignominy. Christians were justified in oppressing Jews and in stealing their property as punishment for the murder of Christ. Pope Innocent III wrote in 1208:

> Though they ought not to be killed, lest the people forget the Divine Law, yet as wanderers ought they to remain upon the earth ... blasphemer of the Christian name ought ... to be forced to servitude of which they made themselves deserving when they raised their sacrilegious hands against Him ... [11]

In the face of this threatening environment, some German Jewish leaders intensified concerns for personal piety. They placed "safeguards around what is already prohibited as to avoid the very possibility of transgressing ... and placed great emphasis on penitential behavior."[12] There is some evidence that these penitential rules were borrowed from twelfth-century monastic sources. Unlike in Christianity, however, penance was not a means of bringing the practitioner closer to God but punishment for engaging in bad behavior.

To some extent, these Jewish religious movements harkened back to the time of the Pharisees. The German pietists protested against their "lawless communal leaders as well as rabbis who pervert justice."[13] Similarly, some Jewish religious leaders in Spain and Provence recoiled at the hedonistic behavior of the wealth-owning class who lorded over the less fortunate members of the Jewish community. The sage Nahmanides became an ally of the anti-aristocratic party and attacked the wealth-owning class for their scandalous religious behavior.[14] These voices, however, represented a small minority. Most important, they emphasized pietist behavior of individuals rather than changing power relationships within Jewish communities.

CATHOLIC ASCETICISM IN IRELAND

By the end of the medieval period, many Catholic communities had embraced ascetic behavior. This tendency was particularly strong in Ireland.

11. Bestul, *Texts of the Passion*, 77-78.
12. Ivan Marcus, *Piety and Society*, 11.
13. Ibid., 7.
14. Septimus, "Piety and Power."

In the sixth century, Saint Columban became the most prominent church leader. His views dominated Irish monasticism for centuries.[15] It proscribed severe bodily austerity:

> The quantity of food and drink is reduced to the barest minimum, and its quality is expected to be extremely unappetizing. Battling with sleep was a common form of asceticism [as] the number and length of night offices of prayer put prolonged rest out of the question. ... Added to these mortifications was exposure to heat and cold, labors undertaken to wear down the body, various individual exercises of asceticism voluntarily undertaken. Again the [Egyptian] desert was the goal held out to every monk, and if he failed to reach it during life he might at least abide there temporarily once or oftener in the year. Austerities of all sorts were expected to accompany these periods of lonely contemplations—fasts, vigils, exposure, nakedness, self-inflicted penances.[16]

Great emphasis is laid on the confession of sin so that Columban Rules simply bristled with punishments. Only by this means, so Columban thought, shall the brother "find the higher way and cling to God."[17] Indeed, punishment of the body was always a marked feature of the Celtic church. One Irish monk, Adamnan of Coldingham, would only touch food twice a week; another, Drythelm of Melrose, would stand up to his neck in winter in the Tweed reciting prayers and psalms.[18]

The asceticism of the Irish system was not lost with the continental triumph of the more moderate Benedictine Rules. They were initially introduced by Benedict of Nursia in the mid-sixth century. The Rules maintained some severity as they were patterned after the writings of John Cassian and Basil of Caesarea.[19] Over time, however, relaxations were gradually introduced in regard to diet and simplicity of life. Also, sources of income were expanded to include rents, tolls, and retainers for actual or anticipated services rendered. Farming operations often produced a profitable commercial spirit. As a result, many of the monasteries became financially prosperous, enabling many monks to abandon fieldwork to serfs.

---

15. Workman, *Monastic Ideal*, 201-202.
16. Ryan, *Irish Monasticism*, 408.
17. Workman, *Monastic Ideal*, 207-208.
18. Ibid., 214.
19. Lynch, *Simoniacal Entry*, xii.

At the end of the tenth century, a group of monks at the French monastery Cluny rebelled against this laxity and founded the Cistercian Order. These monks tried to replicate monastic life exactly as it had been in Saint Benedict's time; indeed, in various points they went beyond it in austerity. The Order desired solitude and divorce from the world, poverty and simplicity. To further these goals, Cistercian houses were to be built remote from habitation and economic transactions were to be kept to a minimum so that they rejected rents, labor services, mills, and tithes. They also demanded a return to manual labor, especially fieldwork.

Given the increased emphasis on the suffering of Christ and the movement to self-mortification, this shift to a more austere monastic lifestyle was inevitable. Indeed, the White Hats of the Cistercian Order dominate monastic growth in the twelfth century, especially in Britain. By mid-century there were over three hundred abbeys throughout Europe tied to the Cistercian Order.[20] In Ireland, when "an influx of new religious life had to be sought from abroad, it was not the Benedictine Rules but the more austere Rules of the Cistercians that appealed to the Irish churchmen." [21] Thus, an adjusted Columban system continued.

The Protestant Reformation had a substantial impact on Irish Catholics. Their rebellion in 1641 was brutally suppressed by Oliver Cromwell. Tens of thousands were slaughtered, including 9,000 inhabitants of Drogheda. When Irish Catholics continued to side with the continental enemies of British rule, a series of penal laws were established that severely restricted their rights. In particular, land was confiscated so that Catholic ownership fell from 21 percent in 1641 to 14 percent in 1700 to only 5 percent in 1775.[22]

With the loss of land, material hardship intensified so that the Irish were reduced to a primitive state. Their diet was so restricted that "bread, meat, grain or corn meal graced only the tables of the better off."[23] This dire poverty was reflected in the virtual absence of basic furnishings. As late as the mid-nineteenth century, it was rare for an Irish peasant family to have a kitchen table or eating utensils. Peasants lived in one-room huts constructed of mud; a whole village might own but one bed or a single chair.[24]

20. Burton, *Monastic and Religious Orders*, 79-80.
21. Ryan, *Irish Monasticism*, 411-412.
22. Ranelagh, *Short History*, 69-70.
23. Ibid., 111.
24. Morris, *American Catholic*, 30.

This austere life and a deeply conservative priesthood only strengthened ascetic tendencies among the faithful. In the eighteenth century, Irish priests were trained in France and Rome at seminaries in which ascetically inclined priests had a prominent role. Some of these priests were among the founding faculty at Maynooth College, which opened in 1795 to enable Irish priests to be trained on Irish soil. This evidence suggests that the establishment of the college was responsible for the introduction of a new and more puritanical tone into the teachings of the Irish Catholic Church, such that "sex was equated for all practical purposes with sin."[25] As Gaelic values were eroded, prudery seeped through Irish society. Sensual Irish love poems were purged.[26]

Support for these puritanical values was aided by the prevailing attitudes among successful Irish Catholic farmers. If they hoped to survive the chaos engulfing rural Ireland, these farmers had to increase the size of their farms, keep them intact, and manage them with great thrift and discipline. They could not give all their sons land, and could not afford dowries for more than one or two daughters. In many Irish tales, when marriages did take place, "the talk was of the bride's heifers and fields, not her charms."[27] These farmers embraced the stem family policy by which landholdings were passed along to only the oldest son. For this system to be successful, family size had to be limited, so late marriage, limited sexual relations within marriage, and celibacy among unmarried children became the norm.[28]

The struggle against pleasurable activities was strengthened when the deeply ascetic Cardinal Cappellari was elected Pope Gregory XVI in 1831. Under his leadership, the Irish Catholic Church began a campaign to eliminate festive events which they considered environments that encouraged drunkenness and immorality. These included the many pilgrimages that blended the sacred and the profane. Typical is a description of the 1813 pilgrimage in celebration of St. John. After partaking of religious activities, the chronicler described the festivities:

> In almost every tent ... twenty to thirty men and women are often huddled together in each, and the circulation of porter and whiskey amongst the various groups is soon evident in its effects ...

25. Connolly, *Priest and People*, 47.
26. Lee, "Women and the Church ," 40.
27. Cahill, *Love of Ireland*, 301.
28. Morris, *American Catholic*, 43.

towards evening the tumult increases, and intoxication becomes almost universal.[29]

Some clergy focused on the Donnybrook Fair, an annual event since 1204. The reforming cleric Fr John Spratt observed the impact of the fair where "many an unfortunate female now rolls in the abyss of prostitution."[30] The fair gradually declined and was gone by the 1860s.

Given the limited Catholic Church infrastructure, these ascetic teachings had only a modest impact on the behavior of the Irish populace before the Great Famine. As a result, the vast majority of the Irish who immigrated to the US during the Great Famine were not practicing Catholics. In the decades immediately after their arrival, "at least half the Irish in New York City's Sixth Ward, including a great majority of the unskilled laborers, hardly ever attended mass. In Ohio, one priest lamented [that among the Irish railroad workers] 'one-half are grown up to 20-25 years and never made their first communion [and] know nothing of their catechism.'"[31]

All this changed in the 1850s when Rome increased resources and appointed Bishop (later Cardinal) Paul Cullen to leadership. Now Ireland had the infrastructure to successfully increase religiosity, broadening the reach of anti-pleasure behaviors. With only a minority of Irish men and women marrying, the historian Joseph Lee surmised, "Sex, therefore, must be denounced as a satanic snare, in even what had been its most innocent pre-famine manifestations. . . . Boys and girls must be kept apart at all costs."[32] Another historian Tom Inglis concluded, "The silencing, hiding, and denial of sex, the confinement of talk about sex to the confessional, significantly influenced the way in which men and women perceived and understood the world."[33] Even among married couples, sex became shameful and fleeting.

This anti-pleasure movement was brought to the US in succeeding immigrant waves. They brought their cultural and religious values with them, which helped to reform those lapsed and non-practicing "shanty" Irish. The American Catholic church itself was transformed by the infusion of personnel—nuns and priests—who had been trained in Ireland. By 1900, three-quarters of US church hierarchy were Irish—officers in the

29. Murphy, *The Irish Bog*, 179.
30. Luddy, *Prostitution*, 24.
31. Miller, *Emigrant and Exile*, 327.
32. Lee, "Women and the Church," 39.
33. Inglis, *Moral Monopoly*, 129.

devotional revolution, whose "mission increasingly was one of 'immigrant uplift,' the tenets of which were as simple as those Cullen's Church had prescribed for the peasantry of Ireland."[34]

Jansenism was the label used by many twentieth-century critics who were angered by these anti-pleasure views. When providing the social context for the Kennedy family, the historian Arthur Schlesinger wrote:

> Jansenism pervaded the Irish Church, encouraging clerical tendencies toward censoriousness and bigotry. . . . It explained that man was weak and life more than a little absurd, unless redeemed by the grace of God mediated through the church. The culture Robert Kennedy's great-grandparents transported to Boston was filled with this conviction of the bloodiness of life. The sense of disorder, tragedy and evil was not unlike that of the Puritans, three centuries earlier. But what the Puritans had placed on the isolated soul in quest of salvation the Irish assigned to the family and the church.[35]

While the Jansenist label is problematic, there is little disagreement that Irish-American Catholicism was severe in its prohibitions against bodily pleasures.[36] For example, Paul Donoghue recounted his mother's behavior: "Laughter and enjoyment, let alone sexual pleasure, are not for God-fearing Jansenists. She gave to every charity but not to herself. She loved flowers but could never buy them for herself."[37] Historian Hasia Diner noted,

> [F]rom pre-Famine days through the early twentieth century, commentators remarked on the lack of popular interest in food. Even when times got better, when the Famine and mass migration had removed the very poorest from the countryside, Irish women and men still said little in memoir and literature about food.[38]

These anti-pleasure attitudes underpinned late nineteenth-century Church attempts to ban Italian-American festivals, which were considered

---

34. Dezell, *Irish America*, 169.

35. Schlesinger, *Robert Kennedy*, 4

36. For an evaluation of the claim that Jansenism was at the root of Irish ascetic behavior, see Cherry, "Was Irish Catholicism Linked to Jansenism?" Morris, *American Catholic*, dismisses the influence of Jansenism in a footnote (44n).

37. Donoghue, *Jesus Advantage*, 96.

38. Diner, *Hungering for America*, 97

"sacrilegious to Irish-American church leaders."[39] Given the scorn heaped upon Italian festivities by the Irish faithful, Italians often had to organize their activities outside the church. For example, when the Italian community observed Saint Donatus festivities in the mid-1890s, they stored the saint's statue in a saloon's loft "lest the priest get hold of him," wrote Jacob Riis. "He was their home patron, and they were not going to give him up. In the saloon they had him safe."[40]

THE JEWISH ABANDONMENT OF ASCETIC TENDENCIES

Within Jewish communities, the traumatic 1492 Spanish expulsion reawakened ascetic impulses. Under the leadership of Isaac Luria, the displaced Jewish Sephardic communities in Palestine developed religious rituals to highlight the losses experienced.[41] During the seventeenth century, Ashkenazi Jewry experienced devastation. The 1640s peasant rebellion against Polish sovereignty, led by Bogdan Chmielnicki, destroyed some seven hundred Ukrainian communities. It caused the deaths of hundreds of thousand Jews, more than had been killed during both the Crusades and the Black Death.[42] For the next century, pogroms were periodically perpetrated by Ukrainian dissidents fighting against continued foreign rule. In addition, the declining power of the Polish state caused economic hardships for much of Polish Jewry.[43]

After the Ukrainian programs, Lurianic views gained adherents among the Eastern European religious elite. Buttressed by the legacy of the German pietists,[44] asceticism complemented a deeply pessimistic worldview in which continual joyfully accepted suffering, both physical and mental, was central to religious perfection. It was essential to withstand all physical pleasures in order to surmount the obstacles that this world perversely presented and to attain the beatitude of the next.

39. Anbinder, *Five Points*, 387.
40. Moses, *Unlikely Union*, 165.
41. For a discussion of Lurianic practices, see Fine, *Safed Spirituality*.
42. Dresner, *The Zaddik*.
43. Etkes, *The Besht*.
44. For a summary of the thirteenth-century German Jewish pietists, see Ivan Marcus, *Piety and Society*.

Forward through the Nineteenth Century

In Eastern Europe, influential treatises began to stress unremitting gloom, pessimism, and oppressive piety. Sukkot would be ignored because its joyfulness "was incompatible with the central themes—weeping, worrying, self-mortification, and despondency. Every possible occasion for critical self-scrutiny accompanied by sorrowful self-mortification is exhaustively expatiated upon."[45] Fasting on Mondays and Wednesdays was advocated. Even the Sabbath was to be, for the truly devout, a day of tearful mourning—despite clear talmudic statements to the contrary.

At the beginning of the eighteenth century, Eastern European Jewish communities privileged the well-to-do and demeaned the uneducated working class. The toiling classes struggled from meal to meal and did not have the luxury of Talmudic study for either themselves or their male offspring. By contrast, the wealthy could provide resources for their sons' Jewish religious education and sometimes their daughters' secular education. The gap between the two social classes grew with the working classes burdened by not only their lack of material resources but also their lack of communal respect. This would give rise to a new Hasidic movement led by the Baal Shem Tov.

Known as the Besht, he began his religious journey by following ascetic Kabbalist practices. For seven years he led a life of solitude in the Carpathian mountains, living apart from his wife for much of the time. After abandoning his solitary life, in 1740, the Besht moved to the town of Miedzyboz, providing advice to Jewish families in need and communing with God on their behalf. Miedzyboz was located in Podolia, the most prosperous region in Poland; a region free from the lingering effects of Jewish "persecutions that had dissipated within one or two generations."[46]

The Besht initiated a new outlook for the Hasidim that attracted a following. He sought to bring God to the common Jew so that over the next decade, he came to forcefully reject and denigrate ascetic behavior. The Besht reasoned that if the whole world is full of God's glory (Isa 6:13), the pious Kabbalists were wrong in thinking that one had to turn one's back on the pleasures of the world. He mandated the use of material pleasures as a means of spiritual elevation. Indeed, it was said that the soul cannot rejoice in the spiritual until the material has rejoiced in the corporeal.

While the distinguishing feature of the Besht's philosophy was his anti-ascetic message to the common Hasid, the ascetic practices by the

---

45. Foxbrunner, *Habad*, 25.
46. Rosman, *Founder of Hasidism*, 62.

Hasidic elite were not forcefully opposed. As a result, some of his followers continued to maintain personal ascetic practices, most prominently, the Maggid of Mezeritch. Like Paul, the Maggid promoted passionless sex among married couples: "Even during intercourse one should ignore the physical in favor of the spiritual."[47] Fortunately, those who faithfully followed the Besht's views were more successful in igniting the religious fervor of the masses. Jacob Joseph of Polnoy strove to bring the Besht's teachings to a broader group within the Jewish community: rabbis, itinerant preachers, learned ritual slaughterers, and teachers. He wished to repair the bridge between the rabbinic elite and the masses.[48]

Jacob Joseph argued that even the common man has a path to commune with God, in contrast to the traditional religious view in which "mystical communion with God had always been regarded as the prerogative of a small minority of spiritually gifted men." His *Toledot Yako Yosepf*, written in 1780, was the first major Hasidic work to be broadly circulated. It transmitted the luminous inner-circle teachings of the Besht and tried to translate them into a clear social directive.

Through the *Tanya*, the first Lubavitch rebbe, Schneur Zalman, also sought to bring the Besht's teachings to the broader Hasidic community. The efforts of Jacob Joseph and Shneur Zalman enabled Beshtian Hasidism to triumph. Allan Nadler noted, "The Besht's emphasis on joyfully serving God with one's physical senses and his insistence that an immanent God completely pervades the created physical universe combined forcefully to eliminate any place for ascetic piety in early Hasidism."[49]

The Hasidim were condemned by traditional Orthodox rabbis for their sacramental indulgences in food, drink, and music which "transformed all of their days into festivities."[50] The merriment that these Jews found so troubling built upon the social norms already in place: the Sabbath meal and religious holidays, Jewish weddings, and the Purim play. Music and entertainment were integral to this performative behavior as evidenced by the joyous celebrations surrounding Jewish weddings. In particular, the wedding day usually began with the wisecracking *badkhn*'s serenade of the groom and then the bride at their respective homes. The wedding party

---

47. Biale, *Eros*, 134.

48. For more on the conflict within the early Hasidic movement, see Cherry, "Hasidic Revolution."

49. Nadler, *Faith of the Mithnagdim*, 80-1.

50. Ibid., 85.

included traditional dances and songs replete with allusions to the tensions between the new in-laws.

The Hasidim glorified spontaneous song and dance, encouraging the creation of simple lyrics in the vocabulary of the masses. Together with the impact of modernity, this joyfulness became embedded in Eastern European Jewish social life. By the mid-nineteenth century, Jewish entertainers were found in popular venues. The Broder singers were essentially secular *badkhomin*. They performed songs and monologues in inns and wine gardens throughout Eastern Europe, becoming the first professional actors and producers in modern Yiddish culture.

Popular culture venues expanded between 1825 and 1875, providing the Jewish public with a group of professional singers, proto-actors, and a knowledgeable audience. While they were partially influenced by the secularization and modernization, these activities remained rooted in the traditional culture that dominated Jewish life. This is most clear when we look at the history of the Yiddish theater. The first Yiddish plays were written by members of the secular *maskilin* community, individuals who were antagonistic to traditional culture. As a result, there was little interest in Yiddish theater until Abraham Goldfaden began producing his plays more than forty years later. Historian Nahma Sandrow wrote: "[I]nstead of making fun of Hasidic tradition, he makes fun of the enlightened younger generation who foolishly go overboard. These plays gave the Jewish people what they needed and were quite successful."[51] These were the cultural norms that Jewish immigrants brought to America at the end of the nineteenth century.

---

51. Sandrow, *Vagabond Stars*, 60.

11

Relevance in the Twentieth Century

THE EVOLUTION OF RELIGIOUS thought during the first four centuries of the Common Era is not only intellectually interesting but has some significant relevance to the twentieth century. It has already been noted that the nineteenth-century Social Gospel movement was inspired by Jesus' Lazarus narrative, whereas the Pauline emphasis on God's grace gave comfort to black sharecroppers in the Jim Crow South. This chapter will demonstrate the ways that Jesus' concern for the poor and oppressed continued to inform sections of the Catholic Church during the twentieth century. In addition, we will find that the Old Testament's prophetic exhortations to support the powerless were embraced by sections of the Jewish community, especially in their support of the black community.

By the twenty-first century, it is hard to see any distinction between the views on bodily pleasure of Christians and Jews. This was not the case, however, a century earlier. Then, Irish Catholicism and Protestant Victorianism maintained anti-pleasure views, especially with regard to female sexuality. By contrast, Jewish immigrants had a positive view of bodily pleasure, including female sexuality. This chapter will detail why these contrasting beliefs are one reason for the ability of Jewish entrepreneurs to break the Protestant stranglehold on big-time vaudeville, and why Irish-American representation declined dramatically.

Relevance in the Twentieth Century

IRISH ENTRY INTO COMMERCIAL VAUDEVILLE

The Irish who first entered America after the Famine were considered no better than black Americans. Indeed, in early vaudeville, the image of these two groups was virtually the same: Both Paddy and Sambo were "childlike, musical, hapless, exuberant, and irrationally loyal to their employers."[1] At his best, "Paddy was a happy-go-lucky buffoon, shiftless and tipsy. At his worst, he was a simian-featured barbarian: childish, emotionally unstable, ignorant, indolent, superstitious, primitive or semi-civilized, dirty, vengeful and violent."[2]

Over the next decades, however, Irish performers help change the presentation of Irish working men and women. Most responsible was Edward Harrigan. In 1873, he teamed with Tony Hart to present short Irish skits in concert saloons. They blended ethnic stereotypes—African Americans, Jews, Italians, and Chinese, as well as Irish—with individualized characterizations taken from the city streets, giving life and vitality to their more realistic performances.[3]

Figure 11.1: Mulligan's Guard Sheet Music Cover

1. Dezell, *Irish America*, 19.
2. Joseph Curran, *Hibernian Green*, 6.
3. Mooney, *Irish Stereotypes*, 160.

In the late 1870s, Harrigan teamed with David Braham to write the first popular songs from musical shows (as opposed to the vaudeville and minstrel stage) to find success in sheet music. Productions featured highly realistic sets depicting the Lower East Side.[4] Most prominent was the Mulligan's Alley series. "Most of Harrigan's characters were working class, and many were poor," noted Jennifer Mooney. "Harrigan's recognition and celebration of the Irish urban community was perhaps one of the most important aspects of his work, for it presented a positive picture of one of the essential realities of Irish-American life."[5]

In the 1880s, vaudeville had become the most desired entertainment in urban areas. In New York City, the most popular venue was Tony Pastor's. As the lights dimmed, the crowd anticipated the entrance of the main attraction, Maggie Cline. It was not to see a stately beauty nor hear a sweet-sounding voice. Maggie was one of their own; a muscular, red-haired, working-class girl, born of Famine Irish parents, destined to work in the New England mills. But she fled the mill life and was now performing to an appreciative audience.

Figure 11.2: Maggie Cline Performing "T'row Him Down McClosky"

4. Ibid., 160.
5. Ibid., 165.

Relevance in the Twentieth Century

Maggie used her physical skills and Irish brogue to sing boisterous, crowd-pleasing songs. She began with her renditions of "How McNulty Carved the Duck" and "Choke Him, Casey, Choke Him." But what brought the house down, what became her trademark song, was "T'row him down McClosky," a comic song about a 47-round prize fight between two Irishmen.

"Now, ladies and gentlemen," Maggie said as she looked to the balcony and pretended to hitch up her trousers in the manner of a brawler readying for a fight, "I will sing the dainty and pathetic little ballad that drove me into this business":

> "T'row him down McCloskey," was to be the battle cry, "T'row him down McCloskey, you can lick him if you try." And future generations with wonder and delight, Will read in history's pages of the great McCloskey fight.

"McCloskey" was typically performed with appropriate loud noises from the audience while Cline shadow-boxed a re-enactment as she sang. When she sang the refrain, everyone backstage would throw whatever they could get their hands on, onto the stage.

Cline and Harrigan exemplified the successful rise of Irish Americans to the dominant position in the nascent vaudeville industry. Indeed, the 1880s was the high point of Irish-American involvement, just as the second-generation of Irish Americans came of age. They were the generation that had embraced the anti-pleasure values promoted by the Church; values that looked askance at the sinful hedonism of popular culture.

One such act was the "Irish Servant Girls," performed by James and John Russell. Outfitted in proper servant girls' dresses and made up to look the part, the Russell Brothers romped through one disaster after another. Their imbecilic characters whacked each other with brooms, drank their employer's booze, started fires, broke fine china, mangled the English language, and inevitably ended up in a tumble with dresses high overhead. John Russell, who played the more restrained of the two sisters, punctuated each disaster with "Oh, Maggie!" which soon became a popular expression.[6]

They had been headliners in major vaudeville houses for more than a decade when they agreed to appear as the Irish Servant Girls at the Victoria Theater in New York City in 1907. The United Irish Societies and the Ancient Order of Hibernians planned an ethnic pride offensive. Over three

---

6. http://irishecho.com/2011/02/the-russell-brothers-sent-packing-2/ For image of Servant Girls see: https://images.search.yahoo.com/search/images

hundred Irishmen stormed the theater in the middle of the Russell Brothers' performance. They pummeled the actors with potatoes and rotten eggs while shouting, "Down with the Russell Brothers. They ridicule the honest, hardworking Irish servant girl."

The show was quickly cancelled.[7] Continued protests drove the Russell Brothers out of the big time and in less than six years they were out of vaudeville altogether.[8] The Russell Brothers were not alone. Over the four decades from 1880 to 1920, references to the combination of drinking, fighting, dancing, and singing declined from 26 percent of the songs for the last two decades of the nineteenth century to an average of 8 percent for the first decades of the new century.[9]

This transformation even affected the career of Maggie Cline. Her stardom was based on her Famine Irish personae, singing boisterous songs. But as the demands of the Irish audiences changed, Cline accommodated by embracing traditional nostalgia, as in her rendering of "Don't Let Me Die Till I See Ireland."[10] Though she discarded most of her once popular songs, older fans would not let her exclude "McClosky" from her repertoire. The number was so popular that when she tried to phase it out of her act, audiences called for it until she gave it to them. When she retired in 1917, Cline estimated that she had performed "McClosky" more than 75,000 times.

More generally, there was steady decline in Irish American performers. On the New England vaudeville circuit, in the field of song and dance, Irish caricatures fell from about 15 percent to 4 percent of identifiable themes in the first decade of the twentieth century.[11] Indeed, Shirley Staples concluded, "fter 1900 the Irish were no longer ubiquitous in American entertainment, as they had been in the 1880s and early 1890s."[12] The pressure exerted by Irish-American groups eventually brought success in this effort, and by the time the United States entered World War I in 1917, "the 'stage Irishman' had all but disappeared from American theaters."[13]

---

7. http://irishecho.com/2011/02/the-russell-brothers-sent-packing-2/

8. DiMeglio, *Vaudeville USA*, 44-45; Staples, *Male-Female Comedy Teams*, 86; and Snyder, "Irish and Vaudeville," 408.

9. Williams. *'Twas Only an Irishman's Dream*, 203.

10. Snyder, "Irish and Vaudeville," 407.

11. Oberdeck, "Contested Cultures," 65.

12. Staples, *Male-Female Comedy Teams*, 89.

13. Joseph M. Curran, *Hibernian Green*, 12.

Relevance in the Twentieth Century
JEWISH ENTREPRENEURS, ENTERTAINERS, AND AUDIENCES

In the last decade of the nineteenth century, Benjamin Franklin Keith and his second-in-command, Edward Franklin Albee, gained a monopoly position in vaudeville. Under their leadership, Victorian standards and Irish-Catholic sensibilities dominated big-time commercial vaudeville. Keith was fanatical in his insistence that audiences behave strictly as ladies and gentlemen. When he opened his first Philadelphia house, Keith actually stood in the gallery during intermission and personally lectured the audience on its behavior. Caps and ladies' hats had to be removed and all stomping, whistling, spitting on the floor, and crunching of peanuts were banned.[14]

Keith and Albee also removed burlesque performances, replacing them with traditionally acted playlets that elevated vaudeville by drawing a more upscale audience. Assured a safe environment, many mothers left their children at the theaters while they went shopping on Saturday afternoons. Leading commentators branded theirs "the Sunday School Circuit."[15]

The dominance of wholesome vaudeville was undermined during the first decade of the twentieth century. In urban areas, young women began to question Victorian values. In addition, many immigrants from eastern and southern Europe not burdened with Victorian values sought pleasurable leisure activities. In particular, Jewish immigrants made up an increasing share of vaudeville audiences, probably one-half in New York and Philadelphia.

Into this changing environment stepped newer, Jewish-owned venues. Since Eastern European Jews came from a cultural tradition that was much more accepting of female sexuality and the value of pleasurable activities, they rejected Victorian values. This more positive view helps explain the ability of Jewish women to dominate one area of early twentieth-century vaudeville: the singing of what were labeled "coon songs;" songs where "Jewish performers sang not only in Negro dialect, but also in blackface."[16] The most prominent coon singers were Fanny Brice and Sophie Tucker. They did not present themselves as traditional beauties. It was their songs,

---

14. Staples, *Male-Female Comedy Teams*, 76.
15. Andrew L. Erdman, *Blue Vaudeville*, 3.
16. Wojcik, "Mae West's Maids," 288.

comic delivery, and open, healthy attitude about sexuality that attracted audiences.

The transformation of vaudeville was furthered by Jewish entrepreneurs. Oscar Hammerstein did not try to make a virtue out of false innocence; his music halls always included a bar and featured provocative acts, including sensual "Oriental dancers" and "Marblesques," voluptuous women posing in varying states of classical undress to represent famous paintings.[17] Similarly, Jesse Lasky promoted musical revues that featured beautiful women in extravagant costumes who relished defying Victorian conventions.[18]

Judaism accommodated the burgeoning anti-Victorian culture. The largest circulating Orthodox Jewish daily, the *Morgn Zhurnal*, took advertisements from Hammerstein's Winter Garden Theatre. One March 17, 1916 advertisement was headlined, "Broadway Vaudeville, The Hanky Panky Girls." An October 19, 1919 advertisement pictured a chorus line of scantily clad girls with the following text: "40 Pretty, Sugar-Sweet Ladies; People (Yidn), Come Seek the Taste of Three Hours of Sweet Pleasure."

While the Catholic Church no longer supported the vaudeville of Keith and Albee, it remained most fearful of the increasing bawdiness of the nickelodeons and vaude-film houses that were dominated by Jewish entrepreneurs. The Church developed a three-pronged approach. First, it sponsored vaudeville shows in order to directly control the content. Second, the Catholic hierarchy encouraged Catholic organizations to safeguard parishioners from offensive productions. With New York City Cardinal Farley's endorsement and the approval of Pope Pius X, the National Catholic Theatre Movement was launched in 1912. Its stated aim was "to bring all classes, irrespective of creed, into a national union for the eradication of immoral drama from the American stage."[19]

Some elements within Catholic Church leadership feared that providing cultural alternatives or guidance would be insufficient to stem the rising tide of immoral popular culture venues. Monsignor Henry Brann stated, "I don't see any remedy for it except civil censorship. They have it in London [and] if we could bring the power of the state and the city to bear on the

---

17. Fields and L. Fields, *From the Bowery to Broadway*, 119.
18. Oberdeck, "Contested Cultures."
19. New York Tribune , "Church to Censor Plays."

subject, we could correct the evil."[20] Thus, increasingly the church shifted to its third alternative: government censorship.

All these efforts proved ineffective. By 1920, Jewish owners dominated both vaudeville and the silent film industry. Their role in undermining Victorian sensibilities upset many. A few Progressives, notably Henry Ford, could not forgive the Jews for their perceived transgressions. In May 1920, he began publishing "The International Jew: The World's Foremost Problem" in his newspaper, *The Dearborn Independent*. In discussing Jewish control, Ford noted, "Frivolity, sensuality, indecency, appalling illiteracy and endless platitude are the marks of the American Stage as it approaches its degeneracy under Jewish control."[21]

A similar process occurred in the silent film industry. As documented by Neal Gabler, the movie moguls were able to outmaneuver the Motion Pictures Patents Company, the Edison combine formed in 1908. Its monopoly power was based on Edison's camera patents and exclusive use of Kodak's motion picture film. By 1914, antitrust legislation had broken these monopoly rights. Before this ruling, however, Jewish movie moguls found ways to circumvent them, particularly by moving their film operations to the Los Angeles area, where they had control of local police enforcement.

Part of the reason for the success of the movie moguls was because they undermined the Victorian themes that dominated the companies in the Edison monopoly. At the most successful of these companies, Biograph, D.W. Griffith produced films depicting helpless waifs living in patriarchal families, waiting to be saved by male heroes. By contrast, the Jewish movie moguls followed the lead of Jewish vaudevillians, presenting women as strong sexual beings.

Before entering the movie business, William Fox combined cheap one-reelers and live vaudeville entertainment, keeping prices low and attendance high. By 1912, he had eighteen vaude-film theaters in the New York City area. Increasingly disappointed with the films produced by Edison's companies, Fox organized his own production company. His first film was a major hit. It starred the Jewish actress, Theda Bara, a voluptuous exotic who was a movie sensation—the vamp. Filmed in risqué, transparent outfits that left little to one's imagination, Bara was probably the first

---

20. New York Tribune, "Cardinal Begins w\War on Immoral Plays."
21. Ford, *International Jew*, Chapter 28.

motion picture sex symbol, a role she reprised in a number of Fox films over the next five years.

Figure 11.3: Theda Bara in "The Sin"

Mary Pickford left Biograph, where she had starred in *The Perils of Pauline*. In those films, the heroine might look at sordid modern life but was always an observer. By contrast, in Paramount films, Pickford "rolled up her sleeves and plunged her hands into previously forbidden realms."[22] Paramount's willingness to embrace more modern views of women was also reflected in the films they produced that were directed by Cecil B. DeMille.

DeMille's early films at Paramount replaced the sentimental Victorian heroine with a "clotheshorse and sexual playmate." Initially, DeMille was reluctant to showcase this type of woman. He changed his position, however, when Paramount executive Jesse Lasky argued, "What the public

22. May, *Screening Out the Past*, 122.

demands today is modern stuff with plenty of clothes, rich sets, and action." At Lasky's insistence, DeMille made a trilogy of films between 1918 and 1920 that captured the "sort of role that the feminists in the country are now interested in . . . the kind of girl that dominates . . . who jumps in and does a man's work." They set the tone at Paramount and made a star out of director DeMille and the actress Gloria Swanson.[23]

By the 1920s, Hollywood was dominated by Jewish film studios. By the 1930s, the movie industry was virtually a Jewish club behind the scenes: Jewish talent agencies represented actors, Jewish lawyers negotiated their contracts, and Jewish writers wrote their dialog. F. Scott Fitzgerald bitterly characterized Hollywood as "a Jewish holiday, a Gentile's tragedy."[24]

THE CATHOLIC STRUGGLE AGAINST ECONOMIC INEQUALITY

The abuses of industrial capitalism reawakened religious efforts to combat economic inequality. While the Social Gospel movement responded to the deteriorating conditions of US farmers, Pope Leo XIII's 1891 encyclical *Rerum Novarum* "confirmed the need for the state to intervene in protection of workers and the poor."[25] He restated the Church's long-standing teaching regarding the crucial importance of private property rights, but recognized that the free operation of market forces must be tempered by moral considerations:

> Let the working man and the employer make free agreements, and in particular let them agree freely as to the wages; nevertheless, there underlies a dictate of natural justice more imperious and ancient than any bargain between man and man, namely, that wages ought not to be insufficient to support a frugal and well-behaved wage-earner. If through necessity or fear of a worse evil the workman accepts harder conditions because an employer or contractor will afford him no better, he is made the victim of force and injustice.[26]

---

23. Correspondences between Lasky and DeMille is referenced in Higashi, "New Woman," 300-301.
24. Gabler, *Empire of Their Own*, 2.
25. Charles E. Curran, *Catholic Social Teaching*, 137.
26. Pope Leo XIII, *Rerum novarum*, 45.

Rerum Novarum vividly depicted the plight of the nineteenth-century urban poor and condemned unrestricted capitalism. To remedy the situation, it supported appropriate unions and other means of collective bargaining.

In the United States, the encyclical had little immediate impact as the drive for instilling religious piety remained the overriding concern of church leadership. However, given the large number of Irish-American workers, the Catholic Church did support some labor efforts. The Church was particularly amenable to involvement with the American Federation of Labor (AFL), as its union affiliates were aggressively anti-socialist.

In 1919, through the efforts of social reformer John A. Ryan, the National Catholic Welfare Conference issued a document that prefigured many New Deal measures. The Bishops' Program of Social Reconstruction endorsed things like a minimum wage, labor unions, public housing, and social insurance. In response to strong criticism, however, the bishops retreated. It became a statement of ideals with "no efforts at implementation."[27]

Sustained social justice initiatives had to wait again until 1933 when Catholic outsiders initiated the Catholic Worker Movement. Its driving force was Dorothy Day, one of its founding members. In her youth, she rejected religion for her new faith of social justice. Becoming a journalist, she began writing muckraking pieces during WWI for various left-wing outlets, including the communist-leaning *The Masses*. Day's deeply rooted pacifism, however, "made her question class struggle as the best means of achieving revolutionary change."[28]

After the war, however, her personal situation was in shambles. Leading a bohemian life, in quick succession she had a stormy relationship that led to an abortion and then a failed one-year marriage. She tramped around the country, taking odd jobs and engaging in political actions that resulted in some arrests. She used these personal experiences to write a novel, *The Eleventh Virgin*, which made enough money for her to return to New York and again write for left-wing magazines, including *The New Masses*.

Day became pregnant again, but this time she had the baby, whom she named Tamar Teresa. Motherhood forced Day to recenter her life away from the bohemian lifestyle and the type of radical politics that she had engaged in for more than a decade. She began to see that the well-being of

---

27. Phiel, *Breaking Bread*, 37.
28. Jordan, *Dorothy Day*, 16-17.

working people depended "less on trade unions, cooperatives, and communes" than on the re-creation of the Catholic family and on a system of distributive justice that did not rely on state funds.[29] This newfound vision led her to convert to Catholicism, having herself and her baby baptized in 1927.

Day continued to sustain herself and her child by writing, but now for the liberal Catholic publications *America* and *Commonweal*. While she rejected the left-wing approach, she was unclear how to pursue social justice from a Catholic perspective. This changed in 1933 when she met a French peasant and social activist, Peter Maurin. He convinced Day to direct her writing talents to produce a monthly paper for ordinary working men and women, *The Catholic Worker*.

Day had a tense relationship with the Catholic leadership. On the one hand, she could be highly critical when it continued to stress religious piety. Her biographers, Mark and Louise Zwick, quote Day as saying, "The moral theology we are taught is to get us into heaven with scorched behinds. What kind of an unwilling, ungenerous love of God is this? We do little enough, and when we try to do more we are lectured on Jansenism."[30] On the other hand, just as Saint Paul, whatever her disagreements with the church hierarchy, she unswervingly followed its rulings.

Figure 11.4: Dorothy Day 1934

29. McKanan, "The Family," 156.
30. Zwick and Zwick, *Catholic Worker Movement*, 149.

Day continued to maintain her activism. In 1936, she was almost expelled from Arkansas after traveling there and writing a muckraking exposé on the plight of tenant farmers. One year later, she traveled to Flint, Michigan, to show solidarity with striking workers who had locked themselves inside a General Motors plant, threatening the company or the National Guard to extract them. When she came, the striking workers "raised her up through an open window."[31]

Day's activism, however, had little in common with the Catholic Worker Movement that her newspaper spawned. It was a loose confederation of communities throughout the United States whose aim was to live in accordance with justice and charity as articulated by Jesus' Sermon on the Mount, which states in part:

> Blessed are the poor in spirit: for theirs is the kingdom of heaven.
>
> Blessed are they that mourn: for they shall be comforted.
>
> Blessed are the meek: for they shall inherit the earth.
>
> Blessed are they which do hunger and thirst after righteousness: for they shall be filled.
>
> Blessed are the merciful: for they shall obtain mercy.
>
> Blessed are the pure in heart: for they shall see God.
>
> Blessed are the peacemakers: for they shall be called the children of God. (Mark 5:2-17)

Rather than political activism, the organization's primary efforts were to set up houses of hospitality in which participants would provide services to the poor, in particular food and beds to the unemployed. The driving vision was to revive the "lay apostolate" by practicing works of mercy. Beyond houses of hospitality, families were encouraged to open up a spare bedroom or "Christ room" to those who might need it. In this regard, this philosophy can be traced to the preaching of John Chrysostom.[32] Recall that he railed against inequality and exhorted the comfortable to do more to aid the poor than symbolic almsgiving.

The Catholic Worker Movement grew to over two hundred autonomous communities. Unfortunately, it never had much of an impact on public policy as its efforts were primarily directed inward toward becoming more faithful Christians by direct involvement in acts of charity. In addition, its strong pacifism put the movement at odds with the American

---

31. Jordan, *Dorothy Day*, 23.

32. McKanan, "The Family," 155.

public and the church hierarchy. Day not only spoke out against the Spanish Civil War but also against US entry into WWII. After Pearl Harbor, in a speech to the Liberal Socialist Alliance in New York, "she called on men to resist the draft and women to resist false patriotism."[33] While many communities were able to sustain themselves through the end of the century, they never were able to become catalysts for societal change.

More recently, many Christians, including Pope Francis have embraced the ideals of liberation theology that puts the Church on the side of the poor and oppressed. In the 1980s, liberation theology spread throughout South America, and the Maryknoll priests and nuns put it into practice with their support for anti-dictator movements. In 1981, Maryknoll Father Edward D. Shellito, who assisted a parish on Mindanao Island in the Philippines, was expelled after he was accused of portraying Jesus as a rebel in his time.

Maryknollers' commitment to the poor and to social justice as integral to Gospel teachings has had grave political consequences, as four nuns were executed in El Salvador. Maryknollers were angered when Jeanne J. Kirkpatrick, United States Ambassador to the United Nations, said of those murdered, "They were not just nuns, they were political activists."[34] Accusations of radical activity also have been made against Maryknoll personnel in Guatemala, in Nicaragua during the Somoza dictatorship, and elsewhere. Despite these setbacks and limited support from the Catholic hierarchy, Maryknollers continue to be active in Central America, pursuing restorative justice.[35]

During the 1980s, the US Council of Catholic Bishops issued a pastoral letter, "Economic Justice for All," which focused on combatting inequality. The letter cited the prophets and the New Testament Gospels, including the Lazarus narrative, to highlight the "dangers of wealth," and how the rich are "prone to violence and oppression." It implored society to follow Jesus and "take the side of the poor" and obey "the prophetic mandate to speak for them, to be defenders of the defenseless, who in biblical terms are the poor."[36]

The letter considered the current unemployment rate "morally unjustified [so that] the most urgent priority for US domestic policy is the

---

33. Jordan, *Dorothy Day*, 23.
34. Austin, "Maryknollers."
35. http://maryknollogc.org/article/central-america-promoting-restorative-justice
36. *Economic Justice for All*, 26-28.

creation of new jobs with adequate pay and decent working conditions."[37] It recommended the creation of long-term public sector jobs and joint government-business programs of job creation. Suggesting the need for government economic planning, it recommended policies "to broaden the sharing of economic power and to make economic decisions more accountable to the common good."[38] Not surprisingly, it was excoriated by conservative Catholic leaders and Catholic businessmen.[39]

Over the next two decades, Catholic bishops who heeded the call of Jesus' ministry to combat the excessive privileges and power of the wealthy were replaced by new bishops who focused instead on personal morality and ignored the pastoral letter, which "attack[ed] the use of religion to avoid the demands of charity and justice."[40] As a result, Pope Francis's recent call for less emphasis on opposing same-sex marriage and more sympathy for Catholic women who have had abortions was not met with wide acceptance.

Instead, there has been a national campaign to fire gay and lesbian employees within the Catholic Church. One of those fired was Fr. Warren Hall, a gay priest and chaplain at Seton Hall University. He wrote to Pope Francis, "Good teachers are being fired, pastoral and compassionate priests and religious women are being silenced . . . and good, faith-filled people are leaving the Church as they witness all this happening."[41]

Pope Francis perceives climate policy to be part of social justice movements. However, his call to combat climate change received a cool reception. Suzanne Goldenberg reported on the response of Archbishop Joseph Kurtz, the Council's leader:

> While ostensibly endorsing the pope's call to action, Kurtz did not join the leader of his faith in condemning pollution as a sin. He did not echo the pope's call for an urgent phasing out of fossil fuels. And Kurtz most definitely did not join the pope in attributing climate change largely to human activities, and calling out powerful vested interests for seeking to conceal the evidence of climate change. In fact, Kurtz did not mention climate at all.[42]

---

37. Crotty and Stormes, "The Bishops," 38.
38. *Economic Justice for All*, Xii.
39. Crotty and Stormes.
40. *Economic Justice for All*, 23.
41. Perriello, "US Bishops."
42. Goldenberg, "Why US Bishops."

About half of the church hierarchy has made official responses to the pope's climate change message. Only a handful of bishops, however, have come out in strong support. This reflects the current priority among the bishops to denounce abortion and same-sex marriage rites. For example, Thomas Tobin, the conservative bishop of Rhode Island, greeted the Supreme Court decision upholding same sex marriages by advocating conscientious objection. By contrast, in response to the pope's climate change message, Tobin wrote, "The pope's message deserves careful study and prudent discussion by Catholics and all those concerned about this issue."[43] Thus, the struggle between changing society to reduce inequalities and focusing on personal piety continues.

JEWISH RESPONSES TO THE PLIGHT OF BLACK AMERICANS

There have been numerous essays and books documenting Jewish involvement in civil rights movements during the first seven decades of the twentieth century. Many of these Jewish activists were inspired by the Jewish prophets' exhortations to aid the powerless who are oppressed by the powerful. This is often captured by the term *tikkun olam*—to repair the world.

Too often, however, these presentations overly emphasize the role of left-wing Jews who had virtually no ties to traditional Jewish communities. This is reflected in the central place that the deaths of Jewish left-wing activists Michael Schwerner and Andrew Goodman have in the discussion of Jewish involvement in civil rights struggles. Along with the black activist James Chaney, they were killed while working on the 1964 Freedom Summer voter registration drive in Mississippi. While not minimizing the efforts of left-wing Jewish activists, this section will demonstrate that the commitment to bettering the lives of black Americans flowed deeply throughout the Jewish community. It will focus on the efforts of Jewish entertainers and Jewish philanthropists during the first half of the twentieth century.

Lynching of blacks in the Jim Crow South was a fact of life during the first half of the twentieth century and left-wing Jews were certainly active in trying to combat it. They were involved with the 1932 Scottsboro Case, where seven black boys were wrongfully convicted of raping two white women, and in campaigning unsuccessfully for federal anti-lynching laws.

---

43. Ibid.

In the entertainment area, left-wing Jews were instrumental in the production and distribution of Billie Holiday's anti-lynching song, "Strange Fruit." Written by the communist songwriter Abel Meeropol, it was released by Commodore Records, owned by Billy Crystal's uncle, Milt Gabler, after Columbia Records refused to record it. Meeropol also wrote "The House We Live In," a song praising multiculturalism that won an Oscar when recorded by Frank Sinatra.

What is often ignored is how this anti-lynching sentiment was widely shared throughout the Jewish community. Many Jews viewed black oppression in the United States through the eyes of their own history of oppression. Not only the left-wing *Forward* but also the two largest Orthodox Jewish newspapers, *Morgen Journal* and *Tageblatt*, were united in their condemnation of the treatment of black Americans. All three newspapers agreed that racism was deeply ingrained in American culture. The *Morgen Journal* published long articles on the deplorable history of slavery, applauding Lincoln "for carrying out the ideas of John Brown." The *Tageblatt* consistently deplored Klan actions. It decried the Klan terrorizing of Camden, New Jersey, residents, "graphically portraying the city's black population fleeing from a burning cross." However, it was lynching that crystallized their thinking on racist violence. Starting in the early 1920s, all three newspapers consistently reported on lynching, always highlighting its bloodiest and most tragic details.[44]

Most telling was Irving Berlin's response to lynchings. Berlin—a patriotic American and the author of "God Bless America"—held traditional Jewish values. By 1933, he was highly successful and was writing another Broadway musical. He sought Ethel Waters to star in his upcoming *As Thousands Cheer*. He made her the first black star to be given equal billing with whites, and made *As Thousands Cheer* the first truly integrated musical as Waters appeared in comedy sketches with white cast members.

Of the four songs Waters sang, none was more poignant than "Suppertime," a musical "monologue of a woman giving her children supper while trying to figure out how to tell them that their father had been lynched by white racists."[45] Berlin's motivation was clear. He told Waters's agent, "We're going to try to inject some serious note into this musical," referring to "Suppertime," a song so troubling it was hard to know where to put it in an

---

44. Diner, *Almost Promised Land*, 94.
45. Dawidoff, *Making History Matters*, 119.

Relevance in the Twentieth Century

otherwise comic show. If someone without Berlin's clout had written it, it almost certainly would have been cut.

Berlin, however, was determined. A wave of lynchings sweeping the South had appalled him. Years later, he said, "People told me I was crazy to write a dirge like that," but he was convinced a musical about the news needed at least one serious song. Waters wrote in her autobiography:

> If one song can tell the whole tragic history of a race it was that song. In singing it, I was telling my comfortable, well-fed, well-dressed listeners about my people . . . When I was through and that big, heavy curtain came down, I was called back again and again. I had stopped the show with a type of song never before heard in a revue.[46]

Today, when the name Al Jolson comes up, people are appalled at his blackface persona, as it harked back to a time when blackface was a vehicle to degrade black Americans. This was certainly the case in the 1880s but not in the 1920s. Indeed, black comedians at the Apollo Theater performed in blackface into the 1940s until the NAACP convinced them to stop.[47]

Figure 11.5: Al Jolson Sheet Music Cover, 1919

---

46. Furia and Lasser, *America's Songs*, 106-107.
47. Fox, *Showtime at the Apollo*, 165.

Jolson was one of the most beloved entertainers by the black community. He was the only white man allowed into Leroy's, an African-American cabaret in Harlem, during the 1910s.[48] The reason was they respected his deep commitment to racial equality. On his return to New York from San Francisco in 1911, he brought with him the Black dance team of Johnny Peters and Mary Dewson. Jolson wanted to feature them in his next show, something that had never been done on Broadway. In the 1920's, Garland Anderson, a black porter who was a fledgling playwright, approached Jolson about a play he had written. Thanks to Jolson's efforts on his behalf, the piece became the first drama with an all-Black cast ever produced on Broadway.

In 1919, Eubie Blake and Noble Sissle were refused service in a Connecticut restaurant. When Jolson heard about this, he promptly tracked them down and told them that he would take them back there and "punch anyone who tried to stop us." Blake and Sissle never forgot Jolson's thoughtfulness. Noble Sissle represented the Negro Actor's Union at Jolson's funeral.[49]

The black community also fully embraced his films. One of the severest critics of blackface, Michael Rogin, conceded, "Audiences at Harlem's Lafayette Theater cried during *The Jazz Singer*, and the black press greeted the film with enthusiasm. *The Amsterdam News* called it 'one of the greatest pictures ever produced' and wrote of Jolson, 'Every colored performer is proud of him.'"[50] When, during the 1940s, L.D. Reddick—a black historian and curator of Harlem's Schomburg Collection of Negro Literature—wrote a scathing exposé of racism in the entertainment business, he had only kind words for Jolson.[51]

These are but two examples of the broad spectrum of traditional Jews in the entertainment industry who helped break down racial barriers. Manager Irving Mills and musician Benny Goodman were instrumental in forcing the integration of big bands and promoting the careers of Duke Ellington and Count Basie in the 1930s. Norman Granz was responsible for the integration of audiences when he organized jazz concerts in the Jim Crow South during the 1940s. Jack Benny made a star of Eddie Anderson, allowing a black man for the first time to get the better of a white man in

---

48. Melnick, *Sing the Blues*, 54.
49. Ciolino,"Al Jolson Defended."
50. Rogin, *Blackface, White Noise*, 196.
51. Ibid., 198.

many of the skits they performed on radio and then television. He also made it possible for Anderson to become the highest-paid black actor in Hollywood in the 1940s.

Now let us turn to the efforts of Jewish philanthropists. Just as Jim Crow was being solidified in the South, and in the nation's capital by President Woodrow Wilson, a group of leading Jewish businessmen and financiers heeded the call of Booker T. Washington to aid black communities. Many of these Jewish philanthropists embraced Washington's focus on vocational training. In particular, Jacob Schiff and Felix Warburg gave generously to Tuskegee and other black vocational training schools throughout the South.

By far the most important figure was Julius Rosenwald. Coming from a lower-middle class upbringing, Rosenwald's entrepreneurial talents led to the presidency of Sears, Roebuck and Company, which he made into the largest retail store in the country. While he supported Jewish institutions and Jewish causes throughout his life, Rosenwald's real passion was furthering the education of black Americans. The Julius Rosenwald Fund supported black colleges and vocational training programs, and provided fellowships to promising black students. Its most important mission, however, was to fund the building of black primary schools throughout the South. Beginning with subsidizing the construction of 300 schools in 1912, by 1932 the Fund had subsidized the construction of 5,357 schools, serving 663,615 students. Indeed, in the 1930s, one-third of all black children in the South had attended a Rosenwald school.[52]

Other Jewish philanthropists focused on improving black colleges, particular Fisk and Howard Universities. Abraham Flexner made sure that the medical training offered at Howard Medical School was as good as any in the country. Julian Mack, Felix Frankfurter, and Rosenwald did the same for Howard's law school.[53] The importance of these supports cannot be overestimated. Given the segregation throughout higher education, black colleges were necessary for the production of black lawyers, doctors, social workers, and other professionals who could serve black communities.

Finally, Jewish philanthropists were key funders of black political organizations. The National Urban League was initiated in 1911 in response to the appalling conditions endured by the first wave of southern migration to northern cities. From the start, Jewish philanthropists were directly

---

52. Heller, "Rosenwald Schools."
53. Diner, *Almost Promised Land*, 172-73.

involved, offering money and administrative expertise. Besides substantial funding to run the organization, funds were also given for specific initiatives and important conferences.

Many Jewish philanthropists provided support for the NAACP. Jews not only gave money but invested their energies in building the organization. Some of the best Jewish lawyers worked for or consulted with the NAACP's legal defense fund, including Louis Brandeis, Louis Marshall, and Herbert Lehman. Virtually all of these Jewish benefactors had strong ties to the Jewish community and used these contacts to raise money for the NAACP. By far the most important Jew involved with the NAACP was Joel Spingarn. From 1914 until his death in 1939, Spingarn was chairman of the board and initiated many of the organization's policies and devised its strategies. When W.E.B. Du Bois published his autobiography in 1940, its dedication read, "To Keep the Memory of Joel Spingarn—A Scholar and a Knight."[54]

Since the 1970s, however, there has been a slow shift by the Jewish community away from social justice concerns. Part of the reason has been the hostility Jews began to experience in social justice organizations and the increasing role that Israel plays within Jewish organizations. However, independent of these political considerations, more Jews are being involved in a religious reawakening, leading them to more pious behavior. Thus, for Jews as well as for contemporary Catholics, the tension between combating inequities and strengthening religious piety continue to exist today as it did two millennia ago.

---

54. Diner, *Almost Promised Land*, 120.

12

Judeo-Christian Myth

THIS BOOK'S OPENING PARAGRAPHS pointed to Republican politicians increasingly referencing Judeo-Christian traditions; traditions that they believe underpin American exceptionalism. There is no question that there are important commonalities between Judaism and Christianity. For some, the fact that both religions have the same Israeli origins and worship the same God is sufficient to justify the term, Judeo-Christian.[1] The conservative radio host Dennis Prager points to the attitudes of some of the founding fathers:

> Christians who founded America saw themselves as heirs to the Hebrew Bible, as much as to theirs. And even more importantly, they strongly identified with the Jews. For example, Thomas Jefferson wanted the design of the seal of the United States to depict the Jews leaving Egypt. Just as the Hebrews left Egypt and its values, Americans left Europe and its values (if only those who admire Jefferson would continue to take his advice).[2]

This book has forcefully demonstrated, however, that Christianity was really a product of the Mediterranean basin not the land of Israel; and more importantly, many early Christian leaders, most notably Marcion, rejected the Old Testament. Indeed, it was included in the Christian cannon primarily because of its value to recruitment and only after Jewish biblical interpretations were totally rejected. While the Church Fathers affirmed

1. Hexter, *Judaeo-Christian Tradtion*.
2. Prager, "What Does Judeo-Christian Mean?"

the historical events in the Old Testament, like the exodus, they had radical different interpretations of its ethical principles.

Prager also points to the fact that Harvard University required Hebrew in its early years. However, this tells us very little about the interpretations of the Old Testament that were taught there. After all, Jerome learned Hebrew not to appreciate Jewish Old Testament beliefs but to better counter them.

Other proponents go back to the monotheistic core of the two religions. As Arthur Cohen noted,

> Jews and Christians affirm an unconditional, universal, and unique God, single and undifferentiated; that that God is believed to have created man, set him in the midst of an ordered nature, appointed him to a destiny of service and trust, brought near a single people—selected arbitrarily, but nevertheless unambiguously—to be His own and to bring His teaching to all the earth. These affirmations respecting the creation, the covenant of God with His elected people-servant, the revelation of His teaching, and the promise of redemption—these truths, schematic, loose, general, archetypal, connect the vision of Judaism and Christianity.[3]

This stance, however, does not distinguish Judaism and Christianity from other religions. Indeed, this has led some to embrace the term "Abrahamic religions" so as to include Islam. As this book has detailed, however, once we look at specific behaviors, rabbinic Judaism and Christianity are in sharp conflict. Through the Middle Ages, Jews were pariahs to Christians not simply because they were Christ killers but because of their commercial behaviors, often motivated by Jewish pleasure principle beliefs.

This book has also pointed to the substantial differences between the Christianity based on Jesus' ministry and that based on the Pauline emphasis on Jesus' death and resurrection. It is the former that provides the religious basis for Christian social justice impulses and, not surprisingly, has much in common with Jewish social justice beliefs. By contrast, it was Pauline Christianity that tried to separate itself as much as possible for Jesus' Jewish roots and his first disciples; and has been in the forefront historically of anti-Jewish Christian beliefs.

Prager correctly notes that it was only in the United States, with its acceptance of entrepreneurial enterprise, that Jews had a reasonable safe haven. While anti-Jewish sentiment in the United States was measured, there

---

3. Arthur Cohen, *Judeo-Christian Tradition*, xii.

was no perception of a Judeo-Christian tradition. Indeed, the nineteenth-century Social Gospel movement highlighted the distinction between the productive labor of Christian workers and their exploitation by the unproductive labor of middlemen which invariably were associated with Jewish entrepreneurs. Moreover, we have seen how the hostility to Jewish values, led Catholic and Protestant leaders to rail against Jewish entertainment industry efforts. This animus climaxed in Henry Ford's anti-Semitic rantings, Joseph Breen's diatribes against Jewish filmmakers, and Father Coughlin's claims that Jewish interests were promoting war with Germany.

These growing anti-Semitic utterances were the context in which the notion of a Judeo-Christian tradition was born. Some Protestant, Catholic, and Jewish leaders came together to embrace unity in the face of social hatred. Forming the National Conference of Christians and Jews (NCCJ) they barnstormed the country in an attempt to rout religious prejudice. Starting in the 1930s, NCCJ held interreligious faith meetings and organized local chapters around the country. In 1934 Brotherhood Day was instituted, enlarged to Brotherhood Week in 1947. As the historian Jonathan Sarna wrote,

> In the face of worldwide anti-Semitic efforts to stigmatize and destroy Judaism, influential Christians and Jews in America labored to uphold it, pushing Judaism from the margins of American religious life toward its very center.[4]

In the 1950s, as the Cold War intensified, many political and religious leaders came to believe that Western religious values were threatened by Godless communism. It was in this new context, that efforts to encourage interfaith celebrations were transformed into notions of a Judeo-Christian tradition to defend US exceptionalism. And it has resurfaced in the twenty-first century among those who believe the mortal threat is now from Islam. Hopeful this book, in a small way, will be an antidote to these harmful efforts.

---

4. Sarna, *American Judaism*, 267.

Appendix

THE BABYLONIAN TALMUD: ITS CONSTRUCTION, CONTENT, AND USE

THE BABYLONIAN TALMUD PROVIDES the central texts for religious education to enable the ethical principles embedded in the Mosaic laws to be applied to concrete, real-world situations. After the Mishnah was produced, comments were compiled at religious academies which, when added, produced the Talmud. In subsequent generations, important religious sages added even more commentary, until the Talmud used today was completed.

COMMENTARIES ARISING FROM THE RELIGIOUS ACADEMIES

There was a similar teaching style in the religious academies in Palestine and Babylonia, owing to the ongoing contact between the two communities. At each academy, the discourse began with a paragraph of Mishnah to which added traditions and discussions from the period prior to the writing of the Mishnah were already attached. These were discussed and new legal statements were added. Each of these developed chunks of material connected to a statement from the Mishnah is called a *sugya*. Each succeeding generation learned the sugya and then added questions, challenges, philosophical arguments, and stories connected to either the actual materials being discussed or to an assumed principle which the legal students believed the previous generations of sages held.

Appendix

Since most teachers had been the students of the previous leaders of the academies, many of their statements were assumed to be direct quotes of their teachers. There are also many examples of noting the behavior of a teacher as proof of that teacher's underlying principles. Some teachers believed in encouraging philosophical arguments; others emphasized close examination of the legal texts themselves.

There was one unique aspect of religious training in Babylonia, the *kallah*. Owing to the great distances between Babylonian Jewish communities, opportunities had to be furnished for those living far from the academies to take part in their deliberations. These meetings of outside students took place during the months of Adar and Elul each year, usually at or near the Sura and Pumbadi academies.

In the kallah months, the disciples journeyed to the meeting, having prepared the treatise announced at the close of the preceding kallah month by the *Resh metibta*, the head of the academy. Upon arrival, they join the assembly of scholars. The first row at the assembly consisted of ten men, heads of the assembly and their assistants. The seventy students, called Sanhedrin, were seated in the next seven rows; and behind them were the remaining members of the academy and the associated disciples.

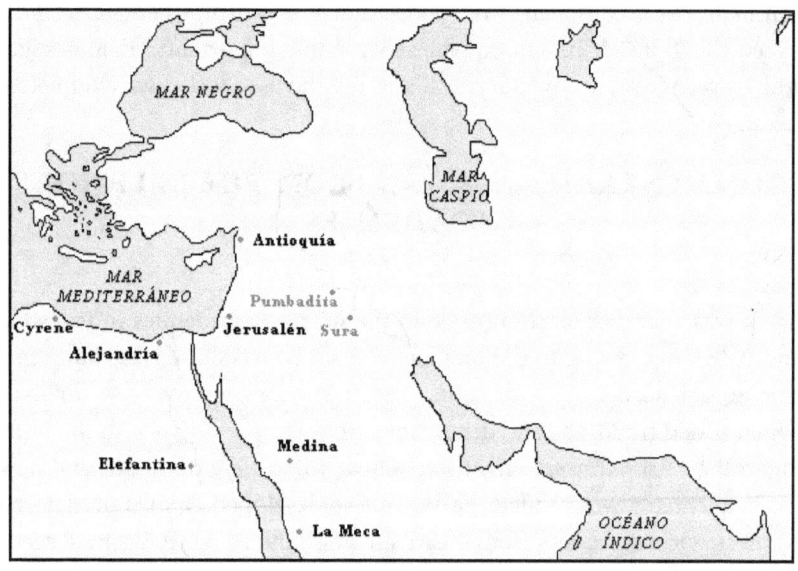

Figure AP.1: Babylonia, 5th Century

APPENDIX

The discourse begins with the ten seated in the first row reciting aloud the subject matter, while the others listen silently. When a passage requiring discussion is reached, they debate it among themselves, the head silently taking note of the subject of the discussion. Then the *reshmetibta* lectures upon the treatise under consideration, and adds an exposition of those passages that have given rise to discussion. Sometimes he addresses a question to those assembled as to how a certain *halakah* is to be explained: this must be answered only by the specific scholar chosen. And when everything has been made clear, one of those in the first row rises and delivers an address intended for the whole assembly, summing up the arguments on the theme they have been considering.

In the fourth week of the kallah month, the members of the Sanhedrin, as well as the other disciples, are examined individually by the head, to determine their knowledge and capacity. Whoever is shown to be insufficiently prepared is reproved by the head and threatened with the withdrawal of the stipend appropriated for his subsistence. The questions that have been received from various quarters are also discussed at these assemblies for final solution. The head lists the opinions of those present and formulates the decision, which is immediately written down. These collective answers are read aloud to the assembly and signed by the head.[1]

STRUCTURE OF THE BABYLONIAN TALMUD

The comments gathered at the academies were collected and organized. They provided the additions to the Mishnah that produced the Babylonian Talmud, completed during the fifth century. Numbering more than sixty books, it is divided into six main parts:

1. ZERAIM: concerning seeds. It treats of seeds, fruits, herbs, trees; of the public and domestic use of fruits, of different seeds, etc.
2. MOED: concerning festivals. It treats of the time when the Sabbath and other festivals are to begin, ended and celebrated.
3. NASCHIM: concerning women. It treats of marrying and repudiating wives, their duties, relations, sicknesses, etc.

---

1. Singer, *Jewish Encyclopedia*.

APPENDIX

4. NEZIKIN: concerning damages. It treats of damages suffered by men and animals, penalties and compensations.
5. KODASCHIM: concerning holiness. It treats of sacrifices and various sacred rites.
6. TOHOROTH: concerning purifications. It treats of the soiling and purifying of vessels, bedclothes and other things.

Each of these six parts, which the Jews call *Schishah Sedarim*—six orders or ordinances—is divided into books or tracts, called *Massiktoth,* and the books into chapters, or *Perakim.*

STUDYING THE BABYLONIAN TALMUD

Let us analyze a page from the Babylonian Talmud on the issue of the importance of blessing everything that is pleasurable. The center column (1) starts with a brief statement of the importance of blessing that appeared in the Mishnah. Since the Mishnah is often very terse and does not give a context for the applications it transmits, the text quickly shifts to Gemara (2): גמ׳; the addenda from the Babylonian academies that were compiled after the Mishnah. In the right column are the commentaries of Rashi (3), a tenth-century Talmudist who attempts to explain uncertainties left unanswered in the Mishnah and Gemara. In the column on the left of the Mishnah are the commentaries by the Tosfes, a group of individuals started by Rashi's grandchildren, who further elaborate. In addition, the notations on the far left (4) identify subsequent sources that discuss the topic, such as Maimonides and Joseph Caro. The notions on the far right (5) identify parallel discussions elsewhere in the Talmud. Finally, notations in the space between the center and the right-hand column of Rashi comments (6) identify biblical sources related to the topic.

On this page, the Gemara begins by enumerating the blessings on the various products consumed: vegetables, grains, etc. It includes dissident minority positions. In particular, it mentions that Rabbi Judah believed that there should be a separate blessing on herbs but all others disagreed. The Gemara then goes on to discuss the sinfulness of those who partake of earthly pleasures without giving a blessing to God. It uses the word לעמ (7) to characterize the illicit pleasure when pleasure is taken without

APPENDIX

making a blessing. Since this word has multiple meanings, Rashi's commentary offers an explanation for its meaning here.

Finally, the Gemara discusses what actions should be taken when someone doesn't give the required blessings (8). It suggests that the person should seek guidance from a respected religious individual. This guidance is meant to help individuals who either out of ignorance or lack of forethought neglected their responsibility.

Note that the Gemara takes a positive view of why individuals may have neglected to offer the required blessings. It does not, moreover, voice

Appendix

condemnation of the individual nor does it require the offending party to do penance. Thus, there is no vengeful attitude toward eradicating actions that could be characterized as sinful.

Bibliography

Albertz, Rainer. *Israel in Exile*. Atlanta: Society of Biblical Literature of Atlanta, 2003.
Anbinder, Tyler. *Five Points*. New York: Plume, 2002.
Antiochian, "The Jewish Quarter(s)." http://libaniusredux.blogspot.com/2009/03/jewish-quarters.html
Applebaum, Shimon. "Economic Life in Palestine." In *The Jewish People in the First Century*, edited by Shmuel Safrai and Menachem Stern, 631-700. Minneapolis: Fortress, 1976.
Aries, Phillippe and Georges Duby. *A History of Private Life, Volume I: From Pagan Rome to Byzantium*. Cambridge, MA: Belknap, 1987.
Aslan, Reza. *Zealot: The Life and Times of Jesus of Nazareth*. New York: Random House, 2013.
Augustine *In John* 33.6 in *Fathers of the Church*. Translated by John W. Rettig. Washington DC: Catholic University of America, 1995.
Austin, Charles. "Maryknollers Pursue Risky Paths in the Third World," *New York Times* (June 21, 1981).
Bean, Jennifer M. and Diane Negra, eds. *A Feminist Reader in Early* Cinema. Durham, NC: Duke University Press, 2002.
Ben Sira, *The Wisdom of Ben Sira*. Cambridge, UK: Cambridge University Press, 1899. http://archive.org/stream/wisdomofbensirapooscheuoft/wisdomofbensirapooscheuoft_djvu.txt
Bestul, Thomas H. *Texts of the Passion*. Philadelphia: University of Pennsylvania Press, 1996.
David Biale, ed. *Culture of* Jews. New York: Schocken, 2002.
———. *Eros and the Jews: From Biblical Israel to Contemporary* America. New York: Basic, 1992.
Blidstein, Gerald J. "Rabbinic Judaism and General Culture: Normative Discussion and Attitudes." In *Judaism's Encounter with Other Cultures*, edited by Jacob J. Schacter. Northvale, NJ: Aronson, 1997, 1-69.
Botticini, Maristella and Zvi Eckstein. *The Chosen Few: How Education Shaped Jewish History, 70-1492*. Princeton, NJ: Princeton University Press, 2012.
Boyarin, Daniel. *Carnal Israel: Reading Sex in Talmudic Literature*. Berkeley, CA: University of California Press, 1993.
———. *The Jewish Gospels: The Story of the Jewish Christ*. New York: New Press, 2012.
Brown, Peter. *The Body and Society*. New York: Columbia University Press, 1988.

Bibliography

———. "Late Antiquity." In *A History of Private Life, Volume I: From Pagan Rome to Byzantium*, edited by Phillippe Aries and Georges Duby. Belknap, 1987, 235-312.

———. *Religion and Society in the Age of St. Augustine*. Eugene, OR: Wipf & Stock, 2007.

———. *Through the Eye of a Needle: Wealth, the Fall of Rome, and the Making of Christianity in the West, 350-550 AD*. Princeton, NJ: Princeton University Press, 2012.

Bultmann, Rudolf. *The History of the Synoptic Tradition*. New York: Harper & Row, 1980.

Burton, Janet. *Monastic and Religious Orders in Britain, 1000-1300*. New York: Cambridge University Press, 1994.

Cahill, Susan. *For the Love of Ireland: A Literary Companion for Readers and Travelers*. New York: Ballantine, 2001.

Cameron, Ron. *The Other Gospels: Non-Canonical Gospel Texts*. Philadelphia, PA: Westminster, 1982.

Carrington, Philip. *The Early Christian Church*, Vol II. Cambridge, UK: Cambridge University Press, 1957.

Casson, Lionel. *Everyday Life in Ancient Rome*. Baltimore: Johns Hopkins, 1998.

Catholic Encyclopedia, "Origen and Origenism": http://www.newadvent.org/cathen/11306b.htm

Cherry, Robert. "The Hasidic Revolution: Foundation of American Popular Culture," *Midstream* 57 (Fall 2011) 12-17.

———. "Was Irish Catholicism Linked to Jansenism?" *Doctrine & Life* 64, no. 7 (Sept 2014) 13-28.

———. *Who Gets the Good Jobs? Combating Race and Gender Disparities*. New Brunswick, NJ: Rutgers University Press, 2001.

Chrysostom, John. *Eight Homilies against the Jews*. Amazon Digital, 2010. http://www.fordham.edu/halsall/source/chrysostom-jews6.html

Ciolino, Joseph. "Al Jolson Defended," *Black Star News* (May 22, 2007) http://blackstarnews.com/?c=120&a=3343.

Clark, Elizabeth. *The Origenist Controversy*. Princeton, NJ: Princeton University Press, 1992.

———. *Reading Renunciation: Asceticism and Scripture in Early Christianity*. Princeton, NJ: Princeton University Press, 1999.

Cohen, Arthur A. *The Myth of the Judeo-Christian Tradition*. New York: Schocken, 1971.

Cohen, Shaye J.D. *From the Maccabees to the Mishnah*. Louisville, KY: Westminster John Knox, 2006.

———. "The Place of the Rabbi in Jewish Society of the Second Century." In *The Galilee in Late Antiquity*, edited by Lee Levine. New York: Jewish Theological Society of America, 1992, 157-173.

———. "Review of *The Fiscus Judaicus and the Parting of the Ways* (Tübingen: Mohr Siebeck, 2010), *Bible History Daily*, October 10, 2012: http://www.biblicalarchaeology.org/reviews/the-fiscus-judaicus-and-the-parting-of-the-ways/

Cohen, Stuart. *The Three Crowns*. New York: Cambridge University Press, 1990.

Cohn, Haim H. *Human Rights in the Bible and Talmud*. Israel: MOD, 1989.

Collins, Eliza. "Kasich Calls for New Federal Agency to Promote Judeo-Christian Values," *Politico* (Nov 17, 2015). http://www.politico.com/story/2015/11/john-kasich-judeo-christian-agency-216001

Connolly, S.J. *Priest and People in Pre-Famine Ireland, 1780-1845*. New York: St. Martin's, 1982.

Contenau, Georges. *Everyday Life in Babylon and Assyria*. New York: St. Martin's, 1954.

Bibliography

Conzelmann, Hans. *History of Primitive Christianity*. Nashville, TN: Abington, 1973.

James R. Crotty and Rev. James R. Stormes, "The Bishops on the US Economy," *Challenge* 28 (Mar-Apr 1985) 36-41.

Crossan, John Dominic and Jonathan Reed. *In Search of Paul: How Jesus' Apostle Opposed Rome's Empire with God's Kingdom*. New York: HarperCollins, 2004.

Curran, Charles E. *Catholic Social Teaching, 1891-Present*. Washington DC: Georgetown University Press, 2002.

Curran, Joseph M. *Hibernian Green on the Silver Screen: The Irish and American Movies*. Westport, CT: Greenwood Press, 1989.

Cruse, Harold. *Crisis of the Black Intellectual*. Acton, MA: Quill, 1984.

Davies, Stevan. *The Revolt of the Widows*. Urbana, IL: University of Southern Illinois Press, 1980.

Dawidoff, Robert. *Making History Matter*. Philadelphia: Temple University Press, 2000.

Della Pergola, Sergio. "Review of *The Chosen Few*," *CDEC Journal* 6 (Dec 2013): http://www.quest-cdecjournal.it/discussion.php?id=64

Dever, William G. *Who Were the Early Israelites and Where Did They Come From?* Grand Rapids, MI: Wm. B. Eerdmans, 2003.

Dezell, Maureen. *Irish America: Coming into Clover*. New York: Doubleday 2001.

Diamond, Eliezer. *Holy Men and Hunger Artists: Fasting and Asceticism in Rabbinic Culture*. New York: Oxford, 2005.

DiMeglio, John. *Vaudeville USA*. Bowling Green, KY: Bowling Green University Press, 1973.

Diner, Hasia R. *Hungering for America* Cambridge, MA: Harvard University Press, 2001.

———. *In the Almost Promised Land*. Baltimore: Johns Hopkins University Press, 1995.

Donfried, Karl Paul, ed. *The Romans Debate*. Peabody, MA: Hendrickson, 1991.

Donoghue, Paul. *The Jesus Advantage: A New Approach to a Fuller Life*. Notre Dame, IN: Ave Maria, 2001.

Dresner, Samuel. *The Zaddik: The Doctrine of the Zaddik According to the Writings of Rabbi Yaakov Yosef of Polnoy*. London: Abelard-Schuman 1960.

Draper, J.A. *The Didache in Modern Research*. Leiden: Brill, 1996.

Dunn, James D.G. *Jesus Remembered: Christianity in the Making*, Vol 1. Grand Rapids, MI: Wm. B. Eerdmans, 2003.

Edwards, Douglas. "The Socio-Economic and Cultural Ethos in the First Century." In *The Galilee in Late Antiquity*, edited by Lee Levine, 53-73. New York: Jewish Theological Seminary, 1992.

Erdman, Andrew L. *Blue Vaudeville: Sex, Morals, and the Mass Marketing of Amusement, 1895-1915*. Jefferson, NC: McFarland, 2004.

Ehrman, Bart D. *Lost Christianities: The Battles for Scripture and the Faiths We Never Knew*. New York: Oxford University Press, 2003.

Etkes, Immanuel. *The Besht: Magician, Mystic, and Leader*. Waltham, MA: Brandeis University Press, 2005.

Feldman, Louis. *Jews and Gentiles in the Ancient World*. Princeton, NJ: Princeton University Press, 1993.

Feldman, Louis and Gohei Hata, eds. *Josephus, Judaism, and Christianity*. Detroit: Wayne State University Press, 1987.

Fields, Armond and L. Marc Fields. *From the Bowery to Broadway: Lew Fields and the Roots of American Popular Theater*. New York: Oxford University Press, 1993.

Bibliography

Fine, Lawrence. *Safed Spirituality: Rules of Mystical Piety, the Beginning of Wisdom.* Mahwah, NJ: Paulist, 1984.

Finkelstein, Louis. *The Pharisees: The Sociological Background of Their Faith.* Philadelphia: Jewish Publication Society of America, 1962.

Flaceliere, Robert. *Daily Life in Greece at the Time of Pericles.* New York: MacMillan, 1965.

Ford, Henry. *The International Jew,* Chapter 28, "Jewish Jazz Becomes Our National Music," *The Dearborn Press* (August 6, 1921).

Fox, Ted. *Showtime at the Apollo.* New York: Holt, Rinehart and Winston, 1983.

Foxbrunner, Roman. *Habad: The Hasidism of R. Schneur Zalman of Lyady.* Lanham, MD: Jason Aronson, 1993.

Fraade, Steven D. "Ascetical Aspects of Ancient Judaism." In *Jewish Spirituality: From the Bible to the Middle Ages,* edited by Arthur Green, 253-288. New York: Crossroad, 1986.

Fredriksen, Paula. *Jesus of Nazareth, King of the Jews.* New York: Alfred A. Knopf, 1999.

Freeman, Charles. *The Closing of the Western Mind.* New York: Vintage, 2005.

Freyne, Sean. "Urban-Rural Relations in First-Century Galilee." In *The Galilee of Late Antiquity,* edited by Lee Levine, 75-91. New York: Jewish Theological Seminary, 1992.

Friedman, Hershey H. and Linda Weiser Friedman. *God Laughed: Sources of Jewish Humor.* New Brunswick, NJ: Rutgers University Press, 2014.

Frymer-Kensky, Tikva. *In the Wake of the Goddesses.* New York: Free Press, 1992.

Furia, Philip and Michael Lasser. *America's Songs: The Stories behind the Songs of Broadway, Hollywood, and Tin Pan Alley.* New York: Routledge, 2006.

Gabler, Neal. *An Empire of Their Own: How the Jews Invented Hollywood.* New York: Anchor, 1988.

Goldenberg, Suzannne. "Why US Bishops Aren't Embracing Pope Francis' Climate Push," *Mother Jones* (Sept. 21, 2015). http://www.motherjones.com/environment/2015/09/pope-francis-climate-change-abortion-gay-marriage

Goodman, Martin. *State and Society in Roman Galilee, AD 132-212.* Totowa, NJ: Rowman & Allanheld, 1983.

Grabbe, Lester L. *A History of Judaism of the Second Temple Period.* London: T & T Clark, 2006.

Green, Arthur, ed. *Jewish Spirituality: From the Bible to the Middle Ages.* New York Crossroad, 1986.

Gruen, Eric. *Heritage and Hellenism: The Reinvention of the Jewish Tradition.* Berkeley, CA: University of California Press, 1998.

Hanson, Paul D. *The Dawn of Apocalyptic: The Historical and Sociological Roots of Jewish Apocalyptic Eschatology.* Minneapolis: Fortress, 1975.

Harper, Kyle. *From Shame to Sin: The Christian Transformation of Sexual Morality in Late Antiquity.* Cambridge, MA: Harvard University Press, 2013.

Hawthorne, Gerald and Ralph Merton. *Dictionary of Paul and His Letters.* Westmount, IL: Intervarsity, 1993.

Heilburt, Tony. *The Gospel Sound.* New York: Simon & Schuster, 1971.

Heller, Karen. "The Enlightened Legacy of the Rosenwald Schools," *Washington Post* (Aug 30, 2015).

Herzog, William. "Why Peasants Responded to Jesus." In *A People's History of Christianity, Vol 1: Christian Origins,* edited by Richard Horsley, 47-70. Minneapolis: Augsburg Fortress, 2005.

Bibliography

Hexter, J.H. *The Judaeo-Christian Tradition*, 2nd ed. New Haven, CT: Yale University Press, 1995.

Higashi, Sumiko. "The New Woman and Consumer Culture: Cecil B. DeMille's Sex Comedies," in *A Feminist Reader in Early Cinema*, edited by Jennifer M. Bean and Diane Negra, 298-332. Durham, NC: Duke University Press, 2002.

Hooper, Richard. *The Crucifixion of Mary Magdelene*. London: Sanctuary, 2005.

Hopkins, Keith. "Christian Number and Its Implications," *Journal of Early Christian Studies* 6 (1998) 185–226.

Horsley, Richard. *Jesus and the Powers: Conflict, Covenant, and the Hope of the Poor*. Minneapolis: Fortress, 2011.

———. *Jesus and the Spiral of Violence*. New York: Harper and Row, 1987.

———. ed. *A People's History of Christianity, Vol 1: Christian Origins*. Minneapolis: Augsburg Fortress, 2005.

———. *Sociology and the Jesus Movement*. New York: Continuum, 1994.

Howe, Irving and Eliezer Greenberg, eds. *A Treasure of Yiddish Stories*. New York: Viking, 1965.

Hunter, David. *Marriage, Celibacy, and Heresy in Ancient Christianity: The Jovianian Controversy*. New York: Oxford University Press, 2007.

Inglis, Tom. *Moral Monopoly: The Rise and Fall of the Catholic Church in Modern Ireland*. Dublin, Ireland: Dublin Press, 1998.

Irshai, Oded. "Confronting a Christian Empire." In *Culture of Jews*, edited by David Biale, 181-221. New York: Schocken, 2002.

Jenkins, Henry, Tara McPherson and Jane Shattuc, eds. *Hop on Pop*. Durham, NC: Duke University Press, 2002.

Jordan, Patrick. *Dorothy Day: Love in Action*. Collegeville, MN: Liturgical, 1989.

Josephus, *Antiquities of the Jews*. London: Aeterna Press, 2015.

Joshel, Sandra R. *Slavery in the Roman World*. New York: Cambridge University Press, 2010.

Just, Felix. "The Deutero-Pauline Letters," Catholic Resources: http://catholic-resources.org/Bible/Paul-Disputedited byhtm

Justin Martyr, "Dialogue with Trypho," *Early Christian Writings*. http://www.earlychristianwritings.com/text/justinmartyr-dialoguetrypho.html

Kaufman, Yehezkel. *Christianity and Judaism: Two Covenants*. Jerusalem: Magnes, 1988.

Koester, Helmut. *Ancient Christian Gospels*. Harrisburg, PA: Trinity Press International, 1990.

Kolatch, Alfred J. *The Second Jewish Book of Why*. Flushing, NY: Jonathan David, 2007.

Koltun-Fromm, Naomi. *Hermeneutics of Holiness*. New York: Oxford University Press, 2010.

———. "Sexuality and Holiness," *Vigiliae Christianae* 54 (2000) 375-395.

Lampe, Peter. "The Roman Christians of Roman 16." In *The Romans Debate*, edited by Karl Paul Donfried, 216-230. Peabody, MA: Hendrickson, 1991.

Lancel, Serge. *Saint Augustine*. London: SCM, 2002.

Joseph Lee, "Women and the Church since the Famine." In *Women in Irish Society: The Historical Dimension*, edited by Margaret MacCurtain and Donncha Ó Corráin, 37-45. Syracuse, NY: Arlen House, 1978.

Lee, Joseph and Marion Casey, editors. *Making the Irish American*. New York: NYU Press, 2006.

Levine, Lee. *The Ancient Synagogue*. New Haven, CT: Yale University Press, 2000.

Bibliography

———. Editor. *The Galilee in Late Antiquity*. New York: Jewish Theological Seminary, 1992.

———. *Jerusalem: Portrait of the City in the Second Temple Period (538 BCE-70 CE)*. Philadelphia: Jewish Publication Society, 2002.

Lewis, Robert, ed. *From Traveling Show to Vaudeville*. Baltimore: Johns Hopkins University Press, 2003.

Libanius. *Antioch as a Centre of Hellenic Culture as Observed*. Translated by A.F. Norman. Liverpool, UK: Liverpool University Press, 2001.

Lichtenstein, Aharon. "Of Marriage: Relationships and Relations." *Tradition: A Journal of Orthodox Jewish Thought* 39 (Summer 2005) 7-35.

Lieberman, Saul. *Hellenism in Jewish Palestine*. New York: Jewish Theological Seminary, 1962.

Lipton, Sara. "Images in the World: Reading the Crucifixion." In *Medieval Christianity in Practice*, edited by Miri Rubin, 173-188. Princeton, NJ: Princeton University Press, 2009.

Luddy, Maria. *Prostitution and Irish Society, 1800-1940*. New York: Cambridge University Press, 2007.

Lynch, Joseph H. *Simoniacal Entry into Religious Life from 1000 to 1260*. Columbus, OH: Ohio State University Press, 1976.

Maccoby, Hyam. *The Mythmaker: Paul and the Invention of Christianity*. New York: Harper & Row, 1986.

MacCurtain, Margaret and Donncha Ó Corráin, eds. *Women in Irish Society: The Historical Dimension*. Syracuse, NY: Arlen House, 1978.

Marcus, Ivan G. *Piety and Society: The Jewish Pietists of Medieval Germany*. Leiden: Brill, 1981.

Marcus, Ralph. "The Challenge of Greco-Roman Culture." In *Great Ages and Ideas of the Jewish People*, edited by Leo W. Schwarz, 95-121. New York: Modern Library, 1977.

Massignon, *Hallaj: Mystic and Martyr*. Translated by Herbert Mason. Princeton, NJ: Princeton University Press, 1994.

May, Lary. *Screening Out the Past: The Birth of Mass Culture and the Motion Picture Industry*. Chicago: University of Chicago Press, 1983.

May, Martha. "The Historical Problem of the Family Wage: The Ford Motor Company and the Five Dollar Day," *Feminist Studies* 8 (1982) 399–424.

McKanan, Daniel. "The Family, the Gospel, and the Catholic Worker," *The Journal of Religion* 87 (April 2007) 153-182.

McMahon, Darrin. *Happiness: A History*. New York: Grove, 2006.

Melnick, Jeffrey. *A Right to Sing the Blues: African Americans, Jews, and American Popular Song*. Cambridge, MA: Harvard University Press, 2001.

Meyers, Eric. "Jewish Culture in Greco-Roman Palestine." In *Culture of* Jews, edited by David Biale, 155-180. New York: Schocken, 2002.

Miller, Kerby. *Emigrant and Exile*. New York: Oxford University Press, 1988.

Montserrat, Dominic. *Sex and Society in Graeco-Roman Egypt*. London: Kegan Paul International, 1996.

Mooney, Jennifer. *Irish Stereotypes in Vaudeville, 1865 to 1905*. New York: Palgrave MacMillan, 2015.

Morris, Charles. *The American Catholic*. New York: Random House, 1997.

Moses, Paul. *An Unlikely Union: The Love-Hate Story of New York's Irish and Italians*. New York: NYU Press, 2015.

Bibliography

Murphy, Frank, ed. *The Irish Bog: Who They Were and How They* Lived. New York: Penguin, 1987.

Murphy-O'Connor, Jerome. *Paul: His Story*. New York: Oxford University Press, 2004.

Nadler, Allan. *The Faith of the Mithnagdim: Rabbinic Responses to Hasidic Rapture*. Baltimore: Johns Hopkins University Press, 1999.

National Council of Bishops, *Economic Justice for All: Pastoral Letter on Catholic Social Teachings and the US Economy*. Washington DC: National Council of Bishops, 1986.

Neusner, Jacob. "Josephus' Pharisees: A Complete Repertoire." In *Josephus, Judaism, and Christianity*, edited by Louis Feldman and Gohei Hata, 274-292. Detroit: Wayne State University Press, 1987.

New York Tribune, "Church to Censor Plays," November 11, 1912.

New York Tribune, "Cardinal Begins War on Immoral Plays," December 19, 1912.

Oberdeck, Kathryn J. "Contested Cultures of American Refinement: Theatrical Manager Sylvester Poli, His Audiences, and the Vaudeville Industry, 1890-1920," *Radical History Review* 66 (1996) 40-91.

Oppenheimer, Aharon. *The 'Am Ha-aretz: A Study in the Social History of the Jewish People in the Hellenistic-Roman Period*. Leiden: Brill, 1977.

Pagels, Elaine. *The Gnostic Paul: Gnostic Exegesis of Pauline Letters*. Minneapolis: Fortress Press, 1975.

Peretz, Isaac Leib. "If Not Still Higher." In *A Treasure of Yiddish Stories*, edited by Irving Howe and Eliezer Greenberg, 231-34. New York: Viking, 1965.

Perriello, Pat. "US Bishops Are Not Responding to Pope Francis' Message," *National Catholic Reporter* (July 30, 2015). http://ncronline.org/blogs/ncr-today/us-bishops-are-not-responding-pope-francis-message

Phiel, Mel. *Breaking Bread: The Catholic Worker and the Origin of Catholic Radicalism in America*. Philadelphia: Temple University Press, 1982.

Pickett, Ray "Conflict in Corinth." In *A People's History of Christianity, Vol 1: Christian Origins*, edited by Richard Horsley. Minneapolis: Augsburg Fortress, 2005, 113-137.

Pirkei Avot (Ethics of Our Fathers). Brooklyn, NY: Mesorah Publication, 1984.

Prager, Dennis. "What Does Judeo-Christian Mean?" *Jewish World Review* (Mar 30, 2004). http://www.jewishworldreview.com/0304/prager_2004_03_30_04.php3

Preston, Andrew. "A Very Young Judeo-Christian Tradition," *Boston Globe* (July 1, 2012).

Prothero, Stephen. "Book review of *Zealot: The Life and Times of Jesus of Nazareth*," *Washington Post* (Aug 2, 2013).

Philo, *The Special Laws*, 1:69. http://www.earlyjewishwritings.com/text/philo/book27.html

Philo, *On The Embassy to Gaius*, http://www.earlychristianwritings.com/yonge/book40.html

Phipps, William. "The Plight of the Song of Songs," *Journal of the American Academy of Religion* 42 (Mar 1974) 82-100.

Pope Leo XIII, *Rerum novarum, Encyclical Letter of Pope Leo XIII on Capital and Labor*, 45: http://w2.vatican.va/content/leo-xiii/en/encyclicals/documents/hf_l-xiii_enc_15051891_rerum-novarum.html

Ranelagh, John O'Beirne. *A Short History of Ireland*, 2nd ed. New York: Cambridge University Press, 1994.

Ranke-Heinemann, Uta. *Eunuchs for the Kingdom of Heaven: Women, Sexuality, and the Catholic Church*. New York: Doubleday, 1990.

Bibliography

Rapp, Claudia. *Holy Bishops in Late Antiquity: The Nature of Christian Leadership in the Age of Transition*. Berkeley, CA: University of California Press, 2013.

Rogin, Michael. *Blackface, White Noise: Jewish Immigrants in the Hollywood Melting Pot*. Berkeley, CA: University of California Press, 1996.

Rosman, Moshe. *Founder of Hasidism: A Quest for the Historical Ba'al Shem Tov*. Berkeley, CA: University of California Press, 1996.

Rubin, Miri, ed. *Medieval Christianity in Practice*. Princeton, NJ: Princeton University Press, 2009.

Ryan, John. *Irish Monasticism*. Ithaca, NY: Cornell University Press, 1972.

Safrai, Shmuel and Menachem Stern, eds. *The Jewish People in the First Century*. Minneapolis: Fortress, 1976.

Sandrow, Nahma. *Vagabond Stars: A World History of Yiddish Theater*. New York: Harper & Row, 1977.

Sanders, E.P. *Jesus and Judaism*. Minneapolis: Fortress Press, 1985.

———. "Jesus in Historical Context." *Theology Today* 50 (Oct 1993) 429-448.

———. *Paul: The Apostle's Life, Letters, and Thought*. New York: Oxford University Press, 1997.

Sarna, Jonathan. *American Judaism*. New Haven, CT: Yale University Press, 2004.

Satlow, Michael L. "And on the Earth You Shall Sleep: Talmud Torah and Rabbinic Asceticism." *Journal of Religion* 83 (April 2003) 204-225.

Schacter, Jacob J. *Judaism's Encounter with Other Cultures*. Lanham, MD: Jason Aronson, 1997.

Schaff, Philipp. *The Sacred Writings of Clement of Alexandria*. Berlin, Germany: Jazzybee Verlag, 2012.

Schiffman, Lawrence. *From Text to Tradition*. Brooklyn, NY: KTAV, 1991.

———. "The Maccabean Revolt: What Really Happened." Lecture, Yeshiva University 2016. http://www.yutorah.org/lectures/lecture.cfm/784855/dr-lawrence-schiffman/the-maccabean-revolt-what-really-happened/

Schlesinger, Arthur M. *Robert Kennedy and His Times*. New York: Mariner Books, 2002.

Schoeps, Hans-Joachim. *Jewish Christianity*. Philadelphia: Fortress Press, 1969.

Schroeder, Jeanne L. *The Vestal and the Fasces: Hegel, Lacan, Property, and the Feminine*. Berkeley, CA: University of California Press, 1998.

Schwarz, Leo W. *Great Ages and Ideas of the Jewish People*. New York: Modern Library, 1977.

Septimus, Bernard. "Piety and Power in Thirteenth-Century Catalonia." In *Studies in Medieval Jewish History and Literature*, edited by Isadore Twersky, 199-209. Cambridge, MA: Harvard University Press, 1979.

Shatz, David and Joel Wolowelsky, eds. *Family Redeemed: Essays on Family Relationships* Brooklyn, NY: KTAV, 2002.

Sheldon, Charles. *Charles Sheldon: His Life Story*. New York: Doran, 1925.

Isidore Singer, *The Jewish Encyclopedia: A Descriptive Record of the History*, Vol 1. Brooklyn, NY: KTAV, 1901. https://books.google.com/books?id=nd4eSjf3X_sC&pg=PA146&lpg=PA146&dq=sura+babylonian+academy&source=bl&ots=1n_VLIveY4&sig=owzNfWt9PubFGAVUpF4e-d5zNbM&hl=en&sa=X&ved=0ahUKEwjXmbKLtOrSAhVozoMKHcf1BiwQ6AEITDAH#v=onepage&q=sura%20babylonian%20academy&f=false

Snyder, Robert. "The Irish and Vaudeville." In *Making the Irish American*, edited by Joseph Lee and Marion Casey, 406-410. New York: NYU Press, 2006.

Bibliography

Spector, Mordecai. "A Meal for the Poor," in *A Treasury of Yiddish Stories*, edited by Irving Howe and Eliezer Greenberg, 250-255. New York: Viking Press, 1965.

Staples, Shirley. *Male-Female Comedy Teams in American Vaudeville, 1865-1932*. Ann Arbor, MI: UMI Research, 1984.

Stark, Rodney. *The Rise of Christianity*. San Francisco: HarperSanFrancisco, 1997.

Steffen, Daniel. *The Messianic Banquet and the Eschatology of Mathew*, Bible.Org (Jan 2004). https://bible.org/article/messianic-banquet-and-eschatology-matthew.

Stillman, Norman. *The Jews of Arab Lands: A History and Source Book*. Philadelphia: Jewish Publication Society of America, 1979.

Sweeney, Marvin A. *Form and Intertextuality in Prophetic and Apocalyptic Literature*. Eugene, OR: Wipf & Stock, 2010.

Tabor, James. "The Strange Ending of the Gospel of Mark and Why It Makes All the Difference," http://www.biblicalarchaeology.org/daily/biblical-topics/new-testament/the-strange-ending-of-the-gospel-of-mark-and-why-it-makes-all-the-difference/

Tertullian, *On Baptism*, Chapter 17 (New Advent): http://www.newadvent.org/fathers/0321.htm

Theissen, Gerd. *Sociology of Early Palestinian Christianity*. Philadelphia: Fortress Press, 1977.

Tkach, Joseph. "Women 'Should Remain Silent'—A Study of 1 Corinthians 14:34-35," *Grace Communion International*, 2005. http://www.gci.org/church/ministry/women9

Toy, Crawford Howell, Carl Siegfried, and Jacob Zallel Lauterbach. "Philo Judaeus: His Methods of Exegesis," *Jewish Encyclopedia*. http://www.jewishencyclopedia.com/articles/12116-philo-judaeus#anchor8

Tuchman, Shera Aranoff and Sandra E. Rapoport. *Moses' Women*. Brooklyn, NY: KTAV, 2008.

Turner, Steve. *Amazing Grace*. New York: HarperCollins, 2002.

Twersky, Isadore, ed. *Studies in Medieval Jewish History and Literature*. Cambridge MA: Harvard University Press, 1979.

Urbach, Ephraim. *The Sages: Their Concepts and Beliefs*. Jerusalem: Magnes, 1995.

Van Groningen, Gerard. *First Century Gnosticism: Its Origin and Motifs*. Leiden: Brill, 1967.

Vermes, Geza. *The Religion of Jesus the Jew*. Minneapolis: Fortress, 1993.

Weiss, Zeev. *Public Spectacles in Roman and Late Antiquities Palestine*. Cambridge, MA: Harvard University Press, 2014.

Wikipedia, "Prostitution in Ancient Rome": http://en.widipedia.org/wiki/Prostitution_in_ancient_Rome

Williams. William H. *'Twas Only an Irishman's Dream: The Image of Ireland and the Irish in American Popular Song Lyrics, 1800-1920*. Urbana, IL: University of Illinois Press, 1996.

Wojcik, Pamela Robertson. "Mae West's Maids: Race, 'Authenticity,' and the Discourse of Camp." In *Hop on Pop*, edited by Henry Jenkins, Tara McPherson and Jane Shattuc, 287-299. Durham, NC: Duke University Press, 2002.

Workman, Herbert. *The Evolution of the Monastic Ideal*. Boston: Beacon, 1962.

Wright, F.A. *Feminism in Greek Literature: From Homer to Aristotle*. Port Washington, NY: Kennikat, 1969.

Wright, Gavin. *Old South, New South*. New York: Basic Books, 1986.

BIBLIOGRAPHY

Wright, William. *Apocryphal Acts of the Apostles*, Volumes 1 and 2, (1871) 156. https://books.google.com/books?id=xilLAAAAYAAJ&pg=PA156&lpg=PA156&dq#v=onepage&q&f=false

Zwick, Mark and Louise Zwick. *The Catholic Worker Movement: Intellectual and Spiritual Origins*. Mahwah, NJ: Paulist, 2005.

Index

A

Aaron, 38, 48
R. Abba Hanan, 121
R. Abbahu, 145
Abdu-Heba, 16
abortion, 44, 186, 190–91
Abraham, 17–18, 56
abstinence, 38, 86–87, 94, 97, 101,108, 119, 139, 150–51
R. Abuyah, Elisha ben, 124
academies, 9, 110–12, 114–15, 146–48, 158, 201–3
Acts of Andrew, 96
Acts of Thecla, 96
Adam, 141–42
Adamnan of Coldingham, 167
adulteries, 52, 65, 101, 104
African-American cabaret, 194
afterlife, 6, 28, 58
Agricultural Adjustment Act (AAA), 60
Ahwaz economy, 158
R. Akiba, 10, 112–13, 115–18, 122–23, 151
Akiban schools, 114, 117
Albee, Edward, 181–82
Alexander the Great, 26
Alexandria, 41, 79, 98–100, 105, 107, 122–23, 214
Alexandrian Jewry, 34, 40, 150
Allegories, 146

Almighty God, 38, 128
Alt, Albrecht, 16
Amarna letters, 16
Amazing Grace, 60–61, 215
Ambrose, 86, 125, 127, 134–37, 140–41
America, xv, 171, 175, 177, 187, 197, 199,
American Catholic, 168–69, 170, 171
American Federation of Labor (AFL), 186
R. Ami, 150
Amidah, 112
ammei ha'aretz, 6, 55, 62, 67, 69, 115–16, 148, 157
Amos, 21, 58
Amsterdam News, 194
Ananus, 5
anchorites, 129–31, 137
Ancient Hebrews, 28
Ancient Judaism, 45, 119
Anderson, Eddie, 194, 195
Anthony, 129–30
anti-ascetic message, 173
anti-Christian actions, 72, 106
Antigonus, 120
anti-Jewish behaviors, 13, 164–65, 198–99
anti-lynching sentiment, 13, 191–92
Antioch, 57, 67–68, 74–75, 77, 90, 98, 133–34, 145
Antioch synagogue, 11
Antiochus III, 26–27
Antiochus IV, 27–28

Index

Aphrahat, 150
Apiru, 16–17
apocalypse, 31, 35, 65–66, 68–69, 81, 87
apocryphal Acts, 96, 98, 131, 100, 129
Apollo Theater, 193
apostles, 63–69, 74, 77, 92–94, 96, 100, 129
Apostolic Tradition, 100, 103
Aramaic languages, 146
Archelaus, 30
Arianism, 138
Aristophanes, 43
Armenia, 96, 134
ascetic behavior, 7–9, 10–12, 37, 41, 51–52, 68, 86–87, 89, 97–98, 103–5, 108–9, 119, 121, 124, 128, 132, 142, 153, 164, 169, 172, 174
asceticism, 4, 9–10, 35, 37–38, 68–69, 71, 86, 88, 94–95, 99, 103–04, 108–09, 117, 119–23, 125, 128, 131, 134, 137, 149, 167, 169–74, 176, 179
Ashkenazi Jewry, 172
Asia Minor, 7, 67, 74, 93, 97, 107, 145, 150, 158–59
Aslan, Reza 3, 5–8, 55, 207
Assyria, 23–24
Athens, 77
Augustine, 2, 53, 123, 125, 127, 138–43
austere life, 101, 133, 169
Av Beit, 46
Avot de-Rabbi Nathan, 111, 120
R. Azzai, 10, 121, 151–52

B

Baal, 15, 24, 37
Baal Shem Tov (Besht), xvi, 13, 172–4
Babylonia, 11–12, 21, 23–25, 32, 39, 47, 49, 94, 113, 125, 144, 147–50, 157, 161, 201–2
Babylonian academies, 149, 159, 204
Babylonian Talmud, 2, 9, 57, 116, 144, 148–49, 201, 203–4
badkhomin, 175

Bagdad, 158
banks, 40, 58–59
Bannon, Steve, 1
banquet, messianic, 6, 36, 69–70
baptism, 36, 51, 53, 64, 99, 142
Bara, Theda, 183
Bar Kochba revolt, 9–10, 70, 113–14, 122, 124
Basil, 132, 135, 167
Beinart, Peter, 2
Beit Din, 48, 112
Benedictine Rules, 167–8
Benny, Jack, 194
Berlin, Irving, 192–93
Biale, David, 10, 37, 152–56, 174
bishops, 90–91, 93, 96, 98–100, 104, 108–9, 124, 127–28, 132, 134–36, 138, 162, 164, 186, 190–91
Black Death, 172
blackface, 181, 193–94, 214
Blake, Eubie, 194
Bonaventure, Saint, 164
Botticini, Maristella, 158, 165
Boyarin, Daniel, 11, 65, 117, 144, 153–56,
Braham, David, 178
Brandeis, Louis, 196
Breen, Joseph, 199
Brice, Fanny, 181
Broadway, 182, 192, 194,
Broder singers, 175
brothels, 44–45, 79, 126–27, 133
brotherhoods, 59, 132, 135–36, 199
Brown, John, 192
Brown, Peter, 40, 128, 141, 156
Bryan, William Jennings, 59
Burial sites, 16, 38, 56, 110
Byzantine Empire, 159

C

Caesar, Julius, 83, 85
Caesarea, 68, 132, 167
Cahill, 169, 208
calendar, 113
Canaan, 14–15, 17–18, 39, 124, 148

Index

Cappadocia, 131, 135
carnality, 123, 157
Cardinal Cappellari, 169
Cardinal Cullen, 12
Cardinal Murphy-O'Connor, 79
Caro, Joseph, 204
Carthage, 98, 103–4, 138–39, 142
Cassian, John, 86, 142, 167
Catholic Church, 165, 176, 182, 186, 190
Catholics, 13, 122–23, 170, 185, 191, 199
Catholic Social Teaching, 13, 185
Catholic Worker Movement, 186–88

celebrations, 10, 13, 18, 127, 136, 169, 174, 178, 199
celibacy, 38, 87, 99, 102–5, 119, 126, 130, 134, 136, 141, 143, 150–52, 162, 169,
Celtic church, 167
Cenchreae, 85
cenobitic organizations, 130
charity, 45, 55, 132–35, 138, 161–62, 171, 188, 190
chastity, 96, 102, 131, 136
Chmielnicki, Bogdan, 172
Christ, 6, 12, 70, 72–74, 76–79, 81–84, 87, 93–94, 97–99, 102–3, 105–6, 109, 133, 164–66, 168
Christian anti-Semitism, 12, 164–65
Christian charismatics, 66–68, 75, 96
Christian communities, xi–xii, xiv, 6–7, 67–68, 70, 83–85, 87, 89–90, 93, 95, 104, 106, 128, 130, 136, 149, 162
Christian evangelists, 48, 68, 72, 74, 86
Christian gnostics, 98
Christianity, xiii–xiv, 2–3, 7–8, 71, 83–84, 86, 89, 93–94, 96–97, 107–9, 123–24, 132, 134–35, 140–41, 159–62, 197–98
 Pauline, 123–24, 198
Christian leaders, 49, 57, 67, 76, 87–88, 93–94, 98–100, 107–09, 122–23, 126–28, 132, 134–38, 197
Christians, xi, 7, 10–13, 50–51, 69–70, 73–78, 84–87, 90, 96–99, 101–4, 106–7, 119–24, 128, 131–32, 140, 165–66, 188, 197–98
Christian thought, 70, 107, 109, 141, 156
Chrysostom, John, 11, 108, 126, 133–35, 138, 142, 156, 188
Church Fathers, xvi, 123, 25, 137, 150, 153, 157, 197
circumcision, 3, 24, 27, 74, 113, 115, 122
Circus Maximus, 75
Cistercian Order, 12, 168
Clement of Alexandria, 79, 95, 99–102, 107, 122–23, 132
Clement of Rome, 90
climate change, 190
Cline, Maggie, 178–80
Cluny monastery, 168
Cold War, 199
Colossae, 77, 83
Columban Rules, 167
Columbia Records, 192
Commodore Records, 192
Commonweal, 187
communion, 8, 97, 120, 170
conception, 64, 135–36, 142
concubines, 16, 139
concupiscence, 141–42, 154
congregants, 11, 66, 107, 109, 124, 134, 136
Constantine, 107, 126
Constantinople, 133–34, 142
continence, 36, 95–96, 99, 102, 106, 108, 131, 136–38, 140
coon singers, 181
Corinth, 77, 82–83, 85
Corinthians, 81, 87, 90, 95
Count Basie, 194
Cromwell, Oliver, 168
Crow, Jim, 195
crucifixion, 52, 61, 67, 103,
Crusades, 172
Crystal, Billy, 192
Cynics, 68
Cyrene, 30
Cyrus, King, 25

Index

D

Daniel, 26, 64–65, 207, 212, 215
David, King, 18, 35, 37, 211, 214
day laborers, 57, 59–60
Day, Dorothy, 13, 186–89
De Bois, W.E.B., 196
Decius persecutions, 105–06
Deep South, 60
degradation, 7, 42, 84, 123, 165
DeMille, Cecil, 184–85
Demiurge, 93, 98
Desert Fathers, 86, 129, 131, 138, 141–42
Deutero Pauline Letters, 82
Dewson, Mary, 194
Diaspora, 3, 7, 50, 62, 78
Didache, 68–69, 89–92, 94
dietary laws, 27, 65, 74–75, 108
Diocletian's persecution, 106–07
disciples, 5, 48, 52–53, 63, 68, 72–74, 81, 92, 97–98, 112, 142, 202–3
Domitian, 93
Donnybrook Fair, 170
Drogheda, 168
dualism, 40–41, 77–78, 86, 108, 120, 128, 153, 157

Emperor Decius, 104
Encratite traditions, 97, 99
Encyclical Letter, 213
end-time, xiv, 4, 8, 63–64, 69, 81–82
Enoch, 65, 70
entertainment, 23, 146, 174, 178, 194
Ephesians, 84
Ephesus, 77, 85
Ephraim, 215
Epicurean philosopher, 100
Epiphanius, 138
Eros, 10, 152–55, 174
erotic art, 40–44, 80, 127, 134
Esther, Queen, 38, 95, 100
Eucharist, 92, 99, 133
eunuchs, 36, 101, 105, 122, 137
Euodia, 84
Europe, 12, 159, 162, 168, 181, 197
Eusebius, 86
Evagrius Ponticus, 138, 142
evangelists, xiv, 3, 6, 8, 67–68, 70, 85, 89–90, 92, 96
Evangelium, 133
evolution, xv–xvi, 2, 7, 12, 70, 125, 157, 161, 176
exodus, 14, 18, 34, 53, 124, 198
Ezekiel, 20–23, 70
Ezra, 20, 22, 25–26, 39, 45, 70, 148

E

Eastern European Jewry, 172–73, 175, 181
economic inequality, 4, 46, 56, 70, 86, 161, 185
Edison, Thomas, 13, 183
Egypt, 14, 16, 18, 21, 26, 30, 39–40, 79, 124, 131, 142, 159, 197
R. Eleazar, 112, 149
R. Eliezer, 117, 150, 153, 156
Elijah, 53
Elisha, 53, 124
Ellington, Duke, 194
El Salvador, 189
Elvira, 127–28
emaciated bodies, 139, 163–64
Emperor Arcadius, 134

F

families, 6, 15, 17, 19, 22, 24, 53, 59, 66–67, 84, 87, 96, 103, 115, 122, 130–31, 133, 151, 162, 171, 183, 188
famine, xv, 20, 22, 171, 177–78
farming, 2, 4, 17, 24, 58, 114, 169, 188
fasting, 38, 41, 52, 71, 119, 130, 136, 138, 167, 173,
Father Coughlin, 199
Fatimids, 159
Felicitas, 103
festivals, 11, 27, 34, 78, 112, 115, 150, 172, 203
films, xv, 183–85, 194
First Temple, 18–19, 20–22, 24

Index

Fitzgerald, Scott, 185
Five Points, 172
flesh, 36, 38, 52, 76, 78, 82, 86, 96–99, 101–2, 123, 135
Flexner, Abraham, 195
Flint (MI), 188
food, 31, 34–35, 37, 66, 78, 94, 100, 105, 131, 139, 146, 149, 154, 167, 171, 174
Ford, Henry, 183, 199
Fox, William, 183–84, 193
Frankfurter, Felix, 195
Freedom Summer, 191

G

Gabler, Neil, xv, 183, 185, 192
Gaelic values, 169
Gaius, 62, 213
Galerius, 106–07
Galilean communities, 55–56, 114–15–6, 148
Galilean peasantry, xiv, 6, 53, 56, 70
Galilee, 2–3, 7, 9, 49–50, 53, 67, 69, 113–15, 124, 145, 148, 210
Gallienus, 106
R. Gamaliel I, 46, 48, 72, 73, 110, 112
R. Gamaliel II, 112, 114, 116
Gedaliah, 22, 24
Gemara, 204–5
gender equality, 6–7, 84, 88, 95, 100, 103
General Motors, 188
Gentiles, 3, 67, 70, 74, 76, 81, 87, 92, 122, 124, 145–46, 150, 185
German pietists, 166, 172
girls, 42–44, 53, 101, 118, 170, 178–79, 182, 185
gluttony, 11, 38, 71
Gnosticism, 39, 98, 108, 139
Gnostics, 99, 106, 123
God, 4–6, 17, 19, 28, 35–38, 52–53, 63–65, 69–70, 78–79, 81–82, 92–95, 99, 102, 104–7, 127, 140–43, 150–52, 171, 173–74, 197–98
God-fearers, 7, 41, 75, 77, 85, 93, 128

good news, 5, 69–70, 72, 86, 93, 103
Goodman, Bennie, 194
gospels, 4, 6, 18, 36, 51, 61–62, 64, 69, 83–84, 91–95, 99–100, 164, 208, 212
Gottwald, Norman, 16
grace, 6, 55, 57, 60, 69–70, 77, 93, 138, 142, 176
Graetz, Heinrich, 149
Granz, Norman, 194
Great Famine, xv, 170
Great Revolt, 45, 48, 110
Greco-Roman world, 27, 39, 44, 78, 109, 124, 140, 145–47, 153
Greeks, 6–7, 39, 43, 49, 55–56, 79, 84, 103, 145–47, 156
Greek Septuagint, 73, 137
Gregory of Nyssa, 52, 105, 123, 132
Guatemala, 189

H

Habad, 173
haberim, 35, 69
halakah, 47, 117, 203
Hallaj, 158
Hammerstein, Oscar, 182
R. Hanna, 122
Hanukkah, 27
happiness, 103, 140, 142–43
Harbor, Pearl, 189
Harlem, 194
harlot, 11, 79, 101
Harrigan, Edward, 177–79
Hart, Tony, 177
Hasidic movement, 12, 173–75
Hasmonean era, 45
Hazor, 15, 17
heaven, 4, 64–66, 105, 111, 120, 122, 187–88
Hebrews, 16, 73, 137, 146, 197–98
Hellenism, 3, 6–7, 26–27, 39, 40–41, 56, 81, 86, 109, 123–24, 145–47, 153
Herod, 30, 32, 46
Herod Antipas, 51, 54–55

Index

Herodotus, 40
Hibernians, 179
Holiday, Billie, 192
holiness, 86, 109, 115, 130, 134, 150–51, 204
Hollywood, 185, 195, 210
Holy Bishops, 90–91, 100, 104, 108, 142
Holy Spirit, 78, 100, 106, 129, 138
homosexuality, 127–28
Hosea, 21
houses, 7–8, 10, 21, 35, 37, 39, 58, 61, 75, 85–86, 92, 95, 145, 149, 179
Howard Medical School, 195
husbands, 42–43, 48, 81, 84, 88, 95–96, 133, 137, 140, 151, 154–56
hymns, 60, 165
Hyrcanus, 117, 150

I

Iconium, 77
Ignatius of Antioch, 90–91, 94, 98
immigrants, 2, 13, 114, 170–71, 175–76, 181
immorality, 43, 79, 81, 99, 117, 169, 182–83
indulgences, 40, 78, 101, 174
industrial capitalism, 161, 185
inequalities, 57–58, 86–87, 161–62, 188, 191
inequities, 4, 6, 19–20, 26, 196
International Jew, 183
Ireland, xv–xvi, 2, 12, 166, 168–71, 180,
Irenaeus, 99–100, 107
Irish America, 171, 177–80, 209
Irish ascetic, 141, 171
Irish Monasticism, 12, 167–68
Isaac, 18
Isaiah, 5, 20–21, 31, 36, 39, 58, 64, 70, 94
Islam, 12, 159–60, 198–99
Israel, 19–20, 22–23, 30–31, 34–36, 39, 46–47, 49, 66–67, 70, 92, 111, 116, 147–48, 196–97, 207–8

Israelites, 2, 8, 15–16, 18–20, 25, 28, 37–38, 103, 121
Italians, 171–72
Italy, 134–35

J

Jacob, 18, 213
R. Jacob Joseph, 174
James, 5, 74
Jansenism, 171, 187
jazz concerts, 194
Jefferson, Thomas, 197
Jehoiachin, 21–22, 24–25
Jehoiakim, 21
Jeremiah, 20–22, 24
Jericho, 15
Jerome, 122–23, 125, 134, 137–38, 141, 150, 198, 213
Jerusalem, xiv, 2–3, 5, 18, 20, 25–28, 30–36, 49, 61, 66–67, 72–74, 93, 110, 115, 211–12, 215
Jerusalem Talmud, 47, 144, 147, 149
Jesus, xi, xiv, xvi, 3–7, 50–53, 55–58, 61–67, 69–71, 73–74, 84, 86–87, 92–93, 95, 135–36, 210–11, 213–15
Jesus' ministry, xi, 2–6, 13–14, 50–51, 53, 57, 61, 67–68, 70–71, 161, 190, 198
Jewish Christians, 48, 72–74, 91–94, 99
Jewish communities, 3, 9, 23, 25–26, 30, 35, 45, 53, 61–63, 67–68, 74–75, 93–94, 113–15, 118, 144–45, 166, 172, 174–176, 191–92, 196
Jewish culture, 41, 67, 75, 111, 145–46
Jewish entertainers, 175, 191, 199
Jewish entrepreneurs, xv, 176, 181–82, 199
Jewish marriage contract, 11, 154
Jewish philanthropists, 13, 191, 195–96
Jewish population in Palestine, 9, 145
Jewish prophets, 13, 58, 64, 124, 151, 191

222

INDEX

Jewish renewal movements, 2, 4, 12, 29–31, 33, 35, 37, 39, 41, 43, 45, 47, 49–50, 68–71
Jim Crow, 60, 176, 191, 194
John the Baptist, 4, 36–37, 50–52, 61, 65–66, 69–70, 86, 96, 99, 129, 164
Jolson, Al, 193–94
Jordan River, 35, 94
Josephus, 5, 35–36, 38, 49, 63, 67
Joshua, 14–16, 18, 46, 111
R. Joshua ben Halafta, 112
Josiah, 19, 22, 24
R. Judah ha Nasi (Rabi), 116–17, 125, 144, 147, 154–55, 157, 204
Judaism, xiii–xiv, 7–10, 14, 17, 23–24, 39–40, 63, 94, 108, 112–13, 157, 160–61, 197–99
Judea, 2, 8–9, 15–17, 19, 21–22, 24–27, 30, 33, 35, 49, 61, 67–69
Judeo-Christian Tradition, 1, 13, 197–99,
Julius Rosenwald Fund, 195
Justin Martyr, 94, 97

K

Kabbalists, 173
Kasich, John, 1
Kennedy, Robert, 171
Kerateion district, 75
Kirkpatrick, Jeanne J., 189
Ku Klux Klan, 192
Kurtz, Joseph, 190

L

labor, 5, 9, 15, 20, 47, 60, 86, 114, 120, 160, 168, 170, 186, 199
labor unions, 186
landowners, 17, 56–57, 59, 132, 159, 169
Lake Mareotis, 129
Lamentations, 22

Lasky, Jesse, 182, 185
Latin Bible, 137–38
laws, 8, 35, 37, 46–47, 52, 55, 65–66, 73, 76–78, 88, 92–94, 115–16, 144–46, 155, 158, 168
Lazarus, 56–58, 69, 82, 97, 161, 189
Lehman, Herbert, 196
Libanius, 75
Liberal Socialist Alliance, 189
liberation theology, 4, 189
Libya, 30
Licinius, 107
lifestyles, 19, 38, 75, 101, 108, 133–34, 149–50, 161, 168, 186
Lipton, Sarah, 164
literacy, 144, 157, 160, 165
love, 11, 39, 66, 74, 93, 100–101, 117–20, 137, 154, 187
Lower East Side, 178
Lubavitch rebbe, 174
Luke, 36, 51–52, 56, 61, 64–65, 67–68, 72, 93, 95, 99, 103
Luria, Isaac, 172
lust, 36, 81, 98, 101, 109, 122, 126–27, 133, 139, 141–42, 154
Lydia's house, 84
lynchings, 191–93

M

Maccabee revolt, 26–27, 45
Maccabees, 27–28, 30, 116
Magdalene, Mary, 52
Maggid, 174
Maimonides, 204
Malachi, 25
Manicheans, 122, 131, 136, 139
manumission, 83, 86
Marcion, 93, 96–99, 122–23, 197
Mark, 4, 51–53, 61, 63–66, 81–82, 99, 187–88
marriage, 11, 25, 79, 81, 87, 96, 99–101, 105–9, 122–23, 126, 132–34, 139–41, 152–55, 156–57, 169, 190
married clergy, 128

INDEX

married householders, 8, 81 108–9, 122, 126, 128, 131–33, 136–37, 140–41, 154–55, 170, 174
martyrdom, 49, 90, 99, 103–4, 110, 113, 128–29, 140–41
Mary, 52, 85, 95, 135–36, 141
Mary Magdalene, 6
Maryknollers, 189
Masada, 49
maskilin community, 175
Matthew, 4, 36–37, 51–52, 57, 61–62, 64–66, 67–68, 92–94, 99, 105, 122
Mattathias, 27, 45
Maximilla, 96
Maynooth College, 169
meat, 19, 34, 46–47, 96–97, 102, 115, 119, 131, 139, 168
medieval period, 12, 159, 161–62, 165–66
Mediterranean basin, xiv, 3, 7, 12, 17, 39, 44, 55–56, 74, 94, 123–24, 145, 158, 197
Meeropol, Abel, 192
R. Meir, 10, 112, 114, 121–22, 125, 150–51, 155
Mendenhall, George, 16–17
Menelaus, 27, 43
Mesopotamia, 39, 97, 158
Micah, 58
Midwestern farmers, 58–59
migration, 9, 39, 149, 158–60, 171, 195
Milan, 107, 126–27, 135, 139
Mills, Irving, 194
Miriam, 38, 151
Mishnah, 47, 116–17, 121, 124, 144–45, 201, 203–4, 208
Mississippi, 60, 191
Mithnagdim, 174,
Moabite women, 25
monasteries, 130, 133, 140, 167
money changers, 4, 61–62, 158, 165
monks, 130–33, 86. 130, 164, 167–68
Montanists, 99
Morgen Journal, 182, 192
Mosaic laws, 3, 6, 9, 19, 24, 28, 31, 34, 46–48, 52, 62, 66–70, 73–74, 76–77, 86, 92–94, 149

Moses, 9, 37–38, 46, 53, 64–65, 92, 150–51, 172, 212
Mosul, 158
Motion Pictures Patents Company, 183
Mount Sinai, 9, 37
Mulligan's Alley, 177–78
murder, 5, 24, 65, 73, 93, 104, 113, 166
music, xv, 10, 55, 150, 174, 178, 182
Muslim caliphates, 158–59

N

NAACP, 193, 196
Nahmanides, 166
National Catholic Theatre Movement, 182
National Catholic Welfare Conference, 186
National Guard, 188
National Urban League, 195
Nazareth, 3, 50, 55–56, 61, 207, 210, 213
Nazirite vows, 119
Nebuchadnezzar, 21, 24
Negro Actor's Union, 194
Nehemiah, 58
neo-Platonism, 107, 153
New Deal policies, 60, 186
New Masses, 186
New Testament, xi, 18, 51, 64, 78, 82, 99, 124, 189
Newton, John, 60–61
New York City, 178–79 181, 183
New York Tribune, 182–83
Nicaragua, 189
Nicea, 126
nickelodeons, 182
Nile, 40, 129–30
North Africa, 39, 113, 139, 141, 145
Northern Kingdom, 23–24
nuns, xv, 12, 133, 140, 170, 189

Index

O

Old South, 60
Old Testament, 18, 26, 28, 37–39, 69, 73, 93–94, 122–24, 162, 176, 197–98
Onah, 155
Onesimus, 83
oppression, 14, 17, 21, 189, 192
Oral Torah, 9, 46–48, 64, 116, 124, 144
Oriental dancers, 182
Origen, 105–8, 105–07, 109, 122–23, 128, 131, 135–38, 141–43
ossuaries, 38, 56

P

Pachomius, 130
paganism, 41, 59, 79, 87, 89, 94, 115, 134, 140, 145
pagans, 7, 39–41, 87, 93, 104, 108, 128, 135, 137–38
Palestine, 9, 12, 25, 27, 105, 113–14, 138, 144–45, 147–49, 153, 157, 159, 172, 201,
 rabbis, 9, 144, 148–49
Palestinian Talmud, 149
parables, 52, 69–70, 146
Paramount films, 81, 184
Passion of Christ, 164
Passover, 14, 34, 39, 61
Pastor, Tony, 178
Pastoral Letters, 6, 82, 86, 88, 91, 94–95, 100–101, 108, 189–90
patriarchy, 6, 83–84, 87, 133, 155
Paul, xiv, 3, 6–10, 66–68, 70–79, 81–89, 91, 93, 95–96, 98–100, 102–03 108–9, 123–24, 131, 176, 184, 198
Paulinus of Nola, 45, 50, 140, 187
Peasants, 56–57, 67–69, 168, 171
pederasty, 43–44, 127
Pelagius, 141–43
Pella, 94
penance, 104, 124, 128, 138, 143, 165–66, 206

perfection, 35, 97–98, 105, 120, 135, 142, 152, 172
persecutions, 5, 27, 73, 103–4, 106, 129, 173
Persia, 25, 39
Peter, 48, 62, 66–67, 73–76, 93, 96, 166,
Pharisaic thought, 45–46, 48, 72–74, 161
Pharisees, 2, 6, 9, 35, 38, 45–47, 49, 52, 55, 61–62, 65–66, 69–70, 72–74, 108, 110, 114–15, 120
Philemon, 83
Philippians, 84
Philippines, 189
Philo, 34, 41, 62, 86, 123, 150–51, 153, 213
Phoebe, 85
Pickford, Mary, 184
piety, 36, 105, 143, 165–66, 166, 172, 214
Pilate, 62–63
pilgrimages, 3, 9, 27, 34, 67, 115, 131, 137, 169
Pirkei Avot, 26, 46–48, 213
Plato, 41, 43, 100, 105
Platonism, 108, 140, 157
Pontius Pilate, 62
Pope Clement V, 165
Pope Francis, 189–90
Pope Gregory XVI, 169
Pope Innocent III, 166
Pope Leo XIII, 185, 213
Pope Pius, 182
popular culture venues, 175, 178, 180, 182
pork, 17, 19, 24, 56
post-Maccabean period, 35
postwar turmoil, 114
pottery, 15–16, 40, 56, 146
poverty, 47, 96, 114, 119–20, 132, 140, 148–49, 168
Prager, Dennis, 197–98, 213
prayer, 39, 45, 61, 91, 100, 112, 167
preaching, 52, 89–90, 132–33, 135–36, 138, 188
predestination, 141

225

Index

priests, 3, 5, 12, 25–27, 31, 34–35, 48, 90, 99, 105–6, 128, 140, 169–70, 190
Priscilla, 85
Procopius, 131
procreation, xi, 37, 41–42, 81, 101, 107, 117, 150–57
Prodigal Son, 52
Progressives, xv, 183
prohibitions, 10, 171
prophetic exhortations, 69, 72, 189, 162, 164
prophets, 20–21, 26, 28, 35, 38, 46, 64–65, 90, 92, 151, 189
proselytizing, 7, 41, 61, 66–67, 70, 74–75, 77, 84–85, 96, 123
prostitutes, 7, 44–45, 80, 86, 126–27, 170
Protestant leaders, 59, 199
Protestant Reformation, 168
protests, 58, 180
Prothero, Stephen, 4–5
Provence, 166
proverbs, 119, 147
psalms, 31, 37, 164, 167
Ptolemy IV, 26
Pumbadi academies, 202
Purim celebrations, 11, 150, 174
Puritans, 171
purity, 6, 19, 34–35, 55, 62, 97, 102, 114–16, 119, 138, 146

Q

Qumran communities, 35–37, 63, 70

R

rabbinic, 38, 47, 112, 114, 116–17, 121, 151–52, 156–58, 174
Rabbinic Judaism, xvi, 2, 12, 110, 119, 121, 123–25, 144, 146–47, 153, 161, 198
rabbinic sages, xiv, xvi, 9, 49, 55, 66, 121, 144, 146
rabbis, 9, 66, 94, 112–17, 119, 124, 145–46, 148–51, 153–54, 156, 166, 174 celibate, 10, 151
race, 99, 128, 142, 192–4
rape, 42, 155
Rashi, 149, 204–05
Rav, see R. Abba Arikha
rebellion, 3, 8–9, 49, 110, 168, 172
redemption, 93, 97, 103, 108, 198
Red Sea, 130
refugees, 17, 22, 25, 114
religions, xi, xiii–xiv, xvi, 12–14, 17, 25–26, 57, 63, 107, 124, 128, 145, 157, 161, 186, 197–98,
religious leaders, 2, 12, 25, 28, 45, 69–70, 99, 102, 111, 123–24, 144, 161–62, 166, 199
religious life, xiv, 31, 168, 212
religious practices, 9, 12, 19, 49, 110, 112–13, 120–21
religious study, xiv, 9, 49, 110–11, 116, 120–21, 147, 149, 154, 157–58, 173, 201–02
remarry, 48, 156
renewal movements, 5–6, 14, 35–37, 51, 65, 161
renunciations, 98, 129–30, 152, 164
repentance, 20, 51–52
Rerum Novarum, 185–86
Resh Lakish, 37, 116, 146, 148
resurrection, 28, 31, 64–65, 71, 198
Revocatus, 103
revolt, xiv, 9, 14, 17, 27, 29, 49, 58, 70, 96–97, 110, 113
Riis, Jacob, 172
ritual bathing, 10, 38, 44, 55–56, 75, 86, 115, 134
rituals, 14, 26, 33, 49, 92, 112–13, 145
Roman aristocracy, 164
Roman army, 49
Roman atrocities, 10
Roman authorities, 4–5, 9, 30, 48, 51, 62, 67, 110, 112–13, 135, 145, 147
Roman Empire, 44, 75, 82, 106, 126, 162

Index

Romans, 4, 49, 52, 56, 63, 65, 67, 69, 74–75, 85, 117, 122, 126, 210–11, 215
Roman theater, 55, 146
Rome, 2, 7, 45, 82, 85, 90, 93, 95, 97–98, 100, 110, 112–13, 126–27, 137, 141, 169–70
Romulus, 44
Rosenwald, Julius, 195
Rufus, 85, 113
ruins, 15, 58, 111
Russell Brothers, 179–80
Ruth, 25, 37
Ryan, John A., 186

S

Sabbath, 7, 19, 24, 27, 52, 66, 77–78, 113, 115, 152, 155, 173–74, 203
sacred writings, 8, 100–102, 118, 214
sacrifices, 17–20, 27, 34, 52, 104, 111, 119
Sadducees, 26, 35, 38, 73
Safed Spirituality, 172
sages, 9–10, 41, 103, 119–22, 124, 145–47, 150, 152–57, 201
Samaritans, 92
Samarra, 158
Sambo, 177
same-sex marriage, 191
Samuel, 18–20, 58, 82, 102
Sandrow, Nahma, 175
Sanhedrin, 25–26, 48, 62, 112, 202–3
Sardi, 145
Sarna, Jonathan, 199
Satan, 81, 109, 170
Saul, 18, 72–73, 82
Savior, 82, 164
sayings, 47, 56, 64
Schiff, Jacob, 195
Schlesinger, Arthur, 171, 192
Schneur Zalman, 174
scholars, 9, 28, 48, 64–65, 82, 85, 88, 112, 114, 144, 147, 149, 151, 196, 202–3
schools, 97, 145, 195

Schwerner, Michael, 191
Scottsboro Case, 191
scribes, 26, 46, 61–62
scriptures, 12, 26, 39, 41, 123, 136, 152
Sea of Galilee, 2
Second Temple, 4–5, 8–9, 12, 24–27, 30, 33–35, 38, 49, 56, 61–63, 102, 106, 110–11, 113, 116–17, 125
secular Jews, xiii, 14
Seleucid Empire, 26–28, 74
self-mortification, 12, 103, 119, 129–30, 138, 143, 165, 168, 173
Seneca, 101
sensual, 41, 143, 118, 182
Septimus, 166
Septuagint, 39, 79
sermons, 66, 92, 133, 135, 146–47
servants, 57, 85, 97–98, 102
settlements, 16–17
Severus, Alexander, 148
sex, xi, 40, 43–45, 79–80, 105, 117, 119, 126, 132, 137, 139, 153–54, 169–70
    marital, 101, 106–07, 136, 155
sexual abstinence, 102, 130, 136, 151–52
    required, 97
sexual act, 7, 12–13, 38, 40–41, 44, 79, 81, 123, 126–28, 137, 139, 142, 151–56
    intercourse, 38, 97, 109, 121, 128, 133, 135–36, 152, 154–55, 174
    passionless, 7, 10, 122, 126, 137, 150
    lovemaking, 11, 91, 118, 154–55
sexuality, 45, 106, 132, 136, 141–42, 150, 153, 155–57, 176, 181–82
sexual relations, xv, 37–38, 43, 79, 81, 109, 113, 116, 118, 126, 132, 140, 148, 150–56, 169
shame, 43, 45, 103, 127, 141, 155
Shammai, 46–48, 112
sharecropper system, 59–60, 176
Shavuot, 34
sheep, 15, 17, 19, 52, 92
shekel, half, 31

INDEX

Sheldon, Charles, 59
Sheshbazzar, 25
Shiva period, 10
R. Shmuel, 149, 214
shopkeepers, 158
Sifre, 146, 151
silk, 133, 150
silver, 20–21
Simeon, 26, 48, 110, 112, 114, 116
Sinatra, Frank, 192
sinfulness, 52, 60, 69, 77, 95, 127, 141, 143, 155, 179, 206
sinners, 6, 31, 52–53, 104, 155
sins, 36, 38, 41, 43, 45, 51–52, 58, 63, 77, 86, 93, 104, 138, 141–42, 167, 169, 184
ben Sira, 26, 31, 45, 78, 123
Sissle, Noble, 194
slaver, 60–61, 85
slaves, 6–7, 16, 18, 43–44, 46, 58, 61, 68, 82–86, 91, 120, 126, 150, 192
Social Gospel, 4, 58–60, 185
social justice, xiii, 4, 6–7, 13, 22, 58, 162, 164, 186–87, 189–90, 196, 198
Socrates, 43, 100
Sokho, 120
soldiers, 5, 38, 63, 128
soldiers fighting, 128
solitary life, 41, 168, 173
Solomon, 18–19, 23, 31, 37, 41
Somoza dictatorship, 189
Song of Songs, 118–19
songs, 118, 123, 127, 175, 179–81, 192–93
sons, 18, 21, 27, 48, 51, 61, 64, 93, 97, 112, 116, 128, 136, 138–39, 150, 169
soul, 10, 36, 41, 82, 86, 106, 108, 120–21, 123, 127, 129, 135, 139, 142, 153, 157
South American Catholics, 4
Spain, 12, 159, 128, 158–59, 166
Spanish Civil War, 189
Spanish expulsion, 12, 159, 172
Spingarn, Joel, 196
Spirit, 5, 77–79, 90, 97, 99–100, 103, 105–6

spiritual leadership, 89, 98, 104
stage Irishman, 180
Stephen, 5, 72
Stoicism, 78–79, 83, 101, 103, 107–8, 156–57
Strabo, 40
Strange Fruit, 192
Sukkot, 34, 124, 173
Sunday School Circuit, 181
Supreme Court, 191
Swanson, Gloria, 185
symplegmata, 80
synagogues, 7, 35, 45–46, 53, 65, 73, 75, 77, 79, 89, 92, 115–16, 146, 150
Synoptic Gospels, 56–57, 61, 103

T

table fellowship, 24, 74–76
Tacitus, 40
Tageblatt, 192
Talmuds, 148–49, 152–53, 155–57, 201, 204
Tanakh, 26
Tanya, 174
R. Tarfon, 112
Tarsus, 72–73, 79
Tatian, 7, 97–98, 131
Taurus, 79
tavern, 44, 80
temple personnel, 27, 34, 61, 70, 73
temptations, 10, 78, 103, 105, 129–30, 142, 146, 148, 152
Teradyon, 122
tikkun olam, 191
Tertullian, 98–100, 107
Teudas, 98
theaters, 11, 56, 75, 134, 146, 180–81, 183
Thecla, 6, 95–96, 98–99, 102
Theissen's claim, 68–69
Theodosian Code, 127
Therapeutae community, 41, 129
Thessalonians, 77, 82
Tiberias, 7, 55–56, 69, 147
Timothy, 77–78, 95

Index

Tin Pan Alley, 210
tithing, 54, 114, 116–17, 168
Titus, 82, 84, 169
Torah, 9, 26, 34–35, 45–48, 62, 92, 111–12, 115, 120–21, 124, 150, 152, 154
Tosefta, 117, 148
traditionalists, 111
tribes, 16, 18, 23, 53, 58, 82
Trump, Donald, 1
Tucker, Sophie, 181
Tunisia, 159
Tuskegee, 195

U

Ukrainian communities, 172
unemployment rate, 189
United Irish Societies, 179
United Nations, 189
United States, 12–13, 58, 180, 186, 188, 192, 197–98
University of Taurus, 79
US Bishops, 13, 190
Usha, 114
utensils, 19, 34, 47, 62, 146
utopian socialist communities, 70

V

Valentinus, 98–99
vaudeville, xv–xvi, 13, 176–78, 180-8
Vespasian, 110
Vibia Perpetua, 103
Victorianism, xv, 181, 183
vineyards, 18, 21, 114, 118
violence, 5, 15, 21, 45, 91, 177, 189, 192
virginity, 7, 10, 86–88, 102–3, 105, 109, 122, 133–37, 140–41, 156
virgins, 86, 96, 99, 102–3, 123, 131–34, 136, 156, 162
visions, 1, 64, 69–70, 137, 151, 188, 198
 apocalyptic, xiv, 31, 64, 81, 86, 89, 97

W

wages, 20, 57, 185–86
war, 38, 58–59, 107, 113–14, 148, 153, 183, 186, 199, 213
Warburg, Felix, 195
Washington, Booker T., 195
Waters, Ethel, 192
wealth, 16, 27, 41, 104, 116, 128, 132, 139, 149, 164, 189
wealth-owning class, 4, 26–27, 31, 114, 166
wealthy, 21, 25, 40, 44, 46, 57–58, 69, 102, 114, 133, 135–36, 138, 149–50, 152, 161–62, 173, 190
weddings, 11, 13, 98, 150, 174
Western Mind, 108, 129, 140
White Noise, 194, 214
widows, 21–22, 81, 91, 96–97, 136, 156, 162, 209
wilderness, 4, 31, 34, 53, 121, 124
wives, 10–11, 25, 37–38, 43, 52, 81, 84, 96, 101–02, 116–19, 128, 133, 135, 137, 140, 151–52, 154–56, 173, 203
Wilson, Woodrow, 195
wine, 96, 51, 71, 92, 101, 114, 116, 118–19, 169
wisdom, 26, 31, 41, 64, 78, 98
women, 6–7, 15, 25, 37–38, 40–45, 48, 52–53, 81, 83–85, 87–88, 95–96, 98–102, 108, 126, 129, 131–33, 135, 137, 139–40, 155, 157, 169–71, 181–84, 187, 189–90, 192
work, xiii, 9–10, 18, 53, 57, 59, 85, 105, 149, 178, 185
workers, 57, 60, 173, 178, 185, 188, 195
World War I, 180, 186
worship, 20, 24, 27, 92, 197
 idol, 113, 124, 145

X

Xenophon, 43

Index

Y

Yahweh, 21, 31
Yavneh, 9, 110–14, 124
Yiddish theaters, 13, 175
R. Yochanan, 147–48
Yom Kippur, 66

Z

Zadokite document, 38
Zakkai, Yohanan ben, 9, 48, 110–12, 114, 117
zealots, 3–5, 8, 49, 55, 103, 110
Zeraim, 203
Zipporah, 38, 151
zugots, 46, 48

www.ingramcontent.com/pod-product-compliance
Lightning Source LLC
Chambersburg PA
CBHW071939240426
43669CB00048B/2319